A Guide to the Missouri Constitution

Greg Casey and Justin Buckley Dyer

A Guide to the Missouri Constitution

Greg Casey
University of Missouri, Columbia

Justin Buckley Dyer
University of Missouri, Columbia

 W. W. NORTON & COMPANY • NEW YORK • LONDON

W. W. Norton & Company has been independent since its founding in 1923, when William Warder Norton and Mary D. Herter Norton first published lectures delivered at the People's Institute, the adult education division of New York City's Cooper Union. The firm soon expanded its program beyond the Institute, publishing books by celebrated academics from America and abroad. By midcentury, the two major pillars of Norton's publishing program—trade books and college texts—were firmly established. In the 1950s, the Norton family transferred control of the company to its employees, and today—with a staff of four hundred and a comparable number of trade, college, and professional titles published each year—W. W. Norton & Company stands as the largest and oldest publishing house owned wholly by its employees.

Editor: Peter Lesser
Project Editor: Tenyia Lee
Associate Editor: Samantha Held
Managing Editor, College: Marian Johnson
Managing Editor, College Digital Media: Kim Yi
Production Manager: Stephen Sajdak
Marketing Manager, Political Science: Erin Brown
Book Designer: Jack Meserole
Permissions Manager: Megan Jackson Schindel
Composition: Westchester Publishing Services
Manufacturing: LSC Communications

ISBN 978-0-393-28327-3

W. W. Norton & Company, Inc., 500 Fifth Avenue, New York, NY 10110-0017

wwnorton.com

W. W. Norton & Company Ltd., 15 Carlisle Street, London W1D 3BS

2   3   4   5   6   7   8   9

To Joan, Denis, Will, Caitlin, and Kennedy Casey;
Joey Berndt; Marcy Harder; Brendan Bowler; Calvin and
Claire Casey-Harder; and the memories of Noëlla Tétrault,
Jack Alphonse ("Gulls") Casey, Méléna Tétrault, and Pierre
Napoléon LaRose

And to our students

CONTENTS

ACKNOWLEDGMENTS

We are greatly obliged to many people who helped us with this project along the way. Kathy Carlsen, W.W. Norton's local college sales representative, encouraged us to take on this project and brought it to the attention of her colleagues. Samantha Held, Associate Editor at W.W. Norton, showed outstanding patience and gave wise guidance at key points. Peter Lesser, Editor and Vice President at W.W. Norton, supported (and occasionally nudged) us as we worked our way toward completion; his interest in this project featuring his native state buoyed and encouraged us on the path. We're also grateful for the good work of Tenyia Lee and Stephen Sajdak, who expeditiously guided the production process. Millie Aulbur, Esq., Director of Citizenship Education of The Missouri Bar, State Coordinator for *We the People* and the James Madison Project, read parts of the text and offered critiques that helped us avoid both terminological and factual error. We are particularly thankful to her also for involving Mr. Eric D. Jennings, Esq., Government Relations Counsel for The Missouri Bar, who gave us similarly valuable suggestions for improving the manuscript. Millie also directed us to Russ Sackreiter, author of *The Voice of the People: Exploring the Missouri Constitution*. Russ has an immense experience in teaching civics in Missouri schools (one of Greg Casey's children studied under him) and in leading students in *We the People* competitions, and we appreciate his suggestions. Founders' Professor (Emeritus) Endsley T. (Terry) Jones of the University of Missouri at St. Louis (Political Science) and author of *Fragmented by Design: Why St. Louis Has So Many Governments* helped us find our way around in the wilderness of local governments in the St. Louis area. We also thank Ryan Resch for providing valuable research assistance.

Finally, in this digital age, we owe thanks to the *St. Louis Post-Dispatch* for digitizing its newspaper from the late 1800s to the present day. Our subscription to this service gave us access to many brilliant political journalists' commentaries and analyses of events affecting the Missouri Constitution from when they were taking place, leading us to a deeper, more historically-based understanding of the origins of constitutional wording. These sources, contemporary in their time, helped confirm our memories of events long past that influenced the development of the Missouri Constitution.

TUCSON, ARIZONA,
GREG CASEY

COLUMBIA, MISSOURI,
JUSTIN BUCKLEY DYER

A Guide to the Missouri Constitution

Greg Casey and Justin Buckley Dyer

Introduction

In the spring of 1820 the 16th U.S. Congress passed a bill to authorize "the people of the Missouri Territory to form a Constitution and State government." According to the bill, the people of Missouri—or at least "all free white male citizens of the United States" who made their residence in the territory—were authorized to vote for a slate of state convention delegates. In September the people's chosen delegates then assembled in St. Louis to establish a "free and independent republic, by the name of 'THE STATE OF MISSOURI.'" Taking the U.S. Constitution as a model, the delegates drafted a document in the name of "WE, the people of Missouri." In seven relatively short articles, the Missouri Constitution of 1820 outlined the geographic boundaries of the state, divided government power between three independent and coequal branches (legislative, executive, and judicial), prescribed a bill of rights, and made provision for future amendments.

The admission of Missouri into the Union was part of a national legislative bargain known as the Missouri Compromise. To maintain a balance of power between free states and slave states, Congress provided for the admittance of Maine (a free state) and Missouri (a slave state) during the same legislative session in 1820. In the bill admitting Missouri into the Union as a slave state, however, Congress also insisted that slavery would be "forever prohibited" from certain federal territories that the United States had acquired from France in the 1803 Louisiana Purchase. This clause was similar to a provision in the Northwest Ordinance, passed under the Articles of Confederation in 1787, prohibiting slavery from the organized Northwest Territory in the Great Lakes region of the United States.

The question of how Congress would treat slavery in the federal territories was enormously important in the antebellum United States. Thomas Jefferson—who had advocated early for the prohibition of slavery in the Northwest Territories and had orchestrated the Louisiana Purchase during his presidency—remarked to a friend not long after the Missouri Compromise had been struck that the

> momentous question, like a fire bell in the night, awakened and filled me with terror. I considered it at once as the knell of the Union. It is hushed indeed for the moment. But this is a reprieve only, not a final sentence. A geographical line, coinciding with a marked principle, moral and political, once conceived and held up to the angry passions of men, will never be obliterated; and every new irritation will mark it deeper and deeper.

Jefferson's prediction that the Missouri Compromise would be a reprieve, and not a final settlement, of the national debate over slavery proved prescient.

In the years after the Missouri Compromise many key events leading to the Civil War centered on the state of Missouri. One such event was a Supreme Court decision involving Dred Scott, a man held in slavery under the laws of Missouri. Scott had traveled with his master, John Emerson, to the Wisconsin Territory where the Missouri Compromise had forever prohibited slavery. After Emerson's death, Scott then filed suit in St. Louis, alleging in part that his extended residence in a free territory had made him legally a free man. Such suits were commonplace in Missouri. Under both Missouri statutory law and Supreme Court precedent, persons held in slavery could petition courts to review the legality of their enslavement, and residence in a free state or territory was often recognized as legal grounds for the freeing of slaves. Dred Scott and the facts of his case thus seemed to line up with numerous precedents in Missouri. As historian Don Fehrenbacher observed, "Again and again, the highest court of the state had ruled that a master who took his slave to reside in a state or territory where slavery was prohibited thereby emancipated him."

Initially successful in the circuit court, Dred Scott eventually lost his case on a writ of error to the Missouri Supreme Court. His attorneys then petitioned the federal courts. In March 1857 the Supreme Court of the United States handed down a sweeping decision in the case in *Dred Scott v. Sandford*, declaring that Dred Scott was not a citizen of the United States and therefore could not bring suit in federal court. In a wide-ranging opinion, Chief Justice Roger Taney went well beyond this initial holding and also insisted, significantly, that (a) "the right of property in a slave is distinctly and expressly affirmed in the Constitution" and (b) the Missouri Compromise was therefore unconstitutional because it deprived citizens of their constitutionally protected slave property in the federal territories without due process of law.

In a high-profile Illinois Senate race the following year, Abraham Lincoln took issue with both points. During his campaign against the sitting Illinois senator Stephen A. Douglas, Lincoln insisted that the framers of the Constitution had sought to "gradually remove the disease [of slavery] by cutting off its source." One way to do this was to treat slavery like a cancer by isolating it geographically and preventing its spread to new territories. Yet the logic of the *Dred Scott* decision, he warned, tended toward the spread of slavery anywhere the American flag flew. Lincoln lost the 1858 Senate race, but he won the presidency on the Republican Party ticket two years later. In 1863, at the height of the Civil War, Lincoln issued the Emancipation Proclamation as a wartime measure, freeing slaves in the rebellious states of the Union. Although the Emancipation Proclamation did not affect slavery in Missouri, the formal legal abolition of slavery nationwide was completed with the passage of the Thirteenth Amendment to the U.S. Constitution in 1865.

THE 1865 AND 1875 MISSOURI CONSTITUTIONS

Under the control of federal troops, the state of Missouri remained in the Union throughout the Civil War. On April 8, 1865—one day before Confederate General Robert E. Lee surrendered to Union General Ulysses S. Grant at Appomattox Courthouse—a constitutional convention in Missouri produced a new, thoroughly nationalist state constitution. Because of the influence of one of the convention delegates, Charles Drake, the 1865 Constitution is often remembered as "Drake's Constitution." (Charles Drake was, incidentally, married to the daughter of one of Dred Scott's previous owners.) Drake's Constitution emphasized Missouri's allegiance to the national government and insisted that Missouri "shall ever remain a member of the American Union." Significantly, and controversially, it also disenfranchised anyone who had supported the Confederate States of America, maintaining in a remarkable and lengthy section that

> [n]o person shall be deemed a qualified voter, who has ever been in armed hostility to the United States, or to the lawful authorities thereof, or to the government of this state, or has ever given aid, comfort, countenance, or support to persons engaged in any such hostility; or has ever, in any manner, adhered to the enemies, foreign or domestic, of the United States, either by contributing to them, or by unlawfully sending within their lines money, goods, letters or information; or has ever disloyally held communication with such enemies; or has ever, by act or word, manifested his adherence to the cause of such enemies, or his desire for their triumph over the arms of the United States, or his sympathy with those engaged in exciting or carrying on rebellion against the United States . . . .

Voters, jurors, officeholders, attorneys, and clergy were required to take a loyalty oath swearing that they had never exhibited disloyalty to the Union and pledging fealty to the U.S. Constitution.

The Iron Clad Oath, as it was called, was abandoned only a decade later under a new constitution passed by Missouri voters in 1875. The 1875 Constitution jettisoned the hard line against Confederates and rebels and put in place the basic constitutional structure maintained today. In it we see a detailed bill of rights, the distribution of political power in three separate departments, rules for apportioning the legislature into districts, and provisions for the local self-government of counties, cities, and towns. We see also sections of the 1875 Constitution that are devoted to revenue and taxation, suffrage and elections, public education, the militia, corporations, railroads, banks, and constitutional amendments.

THE MISSOURI CONSTITUTION OF 1945

The amendment power outlined in the 1875 Constitution was amplified in 1907 when voters adopted an amendment permitting the direct democracy mechanisms of initiative and referendum. Later, in 1920, voters adopted an amendment (Article XII, Section 3[a]) using these procedures that mandated a statewide vote every 20 years on the question: "Shall there be a convention to revise and amend the constitution?" The first such vote, conducted in 1922, was affirmative and resulted in a constitutional convention that proposed a package of 21 amendments (only six of which were ultimately adopted by ballot). In 1942 voters once again responded affirmatively to the call for a convention; it did its work in 1943–44 and reported out a new constitution that voters adopted in a special election in February 1945.[1] Although it has been frequently amended since, the current Missouri Constitution is still partially the product of the debates and convention of the 1940s.

The convention that drafted the 1945 document was composed of 83 delegates representing many paths of life, including two stay-at-home mothers. As the former University of Missouri political scientist and convention delegate William L. Bradshaw noted, the "great majority of delegates were conservative, but constructive in their attitude." The convention made no major changes to Missouri's governing structures—there would still be a governor, bicameral legislature, and independent judiciary—but it did revise and modernize "the entire constitution, eliminating antiquated provisions and much statutory detail, clarifying and simplifying language, and rearranging provisions."

Unlike the federal model, which requires a supermajority of Congress or state legislatures to propose amendments, the Missouri Constitution requires only a bare majority vote in the legislature to propose a new amendment. Significantly, delegates to the 1945 convention also carried forward from the earlier constitution provisions for citizen participation that allow the people to "propose and enact or reject laws and amendments to the constitution" independent of the state legislature. To put a proposed constitutional amendment on the ballot in Missouri, citizens must collect signatures from 8 percent of legal voters in two-thirds of the state's congressional districts. Amendments proposed either by the legislature or by citizen initiative are then put before voters for approval, and a simple majority is enough for the proposed amendment to be adopted.

What these amendment procedures have meant in practice is that the Missouri constitution has grown, and continues to grow, at a fast pace. In a recent August primary, for example, voters in Missouri approved a constitutional amendment to

---

[1]Turnout was poor in voting on the new constitution: less than one-fifth of eligible voters cast ballots. But 63 percent of those exercising their franchise voted for its adoption. See Frederick C. Spiegel, "The Missouri Constitution," in *Missouri Government and Politics*, ed. Richard J. Hardy and Richard R. Dohm (Columbia, MO: University of Missouri Press, 1985), 63.

ensure the right of Missourians to "engage in agricultural production" and, in a separate vote, declared the right to keep and bear arms to be an "inalienable right" that the "state government is obligated to uphold." In a recent November general election, voters were asked whether the state should amend its constitution to allow past criminal acts to be admissible as evidence of new accusations of sexual crimes against children, and, separately, whether to require public teachers' salaries and tenure to be tied to student performance evaluations.

Missouri is *not* unique among states in the ease and frequency with which the state constitution may be amended. In fact, as John Dinan has chronicled, "the fifty states have held 233 constitutional conventions, adopted 146 constitutions, and ratified over 6,000 amendments to their current constitutions." Given the wide variety of issues that remain primarily state-level functions in the U.S. federal system—including education, criminal procedure, property taxation, infrastructure development, voting, child custody, marriage, and social services—state constitutions are an enormously important yet often neglected part of American government. This *Guide to the Missouri Constitution* is intended to aid teachers and students of Missouri government by highlighting the general features and practical importance of the Missouri constitution.

WORKS CONSULTED

Brecke, Ronald, and Greg Plumb. "Missouri Constitutionalism: Meandering toward Progress, 1820–2004." In *The Constitutionalism of American States*, eds. George E. Connor and Christopher W. Hammons (Columbia, MO: University of Missouri Press, 2008), 202–15.

Dinan, John J. *The American State Constitutional Tradition* (Lawrence, KS: University Press of Kansas, 2006).

Fulton, Richard, and Jerry Brekke. *Understanding Missouri's Constitutional Government* (Columbia, MO: University of Missouri Press, 2010).

Karsch, Robert F. *The Government of Missouri*, 14th ed. (Columbia, MO: Lucas Brothers Publishers, 1978).

McCandless, Perry. *Constitutional Government in Missouri* (Iowa City, IA: Sernoll, 1971).

"Missouri Constitutions and Related Documents." University of Missouri Digital Library Collection. http://digital.library.umsystem.edu/cgi/t/text/text-idx?page=home;c=mocon. Accessed January 9, 2017.

"Missouri's Dred Scott Case, 1846–1857." Missouri State Archives. www.sos.mo.gov/archives/resources/africanamerican/scott/scott.asp. Accessed January 9, 2017.

1945 Constitution (Revised 2016) *of the* STATE OF MISSOURI[1]

PREAMBLE

> We, the people of Missouri, with profound reverence for the Supreme Ruler of the Universe, and grateful for His goodness, do establish this Constitution for the better government of the state.

The preamble to the U.S. Constitution reads, "We the People of the United States, in Order to form a more perfect Union, establish Justice, insure domestic Tranquility, provide for the common defence, promote the general Welfare, and secure the blessings of Liberty to ourselves and our Posterity, do ordain and establish this Constitution for the United States of America." Echoing those famous opening lines of the national Constitution, the preamble to Missouri's fundamental law begins in the name of "We, the people of Missouri" but then goes on to identify the "better government of the state" as the document's overarching purpose.

The United States is often portrayed as demonstrating great constitutional stability over time; it is true that the Constitution has lasted since 1789 with little change (only 27 amendments). The state constitutions, however, have experienced great turmoil and shifts. A recent study by Christopher Hammons shows that, in fact, the American states have gone through 145 constitutions since 1776. Louisiana is on its 11th constitution, and Alabama is on its 10th governing document. If one considers that most actual governing took place at the state level until the great expansion of the federal government under President Franklin Roosevelt's New Deal in the 1930s, the conclusion is inevitable that instead of constitutional durability, our country has experienced great waves of constitutional flux.

Hammons notes that of "the 145 constitutions used by the American states since 1776, eighty nine constitutions or sixty one percent contain references to God in

---

[1]"Missouri Constitution," Missouri General Assembly, last modified November 14, 2016, www.moga.mo.gov/mostatutes/moconstn.html (accessed 1/9/2017).

their preambles." In this respect, the Missouri constitution's reference to the "Supreme Ruler of the Universe" in its opening lines places it with the majority of state governing documents.[2]

ARTICLE I
BILL OF RIGHTS

We often refer to the first 10 amendments to the U.S. Constitution as the Bill of Rights. The national Bill of Rights contains protections for religious liberty, freedom of speech, criminal due process, and other fundamental rights and liberties. For most of the nineteenth century, the Supreme Court of the United States interpreted the national Bill of Rights in a way that posed no limitations on the powers of state governments. In the case of *Barron v. Baltimore* (1833), for example, Chief Justice John Marshall proclaimed that the U.S. Constitution "was ordained and established by the people of the United States for themselves, for their own government, and not for the government of the individual States. Each State established a constitution for itself, and in that constitution provided such limitations and restrictions on the powers of its particular government as its judgment dictated."

After the Civil War, however, Congress proposed and the states ratified the Fourteenth Amendment to the U.S. Constitution. Among other things, the wording of this amendment prohibits the states from depriving any person of "life, liberty, or property, without due process of law." Over time, the Supreme Court has gradually interpreted the Fourteenth Amendment's due process clause in a way that applies most of the provisions in the national Bill of Rights against state governments. This is called "incorporating" federal rights (or rights protected against federal government action) into the Fourteenth Amendment so that the state and local governments must also respect the same rights. In other words, the Fourteenth Amendment wording "channels" the national right so that it is a "liberty" that cannot be denied unless there is due process of law. Today, state governments are limited by the national Bill of Rights in a way that they were not for most of the nineteenth century.

In addition to the limitations on state government found in the national Bill of Rights, state constitutions also often have detailed protections for individual rights and liberties. State bills of rights are not identical to the national Bill of Rights, and many state constitutions go beyond what is found in the U.S. Constitution. This is true of the Missouri Constitution. The Missouri bill of rights is much more expansive than the national Bill of Rights, and it lays out a theoretical foundation of government in addition to simply listing certain fundamental rights and liberties.

Article I of the Missouri Constitution builds on the work of political scientists Harry B. Kies and Carl A. McCandless. (Kies and McCandless were professors at

---

[2]Christopher Hammons, "State Constitutions, Religious Protection, and Federalism," *University of St. Thomas Journal of Law & Public Policy* 7.2 (2013): 230.

Rockhurst University and Washington University, respectively.) In September 1943, Kies and McCandless published a manual to guide the state constitutional convention delegates who drafted the state's bill of rights. In their pamphlet, the authors reiterated the natural-rights philosophy of the American founders. According to natural-rights philosophy, human beings are created with the same fundamental rights to things such as life, liberty, and the pursuit of happiness. The state, therefore, exists to secure these rights to promote human well-being. As Kies and McCandless summarize:

1. There is a Creator
2. Men are created equal
3. The state exists for man[3]

What is the practical implication? According to Kies and McCandless, our natural equality imposes on government a duty to respect our rights, and the provisions in the Bill of Rights are therefore designed to limit the power of the state. "Under the Natural Rights philosophy," they write, "the Bill of Rights is an insurance policy against the power of the State."[4]

> In order to assert our rights, acknowledge our duties, and proclaim the principles on which our government is founded, we declare:
>
> SECTION 1. **Source of political power—origin, basis and aim of government.**—That all political power is vested in and derived from the people; that all government of right originates from the people, is founded upon their will only, and is instituted solely for the good of the whole.
>
> SECTION 2. **Promotion of general welfare—natural rights of persons—equality under the law—purpose of government.**—That all constitutional government is intended to promote the general welfare of the people; that all persons have a natural right to life, liberty, the pursuit of happiness and the enjoyment of the gains of their own industry; that all persons are created equal and are entitled to equal rights and opportunity under the law; that to give security to these things is the principal office of government, and that when government does not confer this security, it fails in its chief design.
>
> SECTION 3. **Powers of the people over internal affairs, constitution and form of government.**—That the people of this state have the inherent, sole and exclusive right to regulate the internal government and police thereof, and to alter and abolish their constitution and form of government whenever they may deem it necessary to their safety and happiness, provided such change be not repugnant to the Constitution of the United States.

Sections 1–3 reaffirm the classic theory of American government: that is, that government exists to secure equal natural rights and that political power originates with

---

[3]The words *men* and *man* are not meant to exclude women; a more inclusive contemporary wording would be *human beings* or just *humans*.
[4]Harry B. Kies and Carl A. McCandless, *Manual on the Bill of Rights and Suffrage and Elections* (N.p., 1943), pp. 11–13.

Individual Rights: The U.S. Constitution vs. the Missouri Constitution

MENTIONED EXPLICITLY	U.S. CONSTITUTION	MISSOURI CONSTITUTION
Natural Rights to Life, Liberty, and the Pursuit of Happiness		✓
All Power Is Derived from People	✓	✓
Religious Freedom/ Free Exercise	✓	✓
Freedom of Speech	✓	✓
Right to Assemble and Petition	✓	✓
Due Process of Law	✓	✓
Habeas Corpus	✓	✓
Prohibition of Ex Post Facto Laws	✓	✓
No Unreasonable Search and Seizure	✓	✓
Grand Jury	✓	✓
Access to Charges	✓	✓
No Cruel and Unusual Punishment	✓	✓
Trial by Jury	✓	✓
Right to Bear Arms	✓	✓
Military Subordinate to Civilian Authority	✓	✓
Free Exercise of Right to Suffrage		✓
Limits to Power of Eminent Domain	✓	✓
Collective Bargaining Rights		✓
Limited Delegation to Administrative Agencies		✓
Crime Victim's Rights		✓
Definition of Marriage*		✓
English as Official Language		✓
Right to Farm		✓

*While language remains in the Missouri Constitution that defines marriage as between a man and a woman, this provision has been rendered void by *Obergefell v. Hodges* (2015).

the people and is delegated by the people to the government. Lawful and just government is therefore limited in scope and depends on the consent of the governed. Compare the language used in the Missouri Constitution with the famous second paragraph of the Declaration of Independence:

WE hold these Truths to be self-evident, that all Men are created equal, that they are endowed by their Creator with certain unalienable Rights, that among these are Life, Liberty, and the Pursuit of Happiness—That to secure these Rights, Governments are instituted among Men, deriving their just Powers from the Consent of the Governed, that whenever any Form of Government becomes destructive of these Ends, it is the Right of the People to alter or to abolish it, and to institute new Government, laying its Foundation on such Principles, and organizing its Powers in such Form, as to them shall seem most likely to effect their Safety and Happiness.

SECTION 4. Independence of Missouri—submission of certain amendments to Constitution of the United States.—That Missouri is a free and independent state, subject only to the Constitution of the United States; that all proposed amendments to the Constitution of the United States qualifying or affecting the individual liberties of the people or which in any wise may impair the right of local self-government belonging to the people of this state, should be submitted to conventions of the people.

Section 4's assertion that Missouri is subject *only* to the Constitution of the United States is a plainly unsustainable degree of independence. As a state in the Union, Missouri is subject to types of federal law other than the federal Constitution; as the supremacy clause in Article VI of the U.S. Constitution states: "This [the federal] Constitution, and the Laws of the United States which shall be made in Pursuance thereof; and all treaties made, or which shall be made, under the authority of the United States, shall be the supreme Law of the Land; and the Judges in every State shall be bound thereby, any Thing in the Constitution of Laws of any State to the Contrary notwithstanding" (Art. VI, para. 2).

Thus, not only the U.S. Constitution but also any constitutional federal law (that is, a law "made in pursuance of the federal Constitution") suppresses any conflicting state law. This precedent was set by Chief Justice John Marshall's decision in *McCulloch v. Maryland* (1819) that the state of Maryland's tax on the operations of the national bank created by Congress (the Bank of the United States) set up a "conflict of laws" between the national and state statutes. Marshall and his Court first concluded that Congress possessed the implied power to establish such a bank; thus the act establishing the bank was "in pursuance of the U.S. Constitution" and therefore constitutional. The Court then determined that, since Maryland's law was in conflict with a justifiable federal law, the state had to submit to higher federal law. In Marshall's words, because the "power to tax involves the power to destroy . . . [and] . . . the power to destroy may defeat and render useless the power to create," the state had no right to tax the bank's transactions. Similarly, the state of Missouri, when faced with a conflict of laws between its laws and federal laws, must give in to the federal government's power.

Bad feelings against the primacy of federal law arose in 2013 and 2014 in Missouri. In 2013 the State House of Representatives passed a bill to nullify federal firearms laws within the state of Missouri by a vote of 109–49. Then, in 2014, the State Senate voted up by 23–10 a bill (Senate Bill 613) which would also have nullified federal gun control laws in Missouri. To "nullify" a federal law means that the state government takes steps to prevent the law from being enforced in the state. Thus, the federal law in question would be rendered null and void within the state's boundaries and the state would "interpose" its authority to prevent the law from having sway. These particular bills, which ultimately did not pass the two chambers in the same wording, would have subjected federal agents enforcing federal gun laws against residents of Missouri to fines and/or criminal charges, including imprisonment for up to a year. Such a bill, if ever passed, would engender court challenges, and the first court it came up in (probably federal district court) would issue an injunction against its enforcement.[5]

Not just legislation is involved in potential "conflicts of laws": the Supreme Court decided in a case in 1890 (*In re Neagle*) that presidential executive orders also eclipse state law to the contrary. A federal marshal appointed by executive order to serve as bodyguard to a justice of the Supreme Court shot and killed a man who looked like he was getting ready to shoot the justice, and the California sheriff tried to arrest the marshal for homicide. California challenged the lawfulness of the executive order, but the Supreme Court found that the bodyguard was acting under the authority of the law of the United States. Therefore, an executive order is law, just as much as is legislation passed by Congress. So if the state of Missouri were to face a presidential executive order that conflicted with state law, state law would fall.[6]

Furthermore, a treaty can also suppress state law to the contrary. An important Supreme Court case upholding this principle arose from the state of Missouri in 1920. At the time, Missouri's permissive game laws conflicted with the federal government's desire to protect migratory birds. To that end, Congress passed legislation to regulate the killing of birds. However, that act was held unconstitutional because, at the time, the federal government's power to regulate under the commerce clause of the U.S. Constitution ("power to regulate commerce . . . among the several States") was narrowly interpreted in the courts. The U.S. Department of State then negotiated a treaty with Canada in 1916 to take steps to prevent the killing of birds migrating between the two countries. After ratification of this treaty, Congress

---

[5]Danny Wicentowski, "Missouri Senate Approves Bill That Criminalizes Federal Gun Laws," *Riverfront Times,* February 21, 2014.

[6]As this book goes to press, President Obama's executive orders de-emphasizing enforcement of immigration laws (Deferred Action for Childhood Arrivals, or DACA, and Deferred Action for Parents of Americans, or DAPA) are being contested in court. The case of *United States v. Texas* features the state of Texas arguing that these executive orders cost the state money because of the additional expense of providing drivers' licenses for the extra people staying in the state. (Twenty-five other states have joined Texas in this lawsuit.) The U.S. district court in Texas issued a court order against putting DACA and DAPA into effect, and this injunction was upheld 2–1 by a panel of the U.S. Court of Appeals (Fifth Circuit). The Supreme Court accepted the case, but ultimately delivered a tied verdict. If a multi-member Court ties, the decision of the next lower court is upheld. So the court of appeals' decision, which prevented implementation, is the standing law for the Fifth Circuit (composed of Mississippi, Louisiana, and Texas). The executive orders remained in effect, albeit under a cloud, in states outside the Fifth Circuit. However, President Trump will likely retract these executive orders.

passed essentially the same bill that it had passed earlier. But now a far different situation held sway: the law was backed by a treaty. The state of Missouri sued Holland, the U.S. game warden preparing to take measures to prevent poaching, and the state sought a court order against enforcement. The Supreme Court determined that even if Congress lacks a power under the Constitution, it can gain that power through a treaty "made under the authority of the United States." The treaty does not have to be in "pursuance of the Constitution" either; it can confer upon Congress a power that the Constitution withholds from Congress. So treaties can do an "end run" around the Constitution. In the end, Missouri had to submit to the treaty.

SECTION 5. Religious freedom—liberty of conscience and belief—limitations.—That all men have a natural and indefeasible right to worship Almighty God according to the dictates of their own consciences; that no human authority can control or interfere with the rights of conscience; that no person shall, on account of his religious persuasion or belief, be rendered ineligible to any public office or trust or profit in this state, be disqualified from testifying or serving as a juror, or be molested in his person or estate; but this section shall not be construed to excuse acts of licentiousness, nor to justify practices inconsistent with the good order, peace or safety of the state, or with the rights of others.

The Free Exercise Clause of the First Amendment to the U.S. Constitution stipulates that Congress "shall make no law . . . prohibiting the free exercise" of religion. Article I, Section 5 of the Missouri Constitution gives a much more detailed exposition of religious freedom and its theoretical foundation. The assertion that we each have a "natural and indefeasible right to worship Almighty God according to the dictates of" our consciences echoes many of the arguments for religious freedom made by the U.S. Founders. See, for example, James Madison's famous *Memorial and Remonstrance Against Religious Assessments* (1785). Religion—or the "duty which we owe to our Creator and the manner of discharging it"—Madison argued, "must be left to the conviction and conscience of every man; and it is the right of every man to exercise it as these may dictate. This right is in its nature an unalienable right."

There is, however, a potential tension between the freedom of religion and the rule of law. May devoutly religious citizens invoke the freedom of religion to be exempt from generally applicable laws such as tax assessments, military drafts, or compulsory school attendance? There is no straightforward answer to this question. Article 1, Section 5 of the Missouri Constitution asserts that religious freedom shall not be construed to "justify practices inconsistent with good order, peace or safety of the state, or with the rights of others." In *McDonough v. Aylward*, 500 S.W.2d 721 (Mo. 1973), the supreme court of Missouri held that citizens who send their children to parochial schools are not therefore exempt from paying taxes to support public education in Jackson County. In *Association for Educational Development v. Hayward*, 533 S.W.2d 759 (Mo. 1976), the supreme court of Missouri determined that a religious society was not exempt from single-family residential zoning restrictions in the city of Kirkwood. The U.S. Supreme Court has similarly ruled against First Amendment–based religious exemptions to generally applicable laws. In *Oregon v. Smith* (1990), Justice Antonin Scalia summarized the logic: an "individual's religious beliefs [do not] excuse him from compliance with an otherwise valid law prohibiting conduct that the State is free to regulate."

In response to the decision in *Oregon v. Smith* (1990), Rep. Chuck Schumer (D-NY) and Sen. Ted Kennedy (D-MA) introduced a bill in Congress that would require some religious exemptions to generally applicable laws. In 1993, Congress passed and President Clinton signed the Religious Freedom Restoration Act. Although the Supreme Court subsequently found the Religious Freedom Restoration Act unconstitutional as applied to states, many states have enacted their own state-level religious freedom restoration acts. Mirroring this trend at the national level, the Missouri General Assembly enacted a "religious freedom restoration act" in 2014. Section 1.302.1 of the Missouri Revised Statutes provides:

> A governmental authority may not restrict a person's free exercise of religion, unless:
>
> (1) The restriction is in the form of a rule of general applicability, and does not discriminate against religion, or among religions; and
> (2) The governmental authority demonstrates that application of the restriction to the person is essential to further a compelling governmental interest, and is not unduly restrictive considering the relevant circumstances.

SECTION 6. Practice and support of religion not compulsory—contracts therefor enforceable.—That no person can be compelled to erect, support or attend any place or system of worship, or to maintain or support any priest, minister, preacher or teacher of any sect, church, creed or denomination of religion; but if any person shall voluntarily make a contract for any such object, he shall be held to the performance of the same.

SECTION 7. Public aid for religious purposes—preferences and discriminations on religious grounds.—That no money shall ever be taken from the public treasury, directly or indirectly, in aid of any church, sect or denomination of religion, or in aid of any priest, preacher, minister or teacher thereof, as such; and that no preference shall be given to nor any discrimination made against any church, sect or creed of religion, or any form of religious faith or worship.

Section 7 is a Blaine Amendment, named for James Blaine, a speaker of the U.S. House of Representatives (1869–1875), a U.S. senator, and the Republican candidate for president in the election of 1884 (which he lost to Grover Cleveland). In the post–Civil War era, Blaine proposed the adoption of such amendments across the country at both the state and federal levels to prevent Catholic parochial schools (which, at the time, were being established by Catholic bishops) from being able to make a claim on public funds.

Before the Civil War, Missouri had no public schools; afterward, it struggled to establish them, while the bishops were also setting up Catholic schools. In some places, most notably New York City, public monies (tax revenues) were used to finance both Catholic and public schools, and Missouri Catholics hoped to secure public funding for schools as well. The Catholic bishops set up independent schools because the public schools taught a religiously based morality infused with nondenominational Protestant religious principles, used Protestant prayers, and read selections from the Protestant Bible (the Protestant and Catholic Bibles used different translations and included different "Books"). As taxpayers, the Catholics didn't care to have their children educated in a different faith at taxpayer expense.

Efforts in 1870 to establish both common (public) and Catholic schools centered in St. Louis; members of the General Assembly, under the leadership of State Representative Michael Phelan, authorized the St. Louis School Board to appropriate monies for the city's private schools. The bill passed the lower chamber with only three dissenting votes. This is called the "Phelan Miscalculation": Phelan gambled that the idea of division of funds could carry. And it did—initially. However, after much argument, the bill was brought back up for reconsideration and the House then voted to postpone further consideration, effectively killing the notion of division of funds for schools in the state.

At this point, blowback happened: a constitutional amendment forbidding division of funds was introduced and it came to be seen as a protection for the nascent common school system. The amendment passed both chambers and was put on the ballot along with five other amendments, most dealing with elections and qualifications to vote and to run for office. Unfortunately, election laws at the time did not require nutshell summaries on the ballot of what constitutional amendments would accomplish. The Blaine Amendment was in sixth position among the other amendments proposed, but there was no way for the ordinary voter to know which one it was, in case that voter wanted to vote it down while still voting for the other very popular amendments. All the amendments swept to victory by overwhelming majorities; the amendment to forbid division of funds passed with 92 percent of the vote and even carried in heavily Catholic counties.[7] Like many state constitutional amendments and a few federal constitutional amendments, this amendment had to do with one group flexing its muscles and asserting its superiority over another group by writing its values and way of life into law.

A prime example of this at the federal level is the Prohibition movement, which culminated in the adoption of the Eighteenth Amendment to the U.S. Constitution in 1919. People whose ancestors had migrated to America earlier frowned on

[7]See J. Michael Hoey, "Missouri Education at the Crossroads: The Phelan Miscalculation and the Education Amendment of 1870," *Missouri Historical Review* (2001), 379–93; see also Aaron E. Schwartz, "Dusting off the Blaine Amendment: Two Challenges to Missouri's Anti-Establishment Tradition," *Missouri Law Review* 73 (Winter 2008), 129–76. Thanks to J. Michael Hoey of the Missouri Catholic Conference for detailed explanations of this series of events in a telephone interview on February 29, 2016, with Greg Casey.

consumption of alcoholic beverages, while new Americans tended to come from countries that customarily drank beer and wine with meals. The earlier migrants tried to proselytize their abstemious way of life as thriftier, healthier, wiser, and bound to lead to better personal outcomes, but their ideas were unwelcome among the new Americans. During this "assimilationist reform" phase of the Prohibition movement, Temperance leaders still hoped that the newcomers would voluntarily stop drinking. As it became evident that their campaign wasn't working, Temperance leaders (centered in the Women's Christian Temperance Union [WCTU]) turned to "vindictive reform": if migrant minorities would not voluntarily adopt a more abstemious lifestyle, the WCTU would politicize the issue and use law and the Constitution to force them to stop drinking. Vindictive reform succeeded when the Eighteenth Amendment was ratified and Prohibition began; Congress followed up by passing the Volstead Act, which made virtually all alcoholic products illegal (to manufacture, ship, or sell). Prohibition didn't work out well; the law proved unenforceable, crime rates soared as criminal entrepreneurs served the black market demand for alcoholic beverages, and eventually even some Temperance leaders became supporters of reversing the law. From the middle-class reform perspective, preventing migrants from drinking was a way to show, symbolically, that the migrants of an earlier generation were still superior in status to the newcomers (even though the newcomers were quite numerous in many places).[8]

The Blaine Amendments were an early harbinger of such status politics. Blaine and then President Ulysses S. Grant provided leadership for a campaign to deny all public funds to the Catholic parochial schools. Scapegoating Catholics, many of whom were of foreign origin, became a handy way to distract voters from the corruption and scandals of the Grant administration. Although no Blaine Amendment was ever added to the U.S. Constitution (it is too difficult to amend), Congress did require all new states (post-1876) to incorporate Blaine wording in their constitutions, and many states, including Missouri, adopted such constitutional wording. (In Missouri's case, the Article I, Section 7 wording supplements Article IX, Section 8.)

The Missouri Constitution, like the U.S. Constitution, protects citizens' religious freedom *and* prohibits the government from either aiding religious institutions or preferring particular religious sects. An established religion is not necessarily incompatible with free exercise of religion; the United Kingdom has an established church, but those who adhere to other creeds are free to practice their religious preference. But the American Founders wanted no "law respecting an establishment of religion." Missouri's constitutional provisions are more specific, making it clear that no government monies may support a religious organization "directly or indirectly," and that

---

[8]See Joseph Gusfield, *Symbolic Crusade* (Champaign, IL: University of Illinois Press, 1963).

the government may show neither favoritism nor preference for any particular religious organization.[9]

At the state level, the supreme court of Missouri has recently noted that the Missouri Constitution's reference to the "natural and indefeasible right to worship Almighty God according to the dictates" of conscience "certainly reflects the historical fact that the majority of those who wrote and adopted our constitution felt free to express their own belief in Almighty God, which by text is a reference at least to the deity of monotheistic religions and historically to the Christian or Judeo-Christian deity. Those who wrote and adopted our state's constitution expressed their belief in God, as well, in the preamble to each version of the Missouri Constitution." (See *Oliver v. State Tax Commission of Missouri*, 37 S.W.3d 243 [2001].) At the same time, the supreme court of Missouri has also acknowledged "that the provisions of the Missouri Constitution declaring that there shall be a separation of church and state are not only more explicit but more restrictive" than the First Amendment's establishment clause. In *Paster v. Tussey*, 512 S.W.2d 97 (1974), the supreme court of Missouri struck down a law that would use public money to purchase textbooks at private religious schools, even though the U.S. Supreme Court (in *Board of Education v. Allen* [1968]) had previously upheld similar programs under the U.S. Constitution. In states with Blaine Amendments such as Missouri, state courts can determine that furnishing secular books or transportation to school is an unacceptable aid to religion, even though this might be acceptable under the federal Establishment Clause.

A 1976 effort called the "Fairness in Education" campaign sought to repeal the Blaine Amendment and allow the state to give aid to the private schools for textbooks, services to handicapped students, and transportation; the Missouri Catholic Conference led this drive, while the Missouri Baptist Convention fought it hard. The repeal proposal was put on the primary ballot in August 1976 on the supposition that voter turnout in rural Missouri would be quite low (early August is very busy for farmers and farming communities focused on the harvest). However, a big race for the Democratic nomination for an emptying U.S. Senate seat engulfed the

---

[9]Sorting this out in practical terms has been difficult at both the national and state levels. In *Cochran v. Board of Education* (1930), the Supreme Court upheld making textbooks available to schoolchildren regardless of whether or not they attended religiously affiliated schools, a ruling reaffirmed in *Board of Education v. Allen* (1968), while in *Everson v. Board of Education* (1947) the court allowed public money to fund student transportation to religious schools, arguing that the money flowed to religious organizations as the result of the private choices of individual families. Similarly, religious social service organizations often receive government contracts, and police and fire departments regularly provide service for religious organizations. How, then, do we know when government has given *unconstitutional* aid or preference to religious organizations? An intricate and detailed body of case law has developed around this issue. Perhaps recognizing the difficulties of drawing hard lines in the area of law, the U.S. Supreme Court has tried to delineate guidelines for what constitutes "excessive entanglement" between government and religion. See, for example, *Lemon v. Kurtzman* (1971).

state.[10] The resulting high turnout spelled doom for the Fairness in Education drive; many rural Missourians are unsympathetic to the Catholic Church and 58 percent of the ballots rejected the amendment.[11]

More recently, this jurisprudence has been altered by the Supreme Court's ruling in *Zelman v. Simmons-Harris* (2002) that a publicly-financed school voucher program could be used to subsidize a student's tuition at religiously-affiliated schools as long as the parents of the enrolled child were able to choose between a religious and a secular school. Now, a new view has emerged: states ought not to be able to refuse aid to religious institutions if the aid has nothing to do with religion. A case arising in Columbia, Missouri, may test this question shortly. *Trinity Lutheran Church of Columbia v. Pauley* involves a state program that turns used tires into rubber paving for playgrounds. The state pays for the program by imposing fees on sales of new tires, so state funding is involved, engaging Article I, Section 7 and Article IX, Section 8. This is a grant program: applicants are ranked and awarded the prize on the basis of their ranking. The congregation of Trinity, which runs a daycare for children, applied for the program. The congregation came in at fifth of 44 applicants, so one would think it would get the grant. However, because it is a religious institution, it was turned down on the grounds of the Blaine Amendment. The church sued in federal court, characterizing the rejection as a violation of its First Amendment right to free exercise of religion and the Fourteenth Amendment's equal protection clause. The court of appeals' panel of three judges ruled 2–1 that Trinity was in the wrong, and the case was taken to the full membership of that court,[12] which split 5–5. The case is now on appeal to the U.S. Supreme Court, which took the case on January 15, 2016. The current eight-justice Court might tie in its voting on this case (which would uphold the three-judge panel), or it might defer consideration by slating it for reargument. If President Trump fills the vacant seat promptly, the Court can have reargument, and a full Court can rule decisively.

SECTION 8. Freedom of speech—evidence of truth in defamation actions—province of jury.—That no law shall be passed impairing the freedom of speech, no matter by what means communicated: that every person shall be free to say, write or publish, or otherwise communicate whatever he will on any subject, being responsible for all abuses of that liberty; and that in all suits and prosecutions for libel or slander the truth thereof may

---

[10]A three-way battle for the nomination saw James Symington (son of retiring U.S. Senator Stuart Symington, who had run for President twice and had represented the state in Washington for 24 years), the very popular former governor Warren Hearnes (the first governor to serve two successive terms), and Congressman Jerry Litton (a charismatic farmer and rancher whose plain speech and downhome ways appealed hugely in both rural and urban areas of the state). The race attracted record turnout and Jerry Litton won, but he was killed along with his wife and two children in an airplane crash as they took off for a victory party in Kansas City on the night of the election. Hearnes came in second.

[11]Mark Schlinckmann, "Voters Soundly Reject Aid to Private Schools," *Kansas City Star*, August 4, 1976.

[12]The court of appeals for the Eighth Circuit.

be given in evidence; and in suits and prosecutions for libel the jury, under the direction of the court, shall determine the law and the facts.

SECTION 9. Rights of peaceable assembly and petition.—That the people have the right peaceably to assemble for their common good, and to apply to those invested with the powers of government for redress of grievances by petition or remonstrance.

As with the freedom of religion, the Missouri Constitution's protections for the freedom of speech and assembly are more explicit and more detailed than the protections found in the U.S. Constitution. The First Amendment to the U.S. Constitution prohibits any law "abridging the freedom of speech, or of the press, or the right of the people peaceably to assemble." The Missouri Constitution goes beyond the First Amendment's language and protects speech "no matter by what means communicated" while also acknowledging that individuals are "responsible for all abuses of that liberty." Citing established federal precedent, the supreme court of Missouri explained in *State v. Vollmar*, 389 S.W.2d 20 (1965), that

> [the] protection given speech and press was fashioned to assure unfettered interchange of ideas for the bringing about of political and social changes desired by the people. All ideas having even the slightest redeeming social importance—unorthodox ideas, controversial ideas, even ideas hateful to the prevailing climate of opinion—have the full protection of the guaranties, unless excludable because they encroach upon the limited area of more important interests (quoting *Roth v. United States*, 1957).

There are, however, broad categories of speech that the Missouri and U.S. Supreme Courts have long held are *not* protected. In *Chaplinsky v. New Hampshire* (1942), the U.S. Supreme Court explained that these "include the lewd and obscene, the profane, the libelous, and the insulting or 'fighting' words—those which, by their very utterance, inflict injury or tend to incite an immediate breach of the peace." Consistent with *Chaplinsky*, Missouri Revised Statutes penalize libel and slander (Section 509.210.1); obscenity (Section 573); and threats, breaches of the peace, and fighting words (Section 574.010.1).

Although broken up into a separate section, the language of Missouri's freedom of assembly clause mirrors the First Amendment. In both, citizens have the "right peaceably to assemble" as well as the right to petition their government(s) with a list of "grievances." The right to assemble is not unlimited, however; the supreme court of Missouri has insisted that the state may regulate the right to associate in the interest of the "health, safety and physical well-being of its residents"; see *State v. Allen*, 905 S.W.2d 874 (1995).

One issue emanating from the right to peaceable assembly is "right to work" laws. Unions are one type of peaceable assembly, and their leadership, once a workplace is unionized, represents all employees in dealings with their employer. With unionization comes the question of whether all workers should be obliged to join the union and pay dues, or alternatively, if just those workers who favor union membership should be obliged to do so. If state law permits worker choice on whether or not to join the union, that state is a "right to work" state; otherwise, all workers must join the union and pay dues. Heated arguments surround this issue: some workers who may not believe in unions are forced to join against their better judgment and thus rendered less free, but if it is up to the individual worker whether or not to join the union (and pay dues), the union will possibly have to serve many workers who accept what the union does for them but don't contribute anything toward the union's expenses. This is a typical "free rider" problem. Conservatives generally oppose unions and unionization of the workplace, arguing that unions gum up and bureaucratize the workplace, injuring the prospects of new job creation and economic development. Liberals maintain that unions protect worker rights for all workers, making for a safer workplace and better wages and benefits.

Right to work was thoroughly defeated in Missouri in a referendum in late 1978[13] but was brought up again in the 2015 legislative session. Enjoying solid support from the Republican majority in both chambers of the General Assembly, it passed easily. But Governor Jay Nixon, a Democrat, vetoed it. In the veto session, legislators debated whether the governor's veto would be upheld or overridden, with a two-thirds majority necessary in both chambers to override. The veto was overridden in the Senate but in the House the tally fell 13 votes short. So unions in Missouri can continue to represent and collect dues from workers, even if those workers are opposed to joining the union. However, the election of Governor Eric Greitens in fall of 2016 probably spells imminent victory for the right to work movement under a Republican governor and an overwhelmingly Republican legislature all dedicated to right to work.

SECTION 10. Due process of law.—That no person shall be deprived of life, liberty or property without due process of law.

The U.S. Constitution prohibits the national and state governments from depriving any person of "life, liberty, or property without due process of law" (see the Fifth and Fourteenth Amendments). Article 1, Section 10 of the Missouri Constitution similarly provides that "no person shall be deprived of life, liberty, or property without due process of law." Under the due process clauses of the U.S. Constitution, courts have litigated a variety of important and volatile political issues, including criminal procedure, election law, marriage and family law, abortion rights, and eminent domain. Because the Missouri General Assembly has usually been unfriendly to abortion rights and changes in marriage and family law, groups taking the "liberal" side of these issues often face adverse state legislation, and they tend to flock to federal courts to litigate their claims under the Fourteenth Amendment rather than go to state court to make a claim under the state due process clause. The federal courts are considered a more sympathetic forum and thus have eclipsed the state court sys-

---

[13]Proponents of right to work (i.e., anti-union interests) pushed legislation in the General Assembly but lost when it was voted down; they then moved to the initiative process, gathering signatures to put a right to work law on the ballot. Union interests fought hard to defeat right to work, and it was defeated 60 percent to 40 percent.

Article I | 21

tem in these areas of law. The primacy of the U.S. Constitution does mean that the Constitution suppresses any state claims to the contrary. The wording, bearing repetition, states that "the Laws of the United States which shall be made in Pursuance thereof . . . [of the national constitution] . . . shall be the supreme Law of the Land; and the judges in every state shall be bound thereby, any Thing in the Constitution or Laws of any State to the Contrary notwithstanding" (U.S. Const., Art. IV).

SECTION 11. Imprisonment for debt.—That no person shall be imprisoned for debt, except for nonpayment of fines and penalties imposed by law.

After the racial unrest in Ferguson, Missouri, in the summer of 2014, an investigation conducted by the Department of Justice found that many small suburban municipalities outside the city of St. Louis, including Ferguson, were using their police forces and court systems to fill their treasuries. One way these governments maximized their revenue stream was by ticketing citizens (of their own and surrounding municipalities) for nitpicky offenses such as tall weeds in their yards, broken taillights, or malfunctioning directional signals. The fines for these offenses then were compounded with fees for not paying the fines on time, resulting in poor people being subjected to arrest warrants for nonpayment of the initial fines and facing yet additional fees. The Justice Department report found that people had been imprisoned for their debts, and although the wording of Section 11 exempts fines and penalties imposed by law, the report concluded that suburban St. Louis courts and police forces functioned so unfairly that this exemption should perhaps not be accepted as legitimate. The actions of the Ferguson police department were deemed to violate federally protected rights.[14]

SECTION 12. Habeas corpus.—That the privilege of the writ of habeas corpus shall never be suspended.

Translated literally from Latin as "you may have/hold the body," the writ of habeas corpus is a formal legal document whereby a court reviews the executive branch's legal grounds for an individual's detention. Although the U.S. Constitution allows the suspension of this privilege "in cases of rebellion or invasion [when] the public safety may require it" (Art. I, Sec. 9), the Missouri Constitution significantly requires that the "privilege of the writ of habeas corpus shall never be suspended." As a matter of state law, then, the executive branch in the state of Missouri may not suspend habeas corpus even in cases of rebellion or invasion. The national government, however, may suspend habeas corpus consistent with the U.S. Constitution, and such an act would trump Missouri's noncompliance. Perhaps the best-known historical example of the suspension of the writ of habeas corpus came during the Civil War, when Abraham Lincoln issued an executive order on October 14, 1861, authorizing his military officers to suspend habeas corpus. Lincoln's attorney general,

[14]See generally Wilson Andrews, Alicia Desantis, and Josh Keller, "Justice Department's Report on the Ferguson Police Department," *New York Times*, March 4, 2015.

Edward Bates, a former congressperson from St. Louis, was tasked with putting together a legal opinion about whether it is constitutional for the president to suspend habeas corpus. (Many, both now and at the time, read Article I, Section 9 of the U.S. Constitution as granting the suspension power exclusively to Congress.) According to Attorney General Bates, "It is the plain duty of the President . . . to preserve the Constitution and execute the laws all over the nation." With the state of affairs surrounding the Civil War, Bates argued that the suspension of habeas corpus by the president was a lawful exercise of executive power.[15]

SECTION 13. Ex post facto laws—impairment of contracts—irrevocable privileges.— That no ex post facto law, nor law impairing the obligation of contracts, or retrospective in its operation, or making any irrevocable grant of special privileges or immunities, can be enacted.

The U.S. Constitution prohibits both Congress and state legislatures from enacting ex post facto laws, or laws that apply retroactively (see U.S. Const., Art. I, Sec. 9–10). Section 13 of the Missouri Constitution also prohibits ex post facto laws.

In *Holden v. Antom, Inc.*, 930 S.W.2d 526 (1996), the Missouri Court of Appeals for the Eastern District cited a line of state-level legal precedent and explained that an "ex post facto law is one which denounces as criminal, acts which were non-criminal when committed, or which changes penalties for criminal violations after such violations are committed." The notion that ex post facto laws deal only with criminal matters is consistent with the U.S. Supreme Court's earliest and most noteworthy ex post facto case, *Calder v. Bull* (1798), where the Court ruled that the constitutional prohibition of ex post facto laws applies only to criminal (and not civil) actions.

Section 13 of the Missouri Constitution also prohibits the state from "impairing the obligation of contracts," a prohibition found in the U.S. Constitution as well (Article I, Section 10 of the U.S. Constitution prohibits states from passing any "Law impairing the Obligation of Contracts"). The U.S. Supreme Court, however, has repeatedly read exceptions into this clause during times of national emergency, such as during the Great Depression. See, for example, *Home Building Loan Association v. Blaisdell* (1934).

SECTION 14. Open courts—certain remedies—justice without sale, denial or delay.—That the courts of justice shall be open to every person, and certain remedy afforded for every injury to person, property or character, and that right and justice shall be administered without sale, denial or delay.

The practice of plea bargaining is a relatively common criminal-case handling system whereby a defendant charged with a crime agrees to plead guilty in return for some consideration such as a reduction in sentence, a reduction in the number of

[15]See J. Hubley Ashton, ed., *Official Opinions of the Attorneys General of the United States*, vol. 10 (Washington, DC: W.H. & O.H. Morrison, 1868).

counts on which the defendant is charged (thus producing a lower potential sentence), or a reduction in the gravity of the charged crime. Plea bargaining belies Section 14's guarantee of justice "without sale." Under plea bargaining, justice is for sale, even though the price is not quoted in money, but rather in measures of freedom.

Usually such deals are struck between the defendant's lawyer (defense counsel) and the prosecution[16] and approved by the judge after a courtroom ceremony in which the defendant is asked under oath to attest that he or she has not been promised any consideration in return for pleading guilty. In practice this is a legal fiction, but a recording of it is made, and this renders it nearly impossible for the defendant to challenge the plea bargain later. The benefits of plea bargaining keep the system in place: for the defendant, a lighter sentence or perhaps even probation; for the defense counsel, not having to prepare for a trial; for the prosecution, not having to prove the charges with evidence; and for the judge, not having to conduct a trial. The "trial system" deciding guilt and innocence is often idealized; the true reality of the criminal law system is plea bargaining.[17]

SECTION 15. Unreasonable search and seizure prohibited—contents and basis of warrants.—That the people shall be secure in their persons, papers, homes, effects, and electronic communications and data from unreasonable searches and seizures; and no warrant to search any place, or seize any person or thing, or access electronic communication or data, shall issue without describing the place to be searched, or the person or thing to be seized, as nearly as may be; nor without probable cause, supported by written oath or affirmation.

Both Article 1, Section 15 of the Missouri Constitution and the Fourth Amendment to the U.S. Constitution protect citizens from "unreasonable" searches and seizures by the government. In *State v. Deck,* 994 S.W.2d 527 (1999), the supreme court of Missouri noted that "Missouri's constitutional 'search and seizure' guarantee, article 1, section 15, is co-extensive with the Fourth Amendment." In other words, Missouri's constitutional provision about searches and seizures has the same meaning as the Fourth Amendment. The devil, however, is in the details, and Fourth Amendment jurisprudence is a complex and intricate body of law. As a basic matter, the Fourth Amendment requires police to present probable cause to a judge and receive a warrant before any search they conduct can be considered lawful. Under what is known as the "exclusionary" rule, evidence obtained in unlawful searches is inadmissible in criminal trials. There are, however, exceptions to each of these rules. Under certain exigent circumstances, searches may commence without a warrant

---

[16]In Missouri the prosecution bears the title "prosecuting attorney," except in the city of St. Louis, where the title is "circuit attorney." In many other states the title is "district attorney" (thus the nickname "DA") or "state's attorney." In the federal system the title is "U.S. attorney." Jurisdictions of any consequence have staff attorneys, usually called assistant prosecuting attorneys or assistant DAs.
[17]See generally Lawrence Baum, *American Courts: Process and Policy* (Belmont, CA: Wadsworth, 1986).

(see, for instance, the general discussion of exigency in *Kentucky v. King* [2011]). There also is a "good-faith exception" to the exclusionary rule, which allows some evidence gathered with invalid search warrants to nonetheless be admitted as evidence in court (see, for example, *United States v. Leon* [1984]).

The amendment's original 1875 wording was changed in August 2014; note the addition of "electronic communications and data." These additional protections against warrantless seizure of electronic information enjoyed near unanimous support in the state Senate (31–1) and overwhelming support in the House (114–28). This issue was in part provoked by Edward Snowden's revelations in 2013 that the U.S. government was carrying on extensive global electronic surveillance programs. Other states also saw such efforts to protect electronic privacy. Concerns mounted about warrantless electronic surveillance, and more specifically about law enforcement agencies doing warrantless tracking of cell phone locations. But about a month before the August primary election when this measure was on the ballot in Missouri, the U.S. Supreme Court decided in *Riley v. California* (2014) that police could not search digital information on a cell phone if they seized the device from a person arrested without a warrant. Some commentators then suggested that the need this amendment was meant to address had been met by the Supreme Court's decision. The *St. Louis Post-Dispatch* opposed the amendment on the grounds that since the need was taken care of, the additional verbiage only cluttered the constitution, bloating it further and lengthening it unnecessarily. Other opponents believed that the wording might be construed to make it more difficult for law enforcement to track down perpetrators of cybercrimes. Supporters of the proposed amendment maintained that the Supreme Court decision did not go far enough and failed to protect information on laptops as well as cell phones. The amendment ultimately proved quite popular, earning 75 percent approval by the voting public. So protection from warrantless seizure of electronic data may be stronger against the state of Missouri than against the federal authorities; it will be up to the courts to straighten this out as they decide cases involving seizures of laptops and other electronic devices.

SECTION 16. **Grand juries—composition—jurisdiction to convene—powers.**—That a grand jury shall consist of twelve citizens, any nine of whom concurring may find an indictment or a true bill: Provided, that no grand jury shall be convened except upon an order of a judge of a court having the power to try and determine felonies; but when so assembled such grand jury shall have power to investigate and return indictments for all character and grades of crime; and that the power of grand juries to inquire into the willful misconduct in office of public officers, and to find indictments in connection therewith, shall never be suspended.

SECTION 17. **Indictments and informations in criminal cases—exceptions.**—That no person shall be prosecuted criminally for felony or misdemeanor otherwise than by indictment or information, which shall be concurrent remedies, but this shall not be applied to cases arising in the land or naval forces or in the militia when in actual service in time of war or public danger, nor to prevent arrests and preliminary examination in any criminal case.

A grand jury is a body of citizens convened to determine whether there is enough evidence to bring criminal charges against an individual accused of a crime. In Missouri, grand juries are empaneled from one county or sometimes multiple counties; in federal courts, they are empaneled at a regional level. The charges a grand jury brings against a suspect are called an "indictment." But in Missouri, and in about half of the other states, the formal criminal charge does not have to be an indictment issued by a grand jury. An alternative procedure called the "information" involves the prosecutor presenting evidence of probable cause to a judge and then, with judicial consent, filing the criminal charge. An information is equally as well used to lodge the criminal charge against the suspect (who thereby becomes the defendant). Section 17 shows the legal equivalency between indictment and information as procedures in the judicial process. Indictment and/or information only mean one is charged with a crime; further procedures are necessary to determine guilt and, ultimately, if guilty, sentencing.

Indictment by a grand jury is one of the few protections in the Bill of Rights that is not "incorporated." The U.S. Supreme Court decided the information procedure was in accord with "due process" in *Hurtado v. California* (1884); Hurtado had been convicted of murder and sentenced to death, but the charges were filed via an information. Hurtado maintained his entire trial was flawed by the failure to indict via grand jury, but the Supreme Court rejected his reasoning and conclusion. States can therefore use the information to file charges.

In Missouri, information is ordinarily used to bring the formal charges, but grand juries can be used at the prosecutor's discretion when they are more convenient. For instance, in the urban jurisdictions (Jackson County, St. Louis City, and St. Louis County), grand juries are kept empaneled and can be used to bring charges in cases of heinous crimes. Since neither the defendant's lawyer nor the defendant can appear before the grand jury, while the prosecutor is not just present before it but guides its deliberations, the prosecutor has the upper hand. In a sexual assault case, for instance, the prosecutor can take the victim step-by-step through the testimony identifying the attacker, without her (or his) having to confront the alleged offender; in a murder case, the survivors of the murdered person can testify without having to confront the alleged killer.

One recent high-profile example of the grand jury process is the role of a St. Louis County grand jury in the criminal investigation of Darren Wilson, the white Ferguson police officer who shot and killed Michael Brown, an unarmed 18-year-old black man, in August 2014. In November 2014, St. Louis County Prosecuting Attorney Robert McCulloch announced that a grand jury considered possible criminal charges but decided there was not enough evidence to indict Wilson, sparking a national debate about the use of grand juries in criminal cases involving law enforcement officers. The state of California recently banned the use of grand juries when police officers are involved in lethal altercations with civilians. The bill's legislative sponsor, Sen. Holly Mitchell (D-Los Angeles), cited "the refusal to indict as occurred in Ferguson" as the motivation for the law. Rather than using the grand jury to investigate the accusations against Wilson, McCulloch could easily have used an information to file charges against Wilson.

SECTION 18(a). Rights of accused in criminal prosecutions.—That in criminal prosecutions the accused shall have the right to appear and defend, in person and by counsel; to demand the nature and cause of the accusation; to meet the witnesses against him face to face; to have process to compel the attendance of witnesses in his behalf; and a speedy public trial by an impartial jury of the county.

Sections 16–18 of the Missouri Constitution provide the same protections found in the Fifth and Sixth Amendments to the U.S. Constitution. In both, an accused person cannot face trial unless presented with a formal indictment (or, at the state level, an information), has the right to face his or her accuser (except in grand jury proceedings, where the accused and his or her attorney are not present), has the right to be presented with a formal list of charges, and also has a right to receive a speedy trial. The U.S. Supreme Court and the Missouri Supreme Court have heard hundreds of cases regarding these protections for criminal defendants. Two U.S. Supreme Court cases that have had an enduring effect on state and federal criminal procedure are *Gideon v. Wainwright* (1963) and *Miranda v. Arizona* (1966). In *Gideon*, the Court ruled that states must provide access to legal counsel to a defendant. In *Miranda*, the Court held that the Fifth Amendment protection against self-incrimination requires law enforcement to warn an individual under investigation that he "has the right to remain silent, that any statement he does make may be used as evidence against him, and that he has a right to the presence of an attorney, either retained or appointed."

SECTION 18(b). Depositions in felony cases.—Upon a hearing and finding by the circuit court in any case wherein the accused is charged with a felony, that it is necessary to take the deposition of any witness within the state, other than defendant and spouse, in order to preserve the testimony, and on condition that the court make such orders as will fully protect the rights of personal confrontation and cross-examination of the witness by defendant, the state may take the deposition of such witness and either party may use the same at the trial, as in civil cases, provided there has been substantial compliance with such orders. The reasonable personal and traveling expenses of defendant and his counsel shall be paid by the state or county as provided by law.

SECTION 18(c). Notwithstanding the provisions of sections 17 and 18(a) of this article to the contrary, in prosecutions for crimes of a sexual nature involving a victim under eighteen years of age, relevant evidence of prior criminal acts, whether charged or uncharged, is admissible for the purpose of corroborating the victim's testimony or demonstrating the defendant's propensity to commit the crime with which he or she is presently charged. The court may exclude relevant evidence of prior criminal acts if the probative value of the evidence is substantially outweighed by the danger of unfair prejudice.

The evidence described in this amendment is evidence either missing or sealed in court records showing a defendant's propensity to commit sexual crimes victimizing minors. According to a Missouri Supreme Court ruling in 2007, if this particular sort of evidence has not been tested in open court previously, it cannot be introduced in a later criminal proceeding against the same defendant. (If such a crime is uncharged, meaning there has been neither indictment nor information, the evidence of the crime has never been "tested" in court.)

Prosecutors found this ruling an impediment because so many of their cases are handled by plea bargaining. With plea bargaining, frequently the most serious charges are dropped and the defendant is convicted upon plea (i.e., he or she pleads guilty, avoiding trial) to a lesser includable offense (a misdemeanor instead of a felony, or a lower class of either felony or misdemeanor) so that the actual circumstances of the offense are hidden in the file or only in the memory of the arresting officers.

When adopted in 2014, this amendment overruled the supreme court decision and permitted the introduction of the evidence, but under judicial supervision to avoid unfair prejudice toward the defendant. The amendment was proposed by overwhelming majorities in both chambers of the General Assembly (30–2 in the Senate, 131–26 in the House) and was passed with 72 percent approval by the electorate. The new wording brings Missouri into alignment with federal court rules and those of many other states as well.

> **SECTION 19. Self-incrimination and double jeopardy.**—That no person shall be compelled to testify against himself in a criminal cause, nor shall any person be put again in jeopardy of life or liberty for the same offense, after being once acquitted by a jury; but if the jury fail to render a verdict the court may, in its discretion, discharge the jury and commit or bail the prisoner for trial at the same or next term of court; and if judgment be arrested after a verdict of guilty on a defective indictment or information, or if judgment on a verdict of guilty be reversed for error in law, the prisoner may be tried anew on a proper indictment or information, or according to the law.

The Fifth Amendment to the U.S. Constitution and Section 19 of the Missouri Constitution both protect citizens from the peril of self-incrimination and double jeopardy. Many Americans are familiar with scenes of individuals called to testify in court or in front of legislative committees who "plead the Fifth," a phrase that comes from the Fifth Amendment's protection against self-incrimination. In effect, it is unconstitutional, on both state and federal levels, to force an individual accused of a crime to testify against himself or herself. In *State v. Lindsey*, 578 S.W.2d 903 (Mo. 1979), the Missouri Supreme Court ruled that Section 19 of the Missouri Constitution bars the prosecution from commenting about or otherwise suggesting that the defendant's lack of testimony is itself evidence of guilt.

Prohibition of double jeopardy protects citizens from being tried twice for the same crime after a verdict has been reached. The protection against double jeopardy, however, applies only to those cases where the facts and offenses remain the same, a point the Missouri Supreme Court made clear in *State v. Ross*, 523 S.W.2d 841 (1974) and *State v. Johnson*, 534 S.W.2d 19 (1976). More recently, though, the

U.S. Supreme Court has taken up cases concerning double jeopardy and its strict definition. In *Blueford v. Arkansas* (2011), the Supreme Court determined that a mistrial does not equate to a defendant's acquittal, and the accused can therefore stand trial again for the same crime in the case of a jury's failure to reach a verdict.

SECTION 20. **Bail guaranteed—exceptions.**—That all persons shall be bailable by sufficient sureties, except for capital offenses, when the proof is evident or the presumption great.
SECTION 21. **Excessive bail and fines—cruel and unusual punishment.**—That excessive bail shall not be required, nor excessive fines imposed, nor cruel and unusual punishment inflicted.

Similarly to the Eighth Amendment of the U.S. Constitution, the Missouri Constitution stipulates that no person will be held on excessive bail or be subjected to "cruel and unusual punishment." No strict limit has been set by the either the state or federal courts when it comes to defining excessive bail, but courts have reduced bail requirements in some instances (see *Ex parte Marvin Chandler,* 297 S.W.2d 616 [Mo. 1957]).

Perhaps the most salient issue involving "cruel and unusual punishment" is the imposition of the death penalty. Missouri is one of 31 states that allow death to be inflicted as a punishment for certain crimes. The U.S. Supreme Court has stopped short of saying that the death penalty violates the Eighth Amendment, but it has narrowed the range of persons eligible for the death penalty. In *Roper v. Simmons* (2005), the Supreme Court considered whether the state of Missouri could put to death an individual who committed a heinous murder at the age of 17. In this high-profile case originating in Fenton, Missouri, the Court held for the first time that it is a violation of the Eighth Amendment to impose the death penalty on a defendant who was under the age of 18 at the time of the alleged crime. The Court has also held that the Eighth Amendment prohibits the infliction of death on mentally handicapped individuals (*Atkins v. Virginia* [2002]) and individuals who commit heinous crimes other than murder, such as child rape (*Kennedy v. Louisiana* [2008]). At the state level, the Missouri Supreme Court held in *State v. Eckenfels,* 316 S.W.2d 532 (Mo. 1958), that the imposition of different sentences for different perpetrators of the same crime does not constitute cruel and unusual punishment.

SECTION 22(a). **Right of trial by jury—qualification of jurors—two-thirds verdict.**— That the right of trial by jury as heretofore enjoyed shall remain inviolate; provided that a jury for the trial of criminal and civil cases in courts not of record may consist of less than twelve citizens as may be prescribed by law, and a two-thirds majority of such number concurring may render a verdict in all civil cases; that in all civil cases in courts of record, three-fourths of the members of the jury concurring may render a verdict; and that in every criminal case any defendant may, with the assent of the court, waive a jury trial and submit the trial of such case to the court, whose finding shall have the force and effect of a verdict of a jury.

Both the Missouri Constitution and U.S. Constitution guarantee a trial by jury. According to Federal Rules of Civil Procedure, a federal jury must "begin with at least 6 and no more than 12 members." For cases tried under Missouri law, juries must consist of no fewer than 12 members. However, an individual accused of a crime may waive his or her right to a trial by jury. The trial then proceeds before the judge alone and is called a "bench trial." Although juries are available in both civil and criminal cases, in Missouri certain other courts and court proceedings exist where a trial by jury is neither appropriate nor required. For example, family law (cases involving dissolution of marriages, division of the assets of the married couple, and/or custody of children) is decided in bench trials. Historically, family law was in the hands of the Church (of England) rather than courts of the kingdom, and that tradition came to America, with civil courts substituting for the role of church courts. Similarly, cases involving going to court for a temporary court order or an "injunction" are handled exclusively by judges. The long litigations involving the desegregation of the St. Louis City/County school districts and of the Kansas City Metropolitan School District entailed court orders and were handled in federal district court by judges without jury involvement. Similarly, a "restraining order" or a "protective order" requiring individuals to leave someone alone and maintain a certain distance are court orders or injunctions; if the person under court order violates it, he or she can be immediately incarcerated for contempt of court.

> **SECTION 22(b). Female jurors—optional exemption.**—No citizen shall be disqualified from jury service because of sex, but the court shall excuse any woman who requests exemption therefrom before being sworn as a juror.

This section cannot be enforced constitutionally; it was thrown out by the U.S. Supreme Court in the case of *Duren v. Missouri*, 439 U.S. 357 (1979). In this case, a Kansas City man was convicted of first-degree murder after he shot a woman to death. Jackson County exempted women automatically from jury service, although it called women to participate in the venire for jury empanelment. From the 48 men and 5 women on the jury panel in Duren's case, only men were chosen for the trial jury. The Supreme Court ruled that the jury did not represent a fair cross-section of the state's population as required by the U.S. Constitution.

> **SECTION 23. Right to keep and bear arms, ammunition, and certain accessories—exception—rights to be unalienable.**—That the right of every citizen to keep and bear arms, ammunition, and accessories typical to the normal function of such arms, in defense of his home, person, family and property, or when lawfully summoned in aid of the civil power, shall not be questioned. The rights guaranteed by this section shall be unalienable. Any restriction on these rights shall be subject to strict scrutiny and the state of Missouri shall be obligated to uphold these rights and shall under no circumstances decline to protect against their infringement. Nothing in this section shall be construed to prevent the general assembly from enacting general laws which limit the rights of convicted violent felons or those adjudicated by a court to be a danger to self or others as result of a mental disorder or mental infirmity.

The Second Amendment to the U.S. Constitution provides: "A well regulated Militia, being necessary to the security of a free state, the right of the people to keep and bear Arms, shall not be infringed." In *McDonald v. Chicago* (2010), a sharply divided U.S. Supreme Court held that this provision protects an individual right to possess firearms and that states or localities therefore cannot enact regulatory schemes that effectively ban handgun possession by private citizens. This case "incorporated" the Second Amendment; it had not previously been among the liberties covered under the due process clause of the Fourteenth Amendment.

Section 23 of the Missouri Constitution protects the "right to keep and bear arms" in more detailed and explicit terms than the Second Amendment does, connecting it to the purpose of private home and personal defense. The new Section 23 wording (adopted in 2014) drops the turn of phrase previously included: "this shall not justify the wearing of concealed weapons."[18]

The addition of a new rationale for bearing arms (protection of "family" as well as "home, person, and property" and the incorporation of the words "unalienable" and "strict scrutiny") fortify gun rights in Missouri and make a show of symbolic power for gun rights groups as against groups favoring increased gun control. Democrats in the General Assembly opposed the amendment on the basis that its adoption would render more difficult the task of regulating guns and violent criminals. The Jewish Community Relations Council of St. Louis urged its defeat on the basis of public safety and argued that it would put more guns in the wrong hands. In the polarized politics of gun policy, the measure passed overwhelmingly in the House by a vote of 122–31 and in the Senate by 23–8. In the public balloting, the measure gained the support of 61 percent, with 39 percent opposed—less overwhelming than the margins in the General Assembly, but high enough that we can easily conclude that the legislators knew what their constituents wanted and were able to deliver it.

Difficulties arose later with the complex wording of this provision. The General Assembly is now clearly empowered to limit the gun rights of violent felons and the mentally disordered or infirm. But what about non-violent felons? Does the wording leave them with the right to bear weapons? Before passage of the expanded gun rights amendment, Missouri had a law on the books barring all felons from possessing firearms. In the case of non-violent felons, does the constitutional provision granting the unalienable right to bear weapons take priority over the earlier statute? At first a court challenge charged that the ballot summary was misleading, therefore the election was irregular and the election results ought to be thrown out. But the Missouri Supreme Court upheld the ballot summary.[19] Then as lower courts found that the amendment required strict scrutiny of efforts to take guns away from non-violent felons, they decided that non-violent felons could bear arms.

---

[18]For a detailed treatment of the history and politics that led to up to the adoption of Missouri's conceal and carry law, see William T. Horner, *Showdown in the Show-Me State: The Fight Over Conceal-and-Carry Gun Laws in Missouri* (Columbia, MO: University of Missouri Press, 2005).

[19]Alex Stuckey, "Gun Rights amendment upheld by Missouri Supreme Court," *St. Louis Post-Dispatch*, June 30, 2015.

Prosecutors began to fear that they would be unable to charge non-violent felons for having guns. Three cases involving non-violent felons possessing guns were taken to the state supreme court, and it ultimately found that since the amendment was silent on the topic of non-violent felons, the law forbidding them from having fire-arms was valid. So, in the end, the Missouri Supreme Court made the problem disappear, much to the gratitude of prosecutors and other elected authorities in the urban jurisdictions of Missouri where police and prosecutors try very hard to control gun violence.[20]

> **SECTION 24. Subordination of military to civil power—quartering soldiers.—**That the military shall be always in strict subordination to the civil power; that no soldier shall be quartered in any house without the consent of the owner in time of peace, nor in time of war, except as prescribed by law.

The president of the United States is the commander in chief of the Armed Forces, a title signifying his or her authority over the military. The Founders chose to make the civilian power of the president superior to the power of military leaders to guard against the abuse of military power. Article II, Section 2 of the U.S. Constitution stipulates that the "President shall be commander in chief of the Army and Navy of the United States," a provision similar to Section 24 of the Missouri Constitution's requirement that the "military shall be always in strict subordination to the civil power." To further clarify the relationship of civil and military power, Article IV, Section 6 of the Missouri Constitution makes the governor the "commander in chief" of the state militia.

A protection against quartering of troops—or the forceful housing of soldiers in private residences—is found in both Section 24 of the Missouri Constitution and the Third Amendment to the U.S. Constitution. These provisions are the legacy of the British government forcing American colonists to quarter troops during the Revolutionary Era. Although this provision is rarely the subject of litigation, the U.S. District Court for the District of Nevada found in *Mitchell v. City of Henderson* (2015) that the Third Amendment does not apply to home intrusion by municipal police officers, as they are not strictly soldiers.

> **SECTION 25. Elections and right of suffrage.—**That all elections shall be free and open; and no power, civil or military, shall at any time interfere to prevent the free exercise of the right of suffrage.

Although Section 25 of the Missouri Constitution requires that all elections be "free and open," it does not specify who may exercise the right of suffrage. In *Ellis v. Brown,* 33 S.W.2d 104 (1895), the supreme court of Missouri asserted that the right to suffrage is not a natural right but rather is conventional. The right to suffrage is created, regulated, and limited by the state. Presumably, this is not the case of inherent natural rights such as the right to life; a state does not create natural rights.

[20]Jennifer S. Mann, "Missouri Supreme Court says Amendment 5 did not extend gun rights to non-violent felons," *St. Louis Post-Dispatch*, February 9, 2016.

Article VIII of the Missouri Constitution lists the qualifications of voters in state-level elections. Missouri voters must be citizens of the United States, at least 18 years old, and residents of the state. There are two exceptions to these general qualifications: those deemed legally to suffer from a mental incapacity may not vote, and the legislature may by law deny the right of suffrage to individuals with felony convictions. Missouri Revised Statutes 115.133.1 provides three conditions under which a person may not vote in connection with a felony conviction: (1) while confined under a sentence of imprisonment; (2) while on probation or parole after conviction of a felony, until finally discharged from such probation or parole; or (3) after conviction of a felony or misdemeanor connected with the right of suffrage.

SECTION 26. **Compensation for property taken by eminent domain—condemnation juries—payment—railroad property.**—That private property shall not be taken or damaged for public use without just compensation. Such compensation shall be ascertained by a jury or board of commissioners of not less than three freeholders, in such manner as may be provided by law; and until the same shall be paid to the owner, or into court for the owner, the property shall not be disturbed or the proprietary rights of the owner therein divested. The fee of land taken for railroad purposes without consent of the owner thereof shall remain in such owner subject to the use for which it is taken.

SECTION 27. **Acquisition of excess property by eminent domain—disposition under restrictions.**—That in such manner and under such limitations as may be provided by law, the state, or any county or city may acquire by eminent domain such property, or rights in property, in excess of that actually to be occupied by the public improvement or used in connection therewith, as may be reasonably necessary to effectuate the purposes intended, and may be vested with the fee simple title thereto, or the control of the use thereof, and may sell such excess property with such restrictions as shall be appropriate to preserve the improvements made.

SECTION 28. **Limitation on taking of private property for private use—exceptions—public use a judicial question.**—That private property shall not be taken for private use with or without compensation, unless by consent of the owner, except for private ways of necessity, and except for drains and ditches across the lands of others for agricultural and sanitary purposes, in the manner prescribed by law; and that when an attempt is made to take private property for a use alleged to be public, the question whether the contemplated use be public shall be judicially determined without regard to any legislative declaration that the use is public.

Like the Fifth Amendment of the U.S. Constitution, Article I, Section 26 of the Missouri Constitution prevents the government from taking private property "for public use, without just compensation." The supreme court of Missouri has explained that the right to take private property for public use is a right inherent in every sovereign government (see *Coffman v. Crain*, 308 S.W.2d 451 [1958]). Eminent domain provisions that require "just compensation" are therefore intended to guard against the abuse of the government's inherent power of eminent domain.

In 2005 the U.S. Supreme Court interpreted the phrase "public use" in the Fifth Amendment to allow the taking of private property by states for private economic development (*Kelo v. City of New London*). At issue in *Kelo* was a plan to take private homes—including the home of Suzette Kelo—to sell to private developers in the hope of creating jobs and increasing tax revenues. In response, many states including Missouri passed state-level protections preventing the use of eminent domain for the purpose of economic development. Missouri Revised Statutes 523.271.1 stipulates: "No condemning authority shall acquire private property through the process of eminent domain for solely economic development purposes."

SECTION 29. Organized labor and collective bargaining.—That employees shall have the right to organize and to bargain collectively through representatives of their own choosing.

Although the U.S. Constitution does not mention organized labor, the Missouri Constitution guarantees employees in the state the right to organize as a labor union and bargain with their employers over employment terms and conditions. According to the Missouri Supreme Court, this right applies to both public and private employees (*Independence-National Education Association v. Independence School District*, 223 S.W.3d 131 [Mo. 2007]) and it requires employers to bargain with their employees' representatives (*Coalition of Police v. Chesterfield*, 386 S.W.3d 755 [Mo. 2012]). Additionally, this duty to bargain requires employers to bargain in good faith (*American Federation of Teachers v. Ledbetter*, 387 S.W.3d 360 [Mo. 2012]).

A current debate in Missouri politics involves a proposal to enact a right to work law that would prevent employers from requiring employees to join or pay dues to a labor union as a condition of employment as previously discussed at Section 9, p. 19.

SECTION 30. Treason—attainder—corruption of blood and forfeitures—estate of suicides—death by casualty.—That treason against the state can consist only in levying war against it, or in adhering to its enemies, giving them aid and comfort; that no person can be convicted of treason, unless on the testimony of two witnesses to the same overt act, or on his confession in open court; that no person can be attainted of treason or felony by the general assembly; that no conviction can work corruption of blood or forfeiture of estate; that the estates of such persons as may destroy their own lives shall descend or vest as in cases of natural death; and when any person shall be killed by casualty, there shall be no forfeiture by reason thereof.

This section is modeled on Article III, Section 3 of the U.S. Constitution, which limits the charge of treason to a few discrete circumstances and requires the testimony of two witnesses. In *Cramer v. United States* (1945), the U.S. Supreme Court held that "every act, movement, deed, and word of the defendant charged to constitute treason must be supported by the testimony of two witnesses." Treason prosecutions are therefore difficult and rare in U.S. history. The punishment for treason may not include "corruption of blood or forfeiture of estate." James Madison, writing in *Federalist* No. 43, explains that no punishment shall "extend . . . the consequences of guilt beyond the person of its author." Children, in other words, will not be punished for the treasonous actions of their parents.

SECTION 31. Fines or imprisonments fixed by administrative agencies.—That no law shall delegate to any commission, bureau, board or other administrative agency authority to make any rule fixing a fine or imprisonment as punishment for its violation.

Both the state and federal constitutions separate legislative, judicial, and executive power into distinct branches of government. However, it is common practice for legislative bodies to delegate legislative power to executive branch agencies. This is done when the legislature creates an agency that is empowered to write and enforce regulations. An example of this kind of agency at the federal level is the Environmental Protection Agency, which Congress created with the National Environmental Protection Act (1970). At the state level, many of the executive branch departments—such as the Department of Conservation and the Department of Social Services—exercise rule-making authority as well. The Missouri secretary of state's office makes available a rule making manual that describes the process by which agencies propose, adopt, and promulgate new regulations.[21]

However, Article I, Section 31 of the Missouri Constitution prevents the legislature from delegating its authority to set the punishment for violating a rule or regulation. Only the General Assembly, in other words, can decide that a fine should be levied or imprisonment set as a punishment for the violation of an administrative rule.

SECTION 32. Crime victims' rights.—1. Crime victims, as defined by law, shall have the following rights, as defined by law:

(1) The right to be present at all criminal justice proceedings at which the defendant has such right, including juvenile proceedings where the offense would have been a felony if committed by an adult;

(2) Upon request of the victim, the right to be informed of and heard at guilty pleas, bail hearings, sentencings, probation revocation hearings, and parole hearings, unless in the determination of the court the interests of justice require otherwise;

(3) The right to be informed of trials and preliminary hearings;

(4) The right to restitution, which shall be enforceable in the same manner as any other civil cause of action, or as otherwise provided by law;

(5) The right to the speedy disposition and appellate review of their cases, provided that nothing in this subdivision shall prevent the defendant from having sufficient time to prepare his defense;

(6) The right to reasonable protection from the defendant or any person acting on behalf of the defendant;

(7) The right to information concerning the escape of an accused from custody or confinement, the defendant's release and scheduling of the defendant's release from incarceration; and

---

[21]See www.sos.mo.gov/adrules/manual/manual.asp.

(8) The right to information about how the criminal justice system works, the rights and the availability of services, and upon request of the victim the right to information about the crime.

2. Notwithstanding section 20 of article I of this Constitution, upon a showing that the defendant poses a danger to a crime victim, the community, or any other person, the court may deny bail or may impose special conditions which the defendant and surety must guarantee.

3. Nothing in this section shall be construed as creating a cause of action for money damages against the state, a county, a municipality, or any of the agencies, instrumentalities, or employees provided that the General Assembly may, by statutory enactment, reverse, modify, or supercede any judicial decision or rule arising from any cause of action brought pursuant to this section.

4. Nothing in this section shall be construed to authorize a court to set aside or to void a finding of guilt, or an acceptance of a plea of guilty in any criminal case.

5. The general assembly shall have power to enforce this section by appropriate legislation.

Added to the constitution in 1992, the Missouri Crime Victims' Rights was adopted as part of a broader national movement to protect the victims of violent crime. According to the National Center for Victims of Violent Crime, 32 different states have amended their state constitutions to list the rights of crime victims. A similar federal provision exists in 18 U.S. Code sec. 3771.

Section 33. Marriage, validity and recognition.—That to be valid and recognized in this state, a marriage shall exist only between a man and a woman.

In his 2004 State of the Union address, President George W. Bush urged the country to "defend the sanctity of marriage" as the union of one man and one woman. That same year the state of Missouri amended its constitution to stipulate that "marriage shall exist only between a man and a woman." Just over a decade later, in the summer of 2015, the U.S. Supreme Court ruled in *Obergefell v. Hodges* that it is a violation of the Fourteenth Amendment's due process and equal protection clauses for a state to define marriage exclusively as the union of a man and a woman. So Section 33 of the Missouri Constitution is unconstitutional, null, void, and therefore unenforceable. The decision in *Obergefell* eclipses the Missouri constitutional provision, and same-sex couples in Missouri are now able to legally wed despite this provision in the Missouri Constitution.

Section 34. English to be the official language in this state.—That English shall be the language of all official proceedings in this state. Official proceedings shall be limited to any meeting of a public governmental body at which any public business is discussed, decided, or public policy formulated, whether such meeting is conducted in person or by means of communication equipment, including, but not limited to, conference call, video conference, Internet chat, or Internet message board. The term "official proceeding" shall not include an informal gathering of members of a public governmental body for ministerial or social purposes, but the term shall include a public vote of all or a majority of the members of a public governmental body, by electronic communication or any other means, conducted in lieu of holding an official proceeding with the members of the public governmental body gathered at one location in order to conduct public business.

This amendment established English as the state's official language on November 4, 2008. It reflects "status" or "symbolic" politics, whereby an influential group that feels insecure (in this case, those who believe that U.S.-born Americans are losing ground to immigrants) uses law to show its power by forcing another group (in this case, those whose heritage features a different language) to conform to the culture of the group, thereby symbolically elevating that culture. Supporters of the English-only movement argue that it seeks to use language as a unifying factor, making our nation stronger by ensuring that all can communicate with one another clearly. However, some supporters of "English only" have publicly made disparaging remarks about ethnic minorities, leading some opponents of the movement to call its supporters "linguistic fascists." It's an emotional issue, as most status issues in politics tend to be, and it has been used as a "wedge" issue. Missourians approved the measure with 86.3 percent yeas and 13.7 percent nays; the General Assembly was certainly tuned in to the people's consensual opinion when it put this proposed amendment on the ballot.

Interestingly, Missouri was originally a part of La Nouvelle France, and therefore part of French territory up through 1763, when the French lost the Seven Years' War (also known as the French and Indian War). Spain then took possession of the land that became, in 1803, the Louisiana Purchase. The Spanish, however, did not impose their language on the French-speaking settlers, and French continued as the lingua franca during the Spanish interregnum. The territory was returned to France in 1800.[22] President Thomas Jefferson then purchased the territory in 1803 at a bargain price. There were many Francophones, probably a majority, in the population of the newly added territory. The purchase added the cities of New Orleans and St. Louis to the Union, both of which were largely French-speaking. When Louisiana sought admission as a state, Congress set as a precondition of statehood that it adopt English as its official language.[23] But a heavy French influence remains in both Louisiana and, to a lesser extent, Missouri to this day, and some Spanish influence is also evident. One sees this in street names, place names, and names of early prominent settlers.[24]

---

[22]The Treaty of San Ildefonso accomplished this exchange, but it was a secret treaty because Napoleon wanted to work out a different deal on the European continent. The secret exchange was publicly reaffirmed in the Treaty of Aranjuez in 1801, by which Spain and France publicly acknowledged that the Spanish were ceding Louisiana to France.

[23]In 1847, Louisiana changed its law to allow instruction in both English and French. But after the Civil War French was once again suppressed. Louisiana currently has no law establishing an official state language.

[24]For background, see generally François Furstenberg, *When the United States Spoke French* (New York: The Penguin Press, 2014).

SECTION 35. **Right to farm.**—That agriculture which provides food, energy, health benefits, and security is the foundation and stabilizing force of Missouri's economy. To protect this vital sector of Missouri's economy the right of farmers and ranchers to engage in farming and ranching practices shall be forever guaranteed in this state, subject to duly authorized powers, if any, conferred by article VI of the Constitution of Missouri.

The right to farm was already protected by legislation at the time this constitutional amendment was passed in 2014. It serves to protect farmers against nuisance suits for agricultural practices that bother neighbors such as noise from work in the fields, flies, odors, dust, and so on. Putting the guarantee in the constitution enshrines it more securely, renders it more sacrosanct, and, in terms of symbolic politics, shows the relative power of the agricultural community in Missouri.

This amendment owes its adoption in part to the problem of "puppy mills": Missouri's weak state regulation of dog breeders led to scandalous and cruel conditions and criticisms from the Humane Society of the United States. In 2010 an initiative petition for a law to regulate dog breeders got the requisite number of signatures (5 percent of voters in two-thirds of the state's congressional districts) and was placed on the ballot for the general election in November 2010. It passed with 51.6 percent approval, but immediately afterward lawmakers announced plans for repealing the measure in the next session (2011) of the General Assembly. Legislators disagreed with the new law and expressed great resentment over the national Humane Society's support for the measure; the Humane Society was disdained as an "outside [out-of-state] interest group." Repeal passed the Senate 20–14 and the House 85–71 and headed for the governor's office.

At this point, the governor suggested a compromise between the provisions of the repeal bill and the demands of supporters of the 2010 initiative drive; this pact would keep some parts of the initiative but modify others. The General Assembly adopted the compromise and the governor signed it into law later that year.[25]

Now the fight for the right to farm amendment began in earnest. Resentment of the Humane Society's interference with state government had built up so that supporters of the right to farm amendment used the issue of "out-of-state troublemakers" to counteragitate and advocate support for the proposed amendment. In May 2013 the House approved the amendment by a vote of 132–25, and the Senate approved it 27–7. The Missouri Farm Bureau, a very powerful interest group in the state, backed the amendment, presenting as arguments in its favor the importance of protecting farmers and ranchers from out-of-state interests and the value in protecting the food supply. The importance of helping rural people whose proportion of

[25]In the next legislative session (2012), the Humane Society backed a new constitutional amendment whereby repeal or amendment of a citizen initiative by the General Assembly could only take place with a three-fourths vote of each chamber, or by popular vote. The General Assembly also could repeal if a statute proposed via initiative contained wording granting the General Assembly the power to repeal the law by a majority vote of both chambers. This was an attempt on the part of the Humane Society to show the recalcitrant legislators of the Missouri General Assembly who was boss, and it continued the symbolic dispute that started with the initiative petition of 2010.

the general population had diminished so that most citizens no longer understood rural mores and culture very well was a part of this appeal. In contrast, opponents pointed out that some supporters of right to farm were out of state and even foreign (Smithfield Foods, for example, was now Chinese-owned), and that the state was already failing to protect family farmers. Another argument against the amendment was that it could end up being interpreted as protecting concentrated animal feeding operations (CAFOs), which typically keep pigs crated in cruel conditions and produce overpowering and noxious odors from their excrement. People also expressed worry that the amendment might end up protecting agribusiness from having to label genetically modified organisms (GMOs). Most state newspapers took editorial stands against the measure. Right to farm passed, but barely, garnering 50.12 percent of the votes. The balloting was so close that a recount was held, and the results were upheld. The practical meaning of the amendment, like many recent amendments to the state constitution, will ultimately be worked out by the courts.

ARTICLE II
THE DISTRIBUTION OF POWERS

SECTION 1. **Three departments of government—separation of powers.**—The powers of government shall be divided into three distinct departments—the legislative, executive and judicial—each of which shall be confided to a separate magistracy, and no person, or collection of persons, charged with the exercise of powers properly belonging to one of those departments, shall exercise any power properly belonging to either of the others, except in the instances in this constitution expressly directed or permitted.

Several modern political theorists, such as the French lawyer Charles-Louis de Secondat, Baron La Brède et de Montesquieu (1689–1755) and the English philosopher John Locke (1632–1704), argued that political power ought to be divided into distinct departments as a protection against the abuse of concentrated power. The American Founders argued at length about the most prudent way to separate power in political institutions, and the U.S. Constitution creates a system of "checks and balances" among separate legislative, executive, and judicial departments of government. Similarly, the Missouri Constitution divides the power of government into three distinct departments and provides checks and balances among them.

But on their first tries at self-government, the Founders actually gave only lip service to the notions of separation of powers and checks and balances. Their distrust of executive power was so strong, so inflamed by adverse experiences with British-appointed governors and by their loathing and blaming of King George III, that they initially did not grant the executive branch much power at all. They established no separate executive branch for the government under the Articles of Confederation—only a president who was a presiding officer in the relatively powerless Congress.

After the United States declared independence from Britain, the former colonies designed new state governments that did not rely on the stamp of royal authority. Between 1776 and 1780, the 11 states needing to get rid of remnants of monarchy rewrote their governing documents.[26]

Most states designed constitutions whose underlying principle was legislative supremacy. Governors were weak, usually elected by the legislature to short terms (one or two years); this arrangement made the governors puppets of their legislatures. Moreover, most governors' vetoes could be overridden with a simple majority vote in the legislatures. The appointive power, if not lodged in the legislative branch itself, was denied the governor. One could say, then, that the framers of the early state constitutions honored the tenet of separation of powers in the breach rather than in the observance: the legislative branch with its extensive powers was separated from the other branches, while the executive branch was shut out of power.

Forty years later, corruption in the all-powerful legislatures was common, and various state legislatures passed laws that violated the obligation of contracts. For instance, in 1795, the Georgia legislature, with many of its members receiving "pay for play" bribes, gave land grants along the Yazoo River to certain land companies. The next session of the legislature rescinded the grants, but in the meantime some of the land had been purchased by innocent third parties. Litigation over which parties held clear title to the land came to a head in the Supreme Court in the Yazoo land fraud case (*Fletcher v. Peck* [1810]). The justices decided that the state could not backtrack from its original land grant, because doing so would impair the obligation of contracts. The original land grant was a contract between the state and the grantees that could not be reversed. Many other states committed these violations. These adverse outcomes forced a general rethinking that culminated in a strengthening of the state executives and the imposition of limitations on legislative power. It was in this era that Missouri's first constitution was written, and this general balanced division of power remains a feature of the Missouri Constitution.

ARTICLE III
LEGISLATIVE DEPARTMENT

SECTION 1. **Legislative power—general assembly.**—The legislative power shall be vested in a senate and house of representatives to be styled "The General Assembly of the State of Missouri."

One important difference between the constitutions of state governments and that of the federal government is that states exercise general legislative power, whereas

[26]Only Rhode Island and Connecticut, whose governing documents were compacts (mutual contracts for self-government) rather than royal grants of authority, did not have to change to a new constitution.

the federal government exercises only limited, enumerated powers. Article III, Section 1 of the Missouri Constitution simply states, "the legislative power shall be vested in a senate and house of representatives." Compare this to the language in Article I of the U.S. Constitution: "All legislative Powers herein granted shall be vested in a Congress of the United States, which shall consist of a Senate and House of Representatives." There is a subtle difference: although the Missouri Constitution vests *the* legislative power in the General Assembly, the U.S. Constitution vests only legislative powers *herein granted*. This reflects the theory that state governments exercise general legislative powers while the federal government exercises only powers delegated to the legislature by the U.S. Constitution.

SECTION 2. Election of representatives—apportionment commission, appointment, duties, compensation.—The house of representatives shall consist of one hundred sixty-three members elected at each general election and apportioned in the following manner: Within sixty days after the population of this state is reported to the President for each decennial census of the United States and, in the event that a reapportionment has been invalidated by a court of competent jurisdiction, within sixty days after notification by the governor that such a ruling has been made, the congressional district committee of each of the two parties casting the highest vote for governor at the last preceding election shall meet and the members of the committee shall nominate, by a majority vote of the members of the committee present, provided that a majority of the elected members is present, two members of their party, residents in that district, as nominees for reapportionment commissioners. Neither party shall select more than one nominee from any one state legislative district. The congressional committees shall each submit to the governor their list of elected nominees. Within thirty days the governor shall appoint a commission consisting of one name from each list to reapportion the state into one hundred and sixty-three representative districts and to establish the numbers and boundaries of said districts.

If any of the congressional committees fails to submit a list within such time the governor shall appoint a member of his own choice from that district and from the political party of the committee failing to make the appointment.

Members of the commission shall be disqualified from holding office as members of the general assembly for four years following the date of the filing by the commission of its final statement of apportionment.

For the purposes of this article, the term congressional district committee or congressional district refers to the congressional district committee or the congressional district from which a congressman was last elected, or, in the event members of congress from this state have been elected at large, the term congressional district committee refers to those persons who last served as the congressional district committee for those districts from which congressmen were last elected, and the term congressional district refers to those districts from which congressmen were last elected. Any action pursuant to this section by the congressional district committee shall take place only at duly called meetings, shall be recorded in their official minutes and only members present in person shall be permitted to vote.

The commissioners so selected shall on the fifteenth day, excluding Sundays and holidays, after all members have been selected, meet in the capitol building and proceed to organize by electing from their number a chairman, vice chairman and secretary and shall adopt an agenda establishing at least three hearing dates on which hearings open to the public shall be held. A copy of the agenda shall be filed with the clerk of the house of representatives within twenty-four hours after its adoption. Executive meetings may be scheduled and held as often as the commission deems advisable.

The commission shall reapportion the representatives by dividing the population of the state by the number one hundred sixty-three and shall establish each district so that the population of that district shall, as nearly as possible, equal that figure.

Each district shall be composed of contiguous territory as compact as may be.

Not later than five months after the appointment of the commission, the commission shall file with the secretary of state a tentative plan of apportionment and map of the proposed districts and during the ensuing fifteen days shall hold such public hearings as may be necessary to hear objections or testimony of interested persons.

Not later than six months after the appointment of the commission, the commission shall file with the secretary of state a final statement of the numbers and the boundaries of the districts together with a map of the districts, and no statement shall be valid unless approved by at least seven-tenths of the members.

After the statement is filed members of the house of representatives shall be elected according to such districts until a reapportionment is made as herein provided, except that if the statement is not filed within six months of the time fixed for the appointment of the commission, it shall stand discharged and the house of representatives shall be apportioned by a commission of six members appointed from among the judges of the appellate courts of the state of Missouri by the state supreme court, a majority of whom shall sign and file its apportionment plan and map with the secretary of state within ninety days of the date of the discharge of the apportionment commission. Thereafter members of the house of representatives shall be elected according to such districts until a reapportionment is made as herein provided.

Each member of the commission shall receive as compensation fifteen dollars a day for each day the commission is in session but not more than one thousand dollars, and, in addition, shall be reimbursed for his actual and necessary expenses incurred while serving as a member of the commission.

No reapportionment shall be subject to the referendum.

This provision relates to apportionment of representation in the lower chamber of the Missouri General Assembly, the House of Representatives. Before its adoption, the House was apportioned so that each county had at least one legislator, no matter how small its population. The census of 1900 showed that Missouri was a farm state, with the bulk of the population living in rural areas, so the House was fairly reflective of the state's population in the early 1900s. But despite census results of 1910, 1920, 1930, 1940, and 1950 showing increasing urbanization, the House refused to reapportion itself to give more representation to areas where the population had grown. Self-interest prevailed; rural state representatives would be voting themselves out of a job if they voted to shrink the number of rural legislators. In the 1960s the St. Louis and Kansas City metropolitan areas had about half the population of the state but held only 42 seats in the 163 member House—only 27.5 percent of that chamber's membership. Furthermore, 20 percent of the state's population could elect a majority of members of the lower chamber.[27] On the basis of population, the House was malapportioned.

Such disproportions were the subject of several U.S. Supreme Court decisions in the early 1960s. In the case of *Baker v. Carr* (1962), the Supreme Court ruled that cases involving reapportionment could be brought as lawsuits for judicial resolution because being underrepresented in state legislatures violated equal protection of the laws as guaranteed under the Fourteenth Amendment to the U.S. Constitution.[28] Giving one citizen's vote greater weight than another's was judged to be unequal protection of the laws, and therefore unacceptable. After this doctrinal change, the federal courts could and did consider malapportionment cases from the states and soon ruled in *Reynolds v. Sims* (1964) that all state legislative chambers (both upper and lower) had to be based on population alone, rather than representing geographic divisions such as counties or regions of states. This ruling enshrined the "one man, one vote" doctrine for redistricting (reapportionment) of state legislatures. Missouri had reallocated representation in its Senate (with 34 members) with the adoption of the 1945 Constitution, so representation in the Missouri Senate was fairly well apportioned. In the lower chamber, however, the underrepresentation of the metro areas and the possible majority of a small minority were readily seen as violations of the new doctrine.

In late December 1964 and early January 1965 the federal courts threw out Missouri's districting for seats in the U.S. Congress,[29] the state Senate,[30] and the state House of Representative—a clean sweep of all legislative districted offices at the federal and state levels. Shortly afterward, at the beginning of the legislative session in January 1965, Governor Warren Hearnes recommended a bipartisan commission for House reapportionment similar to the commission in use since 1945 for the state Senate. But House members opposed the commission idea, as they wanted to reapportion themselves, and they passed a reapportionment bill. Hearnes eventually signed the bill despite constitutional misgivings about population variances from equality. His qualms were based on the concern that if the state did nothing to remediate the apportionment problem, the courts might order all members of the state House of Representatives to run state-wide, meaning that every voter would get to (or have to) cast votes for all candidates of the state House, all candidates would have to campaign statewide, ballots (which were then primarily paper) would be the size of Sunday newspapers, and countless incumbents might lose their offices in the turmoil. With these possibilities dogging the General Assembly,

[27]Herbert A. Trask, "The Plan for Redistricting," *St. Louis Post-Dispatch*, August 1, 1965.

[28]Previous cases involving malapportionment had been brought under a different clause of the U.S. Constitution, which put court action out of reach, leaving the situation in the hands of only the legislative branch. But most state legislatures did not want to deal with this problem.

[29]The court's objection here was to the excessive variation in population spread among the 10 congressional districts.

[30]The court had the same objection about excessive population variation as above (in reference to the congressional seats).

Hearnes was able to convince it to apply the bipartisan commission plan for the Senate to the House in the future. Resultantly, the commission scheme was proposed as a constitutional amendment, to be voted on in the August election of 1965.[31]

But the voters rejected the amendment in the August election, with only 41.1 percent approval. So Hearnes called the legislature into special session and it passed a somewhat different commission proposal,[32] which was put up for a special election in January 1966. This time the amendment did pass, scraping by with 51.9 percent approval.

This provision was fine-tuned via constitutional amendment in 1982 with some subtraction and addition of wording. Originally, in 1966, if the redistricting commission failed to reach agreement, the default decision on redistricting was to be made by commissioners of the supreme court, but in 1976 the constitution was amended to phase out the commissioners. Soon there would be no such officers to backstop the redistricting commission. Thus the new wording set up a commission of six appellate judges appointed by the state supreme court as the default decision makers to replace the soon-to-be extinct class of officeholders.

SECTION 3. (Repealed November 2, 1982, L. 1982 SJR 39, § 1 2nd Reg. Sess.)

SECTION 4. Qualifications of representatives.—Each representative shall be twenty-four years of age, and next before the day of his election shall have been a qualified voter for two years and a resident of the county or district which he is chosen to represent for one year, if such county or district shall have been so long established, and if not, then of the county or district from which the same shall have been taken.

SECTION 5. Senators—number—senatorial districts.—The Senate shall consist of thirty-four members elected by the qualified voters of the respective districts for four years. For the election of senators, the state shall be divided into convenient districts of contiguous territory, as compact and nearly equal in population as may be.

SECTION 6. Qualifications of senators.—Each senator shall be thirty years of age, and next before the day of his election shall have been a qualified voter of the state for three years and a resident of the district which he is chosen to represent for one year, if such district shall have been so long established, and if not, then of the district or districts from which the same shall have been taken.

SECTION 7. Senatorial apportionment commission—number, appointment, duties, compensation.—Within sixty days after the population of this state is reported to the President for each decennial census of the United States, and within sixty days after notification by the governor that a reapportionment has been invalidated by a court of competent jurisdiction, the state committee of each of the two political parties casting the highest vote for governor at the last preceding election shall, at a committee meeting duly called, select by a vote of the individual committee members, and thereafter submit to the governor a list of ten persons, and within thirty days thereafter the governor shall

---

[31]The amendment called for a slight increase in the number of House seats, from 163 to 168; no polling data exist to tell whether or not this facet of the proposal was the factor that made it unacceptable to the public.

[32]The new amendment eliminated the wording that increased the number of House seats to 168.

appoint a commission of ten members, five from each list, to reapportion the thirty-four senatorial districts and to establish the numbers and boundaries of said districts.

If either of the party committees fails to submit a list within such time the governor shall appoint five members of his own choice from the party of the committee so failing to act.

Members of the commission shall be disqualified from holding office as members of the general assembly for four years following the date of the filing by the commission of its final statement of apportionment.

The commissioners so selected shall on the fifteenth day, excluding Sundays and holidays, after all members have been selected, meet in the capitol building and proceed to organize by electing from their number a chairman, vice chairman and secretary and shall adopt an agenda establishing at least three hearing dates on which hearings open to the public shall be held. A copy of the agenda shall be filed with the secretary of the senate within twenty-four hours after its adoption. Executive meetings may be scheduled and held as often as the commission deems advisable.

The commission shall reapportion the senatorial districts by dividing the population of the state by the number thirty-four and shall establish each district so that the population of that district shall, as nearly as possible, equal that figure; no county lines shall be crossed except when necessary to add sufficient population to a multi-district county or city to complete only one district which lies partly within such multi-district county or city so as to be as nearly equal as practicable in population. Any county with a population in excess of the quotient obtained by dividing the population of the state by the number thirty-four is hereby declared to be a multi-district county.

Not later than five months after the appointment of the commission, the commission shall file with the secretary of state a tentative plan of apportionment and map of the proposed districts and during the ensuing fifteen days shall hold such public hearings as may be necessary to hear objections or testimony of interested persons.

Not later than six months after the appointment of the commission, the commission shall file with the secretary of state a final statement of the numbers and the boundaries of the districts together with a map of the districts, and no statement shall be valid unless approved by at least seven members.

After the statement is filed senators shall be elected according to such districts until a reapportionment is made as herein provided, except that if the statement is not filed within six months of the time fixed for the appointment of the commission, it shall stand discharged and the senate shall be apportioned by a commission of six members appointed from among the judges of the appellate courts of the state of Missouri by the state supreme court, a majority of whom shall sign and file its apportionment plan and map with the secretary of state within ninety days of the date of the discharge of the apportionment commission. Thereafter senators shall be elected according to such districts until a reapportionment is made as herein provided.

Each member of the commission shall receive as compensation fifteen dollars a day for each day the commission is in session, but not more than one thousand dollars, and, in addition, shall be reimbursed for his actual and necessary expenses incurred while serving as a member of the commission.

No reapportionment shall be subject to the referendum.

We should note that Missouri pioneered the notion of a redistricting commission for redistricting the upper chamber; this was one of the innovations of the

Constitutional Convention of 1942, which produced the Constitution of 1945. As noted above, the original wording of the constitution of 1945 specified that commissioners of the supreme court would be the default decision makers if the redistricting commission failed to meet its deadlines. Since another amendment to the constitution later phased out the commissioners of the supreme court, this amendment had to be fixed to enable some officers whose offices still existed to act as the default decision makers. The arrangement provides that the supreme court should choose six judges of the lower appellate courts (the Missouri Court of Appeals). As a result of the decision in *Reynolds v. Sims* (1964), both the Missouri House and Senate are now apportioned by population. Missouri's congressional districts are also apportioned by population (under the authority of *Wesberry v. Sanders* [1964]). However, the U.S. Senate remains apportioned by geography, with each state maintaining equal representation (two senators each) in the Senate.

> SECTION 8. **Term limitations for members of General Assembly.**—No one shall be elected to serve more than eight years total in any one house of the General Assembly nor more than sixteen years total in both houses of the General Assembly. In applying this section, service in the General Assembly resulting from an election prior to December 3, 1992, or service of less than one year, in the case of a member of the house of representatives, or two years, in the case of a member of the senate, by a person elected after the effective date of this section to complete the term of another person, shall not be counted.

Passed in November of 1992, Article III, Section 8 outlines specific term limits for the Missouri legislature. According to the provision, no person can serve more than eight years in any one house of the General Assembly. The U.S. Constitution, by contrast, does not limit the number of terms individuals may serve in the House of Representatives or Senate. (See below at Article VIII, Section 16 for Missouri's failed state-level attempt to limit the terms of federal officeholders.)

Political theorists have viewed term limits as a check on corruption. Beyond avoiding corruption in office, term limits are also beneficial for democracy because they spread access to political office to more people; rendering officeholders ineligible to succeed themselves makes it easier for new blood to flow into governmental positions.

Term limits for federal congressional representatives became part of the Republican Party platform in the 1994 congressional elections (the famous "Contract with America"). However, after the decision in *U.S. Term Limits, Inc. v. Thornton*, 514 U.S. 779 (1995), in which the Supreme Court ruled that federal term limits could not be adopted by statute but rather only by constitutional amendment, an effort to propose such a constitutional amendment failed by far to get the requisite two-thirds majority in the House of Representatives.

From 1900 through the late 1990s, incumbent legislators who chose to run for reelection almost always won; this epoch is regarded as the "era of incumbency." Congressional tenure in office came to rival tenure on the Supreme Court, where justices have a life appointment. Although term limits for federal legislators (representatives and senators) have not been implemented, the term limits movement spread quickly at the state level, especially in states having the constitutional initiative. Missouri amended its constitution to institute term limits through the initiative process. The Missouri Republican Party was particularly supportive of term limits because the majority in both chambers of the General Assembly was Democratic, and Democratic legislators enjoyed incumbency to such an extent that Republicans felt like a permanent minority. Adoption of term limits helped them gain more than two-thirds of the membership of both chambers, but it took 10 to 12 years before the then incumbent Democrats became ineligible to run again.

Other long-run effects are more detrimental: newly elected legislators can face a long learning curve and, in the meantime, other forces more knowledgeable due to their longer tenure can wield power over amateur legislators. These forces are twofold: (1) interest groups and lobbyists, who often have exceedingly long experience (but are biased toward certain viewpoints), and (2) state bureaucrats, who usually spend their entire careers in the same agency and who adopt an agency viewpoint in their interactions with legislators. In the era of incumbency, legislators were around so long that they had a better chance of becoming immunized against the lobbying efforts of pressure groups and administrators.

Moreover, the theoretical counterforce to corruption that term limits are supposed to provide can fade quickly as legislators catch on to easy means of self-aggrandizement; many scandals have broken out among Missouri legislators in this age of term limits. This may be due in part to weak or nonexistent ethics legislation. From 2008 (when the legislature repealed campaign contribution caps in elections for state offices) until November 2016 (when the voters adopted a constitutional amendment mandating campaign finance reform), Missouri was the only state in the Union with no limit on gifts from lobbyists to legislators, with only a minimal waiting period before retiring legislators may become lobbyists,[33] and with no limit on the amount of money that individuals and corporations can donate to candidates for office. Furthermore, there have been no transparency requirements on donations to office seekers.[34] So the institutionalization of term limits hasn't effectively countered the problem of corruption—at least not in Missouri. See Section 23 of Article VIII for the wording of the constitutional amendment adopted to remedy this deficiency.

SECTION 9, *omitted here, provided for the apportionment of the legislature in 1965–66.*

---

[33]The legislature has now (2016) passed a measure dictating a six-month waiting period before a legislator can become a lobbyist. Before 2016, no waiting period constrained retiring legislators from becoming lobbyists straightaway upon leaving the legislature. The new rule is an exceptionally mild constraint, but it is at least a limitation that would prevent a retiring legislator from lobbying activities in the first regular legislative session after his or her retirement. The governor signed the measure and it took effect in August 2016.

[34]Tony Messenger, "Municipal Elections Are an Ethics-Free Zone This Year," *St. Louis Post-Dispatch*, April 1, 2016.

Missouri Officeholders vs. Federal Officeholders

	MEMBERS (SIZE)	QUALIFICATIONS	TERM	COMPENSATION
Missouri House	163	• At least 24 years old • Qualified voter for two years • District resident for one year	• Two-year term • Restricted to four terms	$35,915/year + per diem
U.S. House	435	• At least 25 years old • U.S. citizen for seven years • Residence in state he/she represents	• Two-year term • No term limits	$174,000/year
Missouri Senate	34	• At least 30 years old • Qualified voter for three years • District resident for one year	• Four-year term • Restricted to two terms	$35,915/year + per diem
U.S. Senate	100	• At least 30 years old • U.S. citizen for nine years • Residence in state he/she represents	• Six-year term • No term limits	$174,000/year
Missouri Governor	1	• At least 30 years old • U.S. citizen for 15 years • MO resident for 10 years	• Four-year term • Restricted to two terms	$133,821/year
U.S. President	1	• At least 35 years old • Natural-born citizen • U.S. resident for 15 years	• Four-year term • Restricted to two terms	$400,000/year
Missouri Supreme Court	7	• 30–70 years old • Licensed to practice law in MO • Qualified voter for 15 years	• Mandatory retirement at age 70	$154,000/year (Chief) $148,000/year (Judge)
U.S. Supreme Court	9	N/A	• Lifetime appointment	$255,500/year (Chief) $244,400/year (Assoc.)

SECTION 10. Basis of apportionment—alteration of districts.—The last decennial census of the United States shall be used in apportioning representatives and determining the population of senatorial and representative districts. Such districts may be altered from time to time as public convenience may require.

SECTION 11, *omitted here, provided for the time and election of state senators and representatives in 1945.*

SECTION 12. Members of general assembly disqualified from holding other offices.—No person holding any lucrative office or employment under the United States, this state or any municipality thereof shall hold the office of senator or representative. When any senator or representative accepts any office or employment under the United States, this state or any municipality thereof, his office shall thereby be vacated and he shall thereafter perform no duty and receive no salary as senator or representative. During the term for which he was elected no senator or representative shall accept any appointive office or employment under this state which is created or the emoluments of which are increased during such term. This section shall not apply to members of the organized militia, of the reserve corps and of school boards, and notaries public.

SECTION 13. Vacation of office by removal of residence.—If any senator or representative remove his residence from the district or county for which he was elected, his office shall thereby be vacated.

SECTION 14. Writs of election to fill vacancies.—Writs of election to fill vacancies in either house of the general assembly shall be issued by the governor.

SECTION 15. Oath of office of members of assembly—administration—effect of refusal to take oath and conviction of violation.—Every senator or representative elect, before entering upon the duties of his office, shall take and subscribe the following oath or affirmation: "I do solemnly swear, or affirm, that I will support the Constitution of the United States and of the state of Missouri, and faithfully perform the duties of my office, and that I will not knowingly receive, directly or indirectly, any money or other valuable thing for the performance or nonperformance of any act or duty pertaining to my office, other than the compensation allowed by law." The oath shall be administered in the halls of the respective houses to the members thereof, by a judge of the supreme court or a circuit court, or after the organization by the presiding officer of either house, and shall be filed in the office of the secretary of state. Any senator or representative refusing to take said oath or affirmation shall be deemed to have vacated his office, and any member convicted of having violated his oath or affirmation shall be deemed guilty of perjury, and be forever disqualified from holding any office of trust or profit in this state.

Although the Missouri Constitution requires public officials to swear or affirm that they will not "knowingly receive, directly or indirectly, any money or other valuable thing" in exchange for legislative favors, the actual ethics regulations are determined by statute.[35]

SECTION 16. Compensation, mileage allowance and expenses of general assembly members.—Senators and representatives shall receive from the state treasury as salary

---

[35]For more information about Missouri's ethics laws, see the Missouri Ethics Commission's *Guide to Ethics Laws: A Plain English Summary* (2015).

such sums as are provided by law. No law fixing the compensation of members of the general assembly shall become effective until the first day of the regular session of the general assembly next following the session at which the law was enacted. Upon certification by the president and secretary of the senate and by the speaker and chief clerk of the house of representatives as to the respective members thereof, the state comptroller shall audit and the state treasurer shall pay such compensation without legislative enactment. Until otherwise provided by law senators and representatives shall receive one dollar for every ten miles traveled in going to and returning from their place of meeting while the legislature is in session, on the most usual route.

Until otherwise provided by law, each senator or representative shall be reimbursed from the state treasury for the actual and necessary expenses incurred by him in attending sessions of the general assembly in the sum of ten dollars ($10.00) per day for each day on which the journal of the senate or house respectively shows the presence of such senator or representative. Upon certification by the president and secretary of the senate and by the speaker and chief clerk of the house of representatives as to the respective members thereof, the state comptroller shall approve and the state treasurer shall pay monthly such expense allowance without legislative enactment.

SECTION 17. **Limitation on number of legislative employees.**—Until otherwise provided by law, the house of representatives shall not employ more than one hundred twenty-five and the senate shall not employ more than seventy-five employees elective, appointive or any other at any time during any session.

SECTION 18. **Appointment of officers of houses—jurisdiction to determine membership—power to make rules, punish for contempt and disorderly conduct and expel members.**—Each house shall appoint its own officers; shall be sole judge of the qualifications, election and returns of its own members; may determine the rules of its own proceedings, except as herein provided; may arrest and punish by fine not exceeding three hundred dollars, or imprisonment in a county jail not exceeding ten days, or both, any person not a member, who shall be guilty of disrespect to the house by any disorderly or contemptuous behavior in its presence during its sessions; may punish its members for disorderly conduct; and, with the concurrence of two-thirds of all members elect, may expel a member; but no member shall be expelled a second time for the same cause.

SECTION 19. **Legislative privileges.**—Senators and representatives shall, in all cases except treason, felony, or breach of the peace, be privileged from arrest during the session of the general assembly, and for the fifteen days next before the commencement and after the termination of each session; and they shall not be questioned for any speech or debate in either house in any other place.

SECTION 20. **Regular sessions of assembly—quorum—compulsory attendance—public sessions—limitation on power to adjourn.**—The general assembly shall meet on the first Wednesday after the first Monday in January following each general election. The general assembly may provide by law for the introduction of bills during the period between the first day of December and the first Wednesday after the first Monday of January.

The general assembly shall reconvene on the first Wednesday after the first Monday of January after adjournment at midnight on May thirtieth of the preceding year. A majority of the elected members of each house shall constitute a quorum to do business, but a smaller number may adjourn from day to day, and may compel the attendance of absent members in such manner and under such penalties as each house may provide. The sessions of each house shall be held with open doors, except in cases which may require secrecy but not including the final vote on bills, resolutions and confirmations. Neither house shall, without the consent of the other, adjourn for more than ten days at any one time, nor to any other place than that in which the two houses may be sitting.

SECTION 20(a). Automatic adjournment—tabling of bills, when.—The general assembly shall adjourn at midnight on May thirtieth until the first Wednesday after the first Monday of January of the following year, unless it has adjourned prior thereto. All bills in either house remaining on the calendar after 6:00 p.m. on the first Friday following the second Monday in May are tabled. The period between the first Friday following the second Monday in May and May thirtieth shall be devoted to the enrolling, engrossing, and the signing in open session by officers of the respective houses of bills passed prior to 6:00 p.m. on the first Friday following the second Monday in May.

The general assembly shall automatically stand adjourned sine die at 6:00 p.m. on the sixtieth calendar day after the date of its convening in special session unless it has adjourned sine die prior thereto.

SECTION 20(b). Special session, procedure to convene—limitations—automatic adjournment.—Upon the filing with the secretary of state of a petition stating the purpose for which the session is to be called and signed by three-fourths of the members of the senate and three-fourths of the members of the house of representatives, the president pro tem of the senate and the speaker of the house shall by joint proclamation convene the general assembly in special session. The proclamation shall state specifically each matter contained in the petition on which action is deemed necessary. No appropriation bill shall be considered in a special session convened pursuant to this section if in that year the general assembly has not passed the operating budget in compliance with Section 25 of this article.

The general assembly shall automatically stand adjourned sine die at 6:00 p.m. on the thirtieth calendar day after the date of its convening in special session under this section unless it has adjourned sine die prior thereto.

The regular session of the General Assembly starts in early January (the Wednesday after the first Monday) and ends on May 30. However, between the first Friday following the second Monday in May and May 30 "enrolling, engrossing, and signing" is the legislature's only activity; legislation has to pass on that first Friday or die. Both the governor and a supermajority (three-fourths) of each chamber in the legislature may call special legislative sessions at other times throughout the year. The Missouri Constitution outlines a specific date and time for the adjournment of its General Assembly when a special session is called: the "thirtieth calendar day after the date of its convening in special sessions" at 6:00 P.M. Under this rule, the Missouri legislature must finish its special session of work and adjourn "sine die" (without a day)—that is, without a definitive date set for a next meeting. See Article III, Section 32 below for details about the legislature's annual veto session.

Legislative Proceedings

SECTION 21. Style of laws—bills—limitation on amendments—power of each house to originate and amend bills—reading of bills.—The style of the laws of this state shall be: "Be it enacted by the General Assembly of the State of Missouri, as follows." No law shall be passed except by bill, and no bill shall be so amended in its passage through either house as to change its original purpose. Bills may originate in either house and may be amended or rejected by the other. Every bill shall be read by title on three different days in each house.

SECTION 22. Referral of bills to committees—recall of referred bills—records of committees—provision for interim meetings.—Every bill shall be referred to a committee of the house in which it is pending.

After it has been referred to a committee, one-third of the elected members of the respective houses shall have power to relieve a committee of further consideration of a bill and place it on the calendar for consideration. Each committee shall keep such record of its proceedings as is required by rule of the respective houses and this record and the recorded vote of the members of the committee shall be filed with all reports on bills.

Each house of the general assembly may provide by rule for such committees of that house as it deems necessary to meet to consider bills or to perform any other necessary legislative function during the interim between the session ending on the thirtieth day of May and the session commencing on the first Wednesday after the first Monday of January.

SECTION 23. Limitation of scope of bills—contents of titles—exceptions.—No bill shall contain more than one subject which shall be clearly expressed in its title, except bills enacted under the third exception in section 37 of this article and general appropriation bills, which may embrace the various subjects and accounts for which moneys are appropriated.

SECTION 24. Printing of bills and amendments.—No bill shall be considered for final passage in either house until it, with all amendments thereto, has been printed and copies distributed among the members. If a bill passed by either house be returned thereto, amended by the other, the house to which the same is returned shall cause the amendment or amendments so received to be printed and copies distributed among the members before final action on such amendments.

SECTION 25. Limitation on introduction of bills.—No bill other than an appropriation bill shall be introduced in either house after the sixtieth legislative day unless consented to by a majority of the elected members of each house or the governor shall request a consideration of the proposed legislation by a special message. No appropriation bill shall be taken up for consideration after 6:00 p.m. on the first Friday following the first Monday in May of each year.

SECTION 26. Legislative journals—demand for yeas and nays—manner and record of vote.—Each house shall publish a journal of its proceedings. The yeas and nays on any question shall be taken and entered on the journal on the motion of any five members. Whenever the yeas and nays are demanded, or required by this constitution, the whole list of members shall be called and the names of the members voting yea and nay and the absentees shall be entered in the journal.

SECTION 27. Concurrence in amendments—adoption of conference committee reports—final passage of bills.—No amendments to bills by one house shall be concurred in by the other, nor shall reports of committees of conference be adopted in either house, nor shall a bill be finally passed, unless a vote by yeas and nays be taken and a majority of the members elected to each house be recorded as voting favorably.

SECTION 28. Form of reviving, reenacting and amending bills.—No act shall be revived or reenacted unless it shall be set forth at length as if it were an original act. No act shall be amended by providing that words be stricken out or inserted, but the words to be stricken out, or the words to be inserted, or the words to be stricken out and those inserted in lieu thereof, together with the act or section amended, shall be set forth in full as amended.

SECTION 29. Effective date of laws—exceptions—procedure in emergencies and upon recess.—No law passed by the general assembly, except an appropriation act, shall take effect until ninety days after the adjournment of the session in either odd-numbered or even-numbered years at which it was enacted. However, in case of an emergency which must be expressed in the preamble or in the body of the act, the general assembly by a two-thirds vote of the members elected to each house, taken by yeas and nays may otherwise direct; and further except that, if the general assembly recesses for thirty days or more it may prescribe by joint resolution that laws previously passed and not effective shall take effect ninety days from the beginning of the recess.

SECTION 30. Signing of bills by presiding officers—procedure on objections—presentation of bills to governor.—No bill shall become a law until it is signed by the presiding officer of each house in open session, who first shall suspend all other business, declare that the bill shall now be read and that if no objection be made he will sign the same. If in either house any member shall object in writing to the signing of a bill, the objection shall be noted in the journal and annexed to the bill to be considered by the governor in connection therewith. When a bill has been signed, the secretary, or the chief clerk, of the house in which the bill originated shall present the bill in person to the governor on the same day on which it was signed and enter the fact upon the journal.

SECTION 31. Governor's duty as to bills and joint resolutions—time limitations—failure to return, bill becomes law.—Every bill which shall have passed the house of representatives and the senate shall be presented to and considered by the governor, and, within fifteen days after presentment, he shall return such bill to the house in which it originated endorsed with his approval or accompanied by his objections. If the bill be approved by the governor it shall become a law. When the general assembly adjourns, or recesses for a period of thirty days or more, the governor shall return within forty-five days any bill to the office of the secretary of state with his approval or reasons for disapproval. If any bill shall not be returned by the governor within the time limits prescribed by this section it shall become law in like manner as if the governor had signed it.

In a bicameral legislative system, bills must pass both the Senate (upper) chamber and the House (lower) chamber in the exact same wording before they are presented to the governor for his or her signature. With minor variations, Sections 21–31 of Missouri Constitution outline a process similar to that found in Article I, Section 7 of the U.S. Constitution.

SECTION 32. Vetoed bills reconsidered, when.—Every bill presented to the governor and returned with his objections shall stand as reconsidered in the house to which it is returned. If the governor returns any bill with his objections on or after the fifth day before the last day upon which a session of the general assembly may consider bills, the general assembly shall automatically reconvene on the first Wednesday following the second Monday in September for a period not to exceed ten calendar days for the sole purpose of considering bills returned by the governor. The objections of the governor shall be entered upon the journal and the house shall proceed to consider the question pending, which shall be in this form: "Shall the bill pass, the objections of the governor thereto notwithstanding?" The vote upon this question shall be taken by yeas and nays and if two-thirds of the elected members of the house vote in the affirmative the presiding officer of that house shall certify that fact on the roll, attesting the same by his signature, and send the bill with the objections of the governor to the other house, in which like proceedings shall be had in relation thereto. The bill thus certified shall be deposited in the office of the secretary of state as an authentic act and shall become a law.

Last amended in 1988, Article III, Section 32 details how and when the Missouri legislature can override a veto by the governor. Every September the Missouri General Assembly gathers to conduct an annual veto session in which the General Assembly decides whether or not to override the governor's various vetoes of legislation. During the veto session—which may last no more than 10 calendar days—each house considers bills that have been returned to it by the governor. A two-thirds vote by the elected members of each chamber is required to override the gubernatorial veto.

SECTION 33. (Repealed August 5, 1986, L. 1986 HCS HJR 4 and 20, Sec. 1, 1st Reg. Sess.)

SECTION 34. Revision of general statutes—limitation on compensation.—In the year 1949 and at least every ten years thereafter all general statute laws shall be revised, digested and promulgated as provided by law.

No senator or representative shall receive any compensation in addition to his salary as a member of the general assembly for any services rendered in connection with said revision.

SECTION 35. Committee on legislative research.—There shall be a permanent joint committee on legislative research, selected by and from the members of each house as provided by law. The general assembly, by a majority vote of the elected members, may discharge any or all of the members of the committee at any time and select their successors. The committee may employ a staff as provided by law. The committee shall meet when necessary to perform the duties, advisory to the general assembly, assigned to it by law. The members of the committee shall receive no compensation in addition to their salary as members of the general assembly, but may receive their necessary expenses while attending the meetings of the committee.

Limitation of Legislative Power

In the U.S. Constitution, specific legislative powers are delegated in Article I, Section 8. The Missouri Constitution, like other state constitutions, vests general legislative power in the state legislature. The first constitutions in the original 13 states called for legislative supremacy, with the executive branch usually chosen by (and therefore a puppet of) the legislature. This worked out poorly as these legislatures succumbed to favoritism and engaged in fraudulent land sales. (See Article II regarding the Yazoo land fraud case, p. 39). In the 1810s and 1820s state constitutional fashion turned to limiting legislative powers and strengthening gubernatorial powers to achieve a better balance between the branches of government. Missouri's first constitution was adopted in this later era of state constitutional change and reflects then-prevailing trends by limiting legislative power in specific ways. Instead of enumerating specific positive legislative powers granted as in the federal constitution, the Missouri Constitution outlines specific limitations on the General Assembly's otherwise plenary legislative power.

SECTION 36. Payment of state revenues and receipts to treasury—limitation of withdrawals to appropriations—order of appropriations.—All revenue collected and money received by the state shall go into the treasury and the general assembly shall have no power to divert the same or to permit the withdrawal of money from the treasury, except in pursuance of appropriations made by law. All appropriations of money by successive general assemblies shall be made in the following order:

First: For payment of sinking fund and interest on outstanding obligations of the state.
Second: For the purpose of public education.
Third: For the payment of the cost of assessing and collecting the revenue.
Fourth: For the payment of the civil lists.
Fifth: For the support of eleemosynary and other state institutions.
Sixth: For public health and public welfare.
Seventh: For all other state purposes.
Eighth: For the expense of the general assembly.

SECTION 37. Limitation on state debts and bond issues.—The general assembly shall have no power to contract or authorize the contracting of any liability of the state, or to issue bonds therefor, except (1) to refund outstanding bonds, the refunding bonds to mature not more than twenty-five years from date, (2) on the recommendation of the governor, for a temporary liability to be incurred by reason of unforeseen emergency or casual deficiency in revenue, in a sum not to exceed one million dollars for any one year and to be paid in not more than five years from its creation, and (3) when the liability exceeds one million dollars, the general assembly as on constitutional amendments, or the people by the initiative, may also submit a measure containing the amount, purpose and terms of the liability, and if the measure is approved by a majority of the qualified electors of the state voting thereon at the election, the liability may be incurred, and the bonds issued therefor must be retired serially and by installments within a period not exceeding twenty-five years from their date. Before any bonds are issued under this section the general assembly shall make adequate provision for the payment of the principal and interest, and may provide an annual tax on all taxable property in an amount sufficient for the purpose.

SECTIONS 37(a) to 37(h), *omitted here, permit the General Assembly to issue bonds to finance specific governmental ends. Sections 37(a), 37(d), and 37(f) allow the government to borrow money to finance the repair, improvement, and construction of state buildings, properties, and parks. Sections 37(b), 37(c), 37(e), 37(g), and 37(h) allow the government to borrow money to finance efforts to control water pollution and improve drinking water and sewer systems.*

These lengthy provisions enable the General Assembly to authorize the floating of general obligation bond issues for particular designated purposes. The public vote to adopt each particular constitutional amendment permits the legislature to begin the process of borrowing money for the designated purpose. Without the constitutional amendment, the state could not borrow money at all. General obligation bonds are repaid on or before their due date; if the state were to fail to repay them by their due date, all property owners in the state would have to pony up the amount owed proportionally. Property taxes would go up as needed to fund payments to the state's creditors. The state office of administration manages the debt and issues a report each year to account for what has been repaid and what is still outstanding. These general obligation bonds are not a deficit like the one that the federal government runs; instead, they mean the government borrows for particular purposes, usually improvements or capital investment, such as a building at one of the state universities.

SECTION 38(a). **Limitation on use of state funds and credit—exceptions—public calamity—blind pensions—old age assistance—aid to children—direct relief—adjusted compensation for veterans—rehabilitation—participation in federal aid.—** The general assembly shall have no power to grant public money or property, or lend or authorize the lending of public credit, to any private person, association or corporation, excepting aid in public calamity, and general laws providing for pensions for the blind, for old age assistance, for aid to dependent or crippled children or the blind, for direct relief, for adjusted compensation, bonus or rehabilitation for discharged members of the armed services of the United States who were bona fide residents of this state during their service, and for the rehabilitation of other persons. Money or property may also be received from the United States and be redistributed together with public money of this state for any public purpose designated by the United States.

The last sentence of Section 38(a) permits the state to receive monies from the federal government to spend on specific purposes; these are called "grant-in-aid" programs (highway programs are one example). In accepting the federal handout, the state agrees to comply with federal guidelines and usually also puts up some "match," some state contribution to the funding for the program.

SECTION 38(b). **Tax levy for blind pension fund.—**The general assembly shall provide an annual tax of not less than one-half of one cent nor more than three cents on the one hundred dollars valuation of all taxable property to be levied and collected as other taxes, for the purpose of providing a fund to be appropriated and used for the pensioning of the deserving blind as provided by law. Any balance remaining in the fund after the payment of the pensions may be appropriated for the adequate support of the commission for the blind, and any remaining balance shall be transferred to the distributive public school fund.

SECTION 38(c). **Neighborhood improvement districts, cities and counties may be authorized to establish, powers and duties—limitation on indebtedness.—**1. The general assembly may authorize cities and counties to create neighborhood improvement districts and incur indebtedness and issue general obligation bonds to pay for all or part of the cost of public improvements within such districts. The cost of all indebtedness so incurred shall be levied and assessed by the governing body of the city or county on the property benefited by such improvements. The city or county shall collect the special assessments so levied and use the same to reimburse the city or county for the amount paid or to be paid by it on the general obligation bonds issued for such improvements.

2. Neighborhood improvement districts may be created by a city or county only when approved by the vote of a percentage of electors voting thereon within such district, or by a petition signed by the owners of record of a percentage of real property located within such district, that is equal to the percentage of voter approval required for the issuance of general obligation bonds under article VI, section 26.

3. The total amount of city or county indebtedness for all such districts shall not exceed ten percent of the assessed valuation of all taxable tangible property, as shown by the last completed property assessment for state or local purposes, within the city or county.

SECTION 38(d). **Stem cell research—title of law—permissible research—violations, penalty—report required, when—prohibited acts—definitions.—**1. This section shall be known as the "Missouri Stem Cell Research and Cures Initiative."

2. To ensure that Missouri patients have access to stem cell therapies and cures, that Missouri researchers can conduct stem cell research in the state, and that all such research is conducted safely and ethically, any stem cell research permitted under federal law may be conducted in Missouri, and any stem cell therapies and cures permitted under federal law may be provided to patients in Missouri, subject to the requirements of federal law and only the following additional limitations and requirements:

(1) No person may clone or attempt to clone a human being.

(2) No human blastocyst may be produced by fertilization solely for the purpose of stem cell research.

(3) No stem cells may be taken from a human blastocyst more than fourteen days after cell division begins; provided, however, that time during which a blastocyst is frozen does not count against the fourteen-day limit.

(4) No person may, for valuable consideration, purchase or sell human blastocysts or eggs for stem cell research or stem cell therapies and cures.

(5) Human blastocysts and eggs obtained for stem cell research or stem cell therapies and cures must have been donated with voluntary and informed consent, documented in writing.

(6) Human embryonic stem cell research may be conducted only by persons that, within 180 days of the effective date of this section or otherwise prior to commencement of such research, whichever is later, have

(a) provided oversight responsibility and approval authority for such research to an embryonic stem cell research oversight committee whose membership includes representatives of the public and medical and scientific experts;

(b) adopted ethical standards for such research that comply with the requirements of this section; and

(c) obtained a determination from an Institutional Review Board that the research complies with all applicable federal statutes and regulations that the Institutional Review Board is responsible for administering.

(7) All stem cell research and all stem cell therapies and cures must be conducted and provided in accordance with state and local laws of general applicability, including but

not limited to laws concerning scientific and medical practices and patient safety and privacy, to the extent that any such laws do not (i) prevent, restrict, obstruct, or discourage any stem cell research or stem cell therapies and cures that are permitted by the provisions of this section other than this subdivision (7) to be conducted or provided, or (ii) create disincentives for any person to engage in or otherwise associate with such research or therapies and cures.

3. Any person who knowingly and willfully violates in this state subdivision (1) of subsection 2 of this section commits a crime and shall be punished by imprisonment for a period of up to fifteen years or by the imposition of a fine of up to two hundred fifty thousand dollars, or by both. Any person who knowingly and willfully violates in this state subdivisions (2) or (3) of subsection 2 of this section commits a crime and shall be punished by imprisonment for a period of up to ten years or by the imposition of a fine of up to one hundred thousand dollars, or by both. A civil action may be brought against any person who knowingly and willfully violates in this state any of subdivisions (1) through (6) of subsection 2 of this section, and the state in such action shall be entitled to a judgment recovering a civil penalty of up to fifty thousand dollars per violation, requiring disgorgement of any financial profit derived from such violation, and/or enjoining any further such violation. The attorney general shall have the exclusive right to bring a civil action for such violation. Venue for such action shall be the county in which the alleged violation occurred.

4. Each institution, hospital, other entity, or other person conducting human embryonic stem cell research in the state shall (i) prepare an annual report stating the nature of the human embryonic stem cells used in, and the purpose of, the research conducted during the prior calendar year, and certifying compliance with subdivision (6) of subsection 2 of this section; and (ii) no later than June 30 of the subsequent year, make such report available to the public and inform the Secretary of State how the public may obtain copies of or otherwise gain access to the report. The report shall not contain private or confidential medical, scientific, or other information. Individuals conducting research at an institution, hospital, or other entity that prepares and makes available a report pursuant to this subsection 4 concerning such research are not required to prepare and make available a separate report concerning that same research. A civil action may be brought against any institution, hospital, other entity, or other person that fails to prepare or make available the report or inform the Secretary of State how the public may obtain copies of or otherwise gain access to the report, and the state in such action shall be entitled as its sole remedy to an affirmative injunction requiring such institution, hospital, other entity, or other person to prepare and make available the report or inform the Secretary of State how the public may obtain or otherwise gain access to the report. The attorney general shall have the exclusive right to bring a civil action for such violation.

5. To ensure that no governmental body or official arbitrarily restricts funds designated for purposes other than stem cell research or stem cell therapies and cures as a means of inhibiting lawful stem cell research or stem cell therapies and cures, no state or local governmental body or official shall eliminate, reduce, deny, or withhold any public funds provided or eligible to be provided to a person that (i) lawfully conducts stem cell research or provides stem cell therapies and cures, allows for such research or therapies and cures to be conducted or provided on its premises, or is otherwise associated with such research or therapies and cures, but (ii) receives or is eligible to receive such public funds for purposes other than such stem cell-related activities, on account of, or otherwise for the

purpose of creating disincentives for any person to engage in or otherwise associate with, or preventing, restricting, obstructing, or discouraging, such stem cell-related activities.

6. As used in this section, the following terms have the following meanings:

(1) "Blastocyst" means a small mass of cells that results from cell division, caused either by fertilization or somatic cell nuclear transfer, that has not been implanted in a uterus.

(2) "Clone or attempt to clone a human being" means to implant in a uterus or attempt to implant in a uterus anything other than the product of fertilization of an egg of a human female by a sperm of a human male for the purpose of initiating a pregnancy that could result in the creation of a human fetus, or the birth of a human being.

(3) "Donated" means donated for use in connection either with scientific or medical research or with medical treatment.

(4) "Fertilization" means the process whereby an egg of a human female and the sperm of a human male form a zygote (i.e., fertilized egg).

(5) "Human embryonic stem cell research," also referred to as "early stem cell research," means any scientific or medical research involving human stem cells derived from in vitro fertilization blastocysts or from somatic cell nuclear transfer. For purposes of this section, human embryonic stem cell research does not include stem cell clinical trials.

(6) "In vitro fertilization" means fertilization of an egg with a sperm outside the body.

(7) "Institutional Review Board" means a specially constituted review board established and operating in accordance with federal law as set forth in 42 U.S.C. 289, 45 C.F.R. Part 46, and any other applicable federal statutes and regulations, as amended from time to time.

(8) "Permitted under federal law" means, as it relates to stem cell research and stem cell therapies and cures, any such research, therapies, and cures that are not prohibited under federal law from being conducted or provided, regardless of whether federal funds are made available for such activities.

(9) "Person" means any natural person, corporation, association, partnership, public or private institution, or other legal entity.

(10) "Private or confidential medical, scientific, or other information" means any private or confidential patient, medical, or personnel records or matters, intellectual property or work product, whether patentable or not and including but not limited to any scientific or technological innovations in which an entity or person involved in the research has a proprietary interest, prepublication scientific working papers, research, or data, and any other matter excepted from disclosure under Chapter 610, RSMo, as amended from time to time.

(11) "Solely for the purpose of stem cell research" means producing human blastocysts using in vitro fertilization exclusively for stem cell research, but does not include producing any number of human blastocysts for the purpose of treating human infertility.

(12) "Sperm" means mature spermatozoa or precursor cells such as spermatids and spermatocytes.

(13) "Stem cell" means a cell that can divide multiple times and give rise to specialized cells in the body, and includes but is not limited to the stem cells generally referred to as (i) adult stem cells that are found in some body tissues (including but not limited to adult stem cells derived from adult body tissues and from discarded umbilical cords and placentas), and (ii) embryonic stem cells (including but not limited to stem cells derived from in vitro fertilization blastocysts and from cell reprogramming techniques such as somatic cell nuclear transfer).

(14) "Stem cell clinical trials" means federally regulated clinical trials involving stem cells and human subjects designed to develop, or assess or test the efficacy or safety of, medical treatments.

(15) "Stem cell research" means any scientific or medical research involving stem cells. For purposes of this section, stem cell research does not include stem cell clinical trials.

(16) "Stem cell therapies and cures" means any medical treatment that involves or otherwise derives from the use of stem cells, and that is used to treat or cure any disease or injury. For purposes of this section, stem cell therapies and cures does include stem cell clinical trials.

(17) "Valuable consideration" means financial gain or advantage, but does not include reimbursement for reasonable costs incurred in connection with the removal, processing, disposal, preservation, quality control, storage, transfer, or donation of human eggs, sperm, or blastocysts, including lost wages of the donor. Valuable consideration also does not include the consideration paid to a donor of human eggs or sperm by a fertilization clinic or sperm bank, as well as any other consideration expressly allowed by federal law.

7. The provisions of this section and of all state and local laws, regulations, rules, charters, ordinances, and other governmental actions shall be construed in favor of the conduct of stem cell research and the provision of stem cell therapies and cures. No state or local law, regulation, rule, charter, ordinance, or other governmental action shall (i) prevent, restrict, obstruct, or discourage any stem cell research or stem cell therapies and cures that are permitted by this section to be conducted or provided, or (ii) create disincentives for any person to engage in or otherwise associate with such research or therapies and cures.

8. The provisions of this section are self-executing. All of the provisions of this section are severable. If any provision of this section is found by a court of competent jurisdiction to be unconstitutional or unconstitutionally enacted, the remaining provisions of this section shall be and remain valid.

In the late 1990s and early 2000s citizens in Missouri and throughout the country vigorously debated the benefits and ethics of scientific research on stem cells derived from destroyed human embryos. In response, citizens of Missouri put a constitutional amendment offering guidelines for stem cell research on the ballot through an initiative petition drive; the amendment passed in November 2006 and is now found in Article III, Section 38d. While no longer at the forefront of Missouri politics, debate over this issue was contentious and the amendment passed with only 51 percent of the vote. Now known as the Missouri Stem Cell Research and Cures Initiative, the amendment allows any research and use that is also allowed by federal law, but prohibits the use of stem cells in human cloning procedures. This issue took on the proportions of a wedge issue.

SECTION 39. Limitation of power of general assembly.—The general assembly shall not have power: (1) To give or lend or to authorize the giving or lending of the credit of the state in aid or to any person, association, municipal or other corporation;

(2) To pledge the credit of the state for the payment of the liabilities, present or prospective, of any individual, association, municipal or other corporation;

(3) To grant or to authorize any county or municipal authority to grant any extra compensation, fee or allowance to a public officer, agent, servant or contractor after service has been rendered or a contract has been entered into and performed in whole or in part;

(4) To pay or to authorize the payment of any claim against the state or any county or municipal corporation of the state under any agreement or contract made without express authority of law;

(5) To release or extinguish or to authorize the releasing or extinguishing, in whole or in part, without consideration, the indebtedness, liability or obligation of any corporation or individual due this state or any county or municipal corporation;

(6) To make any appropriation of money for the payment, or on account of or in recognition of any claims audited or that may hereafter be audited by virtue of an act entitled "An Act to Audit and Adjust the War Debts of the State," approved March 19, 1874, or any act of a similar nature, until the claim so audited shall have been presented to and paid by the government of the United States to this state;

This is one of several archaic provisions remaining in the state constitution long after its appropriate or necessary use has faded into the mists of time. The War Debts were incurred during the Civil War, now more than 150 years ago—but not forgotten.

(7) To act, when convened in extra session by the governor, upon subjects other than those specially designated in the proclamation calling said session or recommended by special message to the general assembly after the convening of an extra session;

(8) To remove the seat of government from the City of Jefferson;

(9) Except as otherwise provided in section 39(b), section 39(c), section 39(e) or section 39(f) of this article, to authorize lotteries or gift enterprises for any purpose, and shall enact laws to prohibit the sale of lottery or gift enterprise tickets, or tickets in any scheme in the nature of a lottery; except that, nothing in this section shall be so construed as to prevent or prohibit citizens of this state from participating in games or contests of skill or chance where no consideration is required to be given for the privilege or opportunity of participating or for receiving the award or prize and the term "lottery or gift enterprise" shall mean only those games or contests whereby money or something of value is exchanged directly for the ticket or chance to participate in the game or contest. The general assembly may, by law, provide standards and conditions to regulate or guarantee the awarding of prizes provided for in such games or contests under the provision of this subdivision;

(10) To impose a use or sales tax upon the use, purchase or acquisition of property paid for out of the funds of any county or other political subdivision.

Section 39, part 9 permits gambling in Missouri. Previous to its adoption, the state legislature was forbidden to allow gambling of any sort—and gambling was considered a criminal activity. A series of public votes on constitutional amendments to permit increasing degrees of gambling (and, later, to adjust for problems in wording of previous gambling-related amendments) unfolded between 1978 and 2004.

First, a 1978 amendment permitted the legislature to authorize games in which nothing of value was at stake. Before the passage of this amendment, grocery stores and banks would give away items of value (such as turkeys at Thanksgiving time, or toasters for opening a bank account) but the customer had to enter the business and sign up to win—a technically illegal type of "lottery" according to the state's attorney general. The attorney general's office would not actively enforce the statute but would send warning letters to businesses in cases where someone complained or notified authorities of infractions. The 1978 amendment allowed the legislature to permit such minimal "lottery" activity.

SECTION 39(a). **Bingo may be authorized—requirements.**—The game commonly known as bingo when conducted by religious, charitable, fraternal, veteran or service organizations is not a lottery or gift enterprise within the meaning of subdivision (9) of section 39 of this article if the general assembly authorizes by law that religious, charitable, fraternal, service, or veteran organizations may conduct the game commonly known as bingo, upon the payment of the license fee and the issuance of the license as provided for by law. Any such law shall include the following requirements:

(1) All net receipts over and above the actual cost of conducting the game as set by law shall be used only for charitable, religious or philanthropic purposes, and no receipts shall be used to compensate in any manner any person who works for or is in any way affiliated with the licensed organization;

(2) No license shall be granted to any organization unless it has been in continuous existence for at least five years immediately prior to the application for the license. An organization must have twenty bona fide members to be considered to be in existence;

(3) No person shall participate in the management, conduct or operation of any game unless that person:

(a) Has been a bona fide member of the licensed organization for the two years immediately preceding such participation, and volunteers the time and service necessary to conduct the game;

(b) Is not a paid staff person for the licensed organization;

(c) Is not and has never been a professional gambler or gambling promoter;

(d) Has never purchased a tax stamp for wagering or gambling activity;

(e) Has never been convicted of any felony;

(f) Has never been convicted of or pleaded nolo contendere to any illegal gambling activity;

(g) Is of good moral character;

(4) Any person, any officer or director of any firm or corporation, and any partner of any partnership renting or leasing to a licensed organization any equipment or premises for use in a game shall meet all of the qualifications of paragraph (3) except subparagraph (a);

(5) No lease, rental arrangement or purchase arrangement for any equipment or premise for use in a game shall provide for payment in excess of the reasonable market rental rate for such premises and in no case shall any payment based on a percentage of the gross receipts or proceeds be permitted;

(6) No person, firm, partnership or corporation shall receive any remuneration or profit for participating in the management, conduct or operation of the game;

(7) No advertising of any game shall be permitted except on the premises of the licensed organization or through ordinary communications between the organization and its members;

(8) Any other requirement the general assembly finds necessary to insure that any games are conducted solely for the benefit of the eligible organizations and the general community.

The adoption of Section 39(a) in 1980 allowed the legislature to authorize bingo, a gambling game involving small stakes and often sponsored by churches, fraternal organizations, and service groups. Bingo games had gone on in the St. Louis area for decades, quite often in Catholic parish church facilities. However, these games technically were forbidden by law, and the General Assembly was not authorized by the constitution to give them a legal basis. Eventually, St. Louis–area authorities forced the issue with police raids of church basement bingo players. This was particularly offensive to the Catholic population of the state because the raids seemed aimed at one religion. Many elderly women whose social lives centered on bingo games were arrested, booked, and prosecuted for felony violations of the law.

But the bingo games continued; their location and time were announced in countless advertisements in area newspapers under the label of "green social." "Green" meant money, money meant bingo, and "social" meant play bingo! Law enforcement put pressure on the Catholic Cardinal of St. Louis to punish parish pastors who permitted the games. But bingo continued; it had too large a following. Police were embarrassed to arrest the elderly ladies—one police officer had to arrest his own grandmother—and judges apologized to bingo players as they sentenced the accused, usually to probation.[36]

These actions showed the futility of outlawing bingo, so this amendment gave the legislature the power to decriminalize and authorize the game in the November 1980 election. The popular amendment garnered 72.7 percent of the vote. The Missouri Baptist Convention spoke out against adoption of this amendment, out of fear of a slippery slope downward toward other forms of gambling, but fraternal and veterans' organizations supported bingo legalization because such organizations desired the opportunity to raise money-running bingo games.[37]

State Lottery

SECTION 39(b). State lottery, authority to establish—lottery proceeds fund established, purpose.—1. The general assembly shall have authority to authorize a Missouri state lottery by law. If such legislation is adopted, there shall be created a "State Lottery Commission" consisting of five members who shall be appointed by the governor with the advice and consent of the senate and who may be removed, for cause by the governor and who shall be chosen from the state at large and represent a broad geographic spectrum with no more than one member chosen from each federal congressional district. Each member at the time of his appointment and qualification shall have been a resident of this state for a period of at least five years next preceding his appointment and qualification and shall also be a qualified elector therein and be not less than thirty years of age. No more than three members of the commission shall be members of the same political party. Members of the commission shall have three-year terms as provided by law. Members of

[36]Elaine Viets, "Stamp Out Crime in Our Churches," *St. Louis Post-Dispatch*, April 11, 1978.
[37]Fred W. Lindecke, "Under the Propositions, No. 3 Would Legalize Bingo," *St. Louis Post-Dispatch*, September 23, 1980.

the commission shall receive no salary but shall receive their actual expenses incurred in the performance of their responsibilities. The commission shall employ such persons as provided by law. The commission shall have the authority to join other states and jurisdictions for the purpose of conducting joint lottery games.

2. The money received by the Missouri state lottery commission from the sale of Missouri lottery tickets, and from all other sources, shall be deposited in the "State Lottery Fund", which is hereby created in the state treasury.

3. The monies received from the Missouri state lottery shall be governed by appropriation of the general assembly. Beginning July 1, 1993, monies representing net proceeds after payment of prizes and administrative expenses shall be transferred by appropriation to the "Lottery Proceeds Fund" which is hereby created within the state treasury and such monies in the lottery proceeds fund shall be appropriated solely for public institutions of elementary, secondary and higher education.

4. A minimum of forty-five percent of the money received from the sale of Missouri state lottery tickets shall be awarded as prizes.

5. The commission shall have the authority to purchase and hold title to any securities of the United States government or its agencies and instrumentalities thereof for prizes, as provided by law.

6. Until July 1, 1993, any person possessing a department of revenue retail sales license as provided by law or any chartered civic, fraternal, charitable or political organization or labor organization shall be eligible to obtain a license to act as a lottery ticket sales agent except a license to act as an agent to sell lottery tickets shall not be issued to any person primarily engaged in business as a lottery ticket sales agent. Until July 1, 1993, the general assembly may impose additional qualifications on such persons to obtain a lottery ticket sales agent license as it deems appropriate. Until July 1, 1993, the commission is also authorized to sell lottery tickets at its office and at special events as provided by law. Beginning July 1, 1993, the general assembly shall enact laws governing lottery ticket sales.

7. Revenues produced from the conduct of a state lottery shall not be part of "total state revenues" as defined in sections 17 and 18 of article X of this constitution and the expenditure of such revenue shall not be an "expense of state government" under section 20 of article X of this constitution.

It turned out that the Baptist Convention was correct in fearing that bingo legalization would be a foot in the door for other forms of gambling. In November 1984 two more proposals for gambling legalization appeared on the ballot. One came directly from the legislature, which referred an amendment authorizing the state to run a lottery. Context helps explain why this form of gambling appealed to the General Assembly. First, the election of 1980 saw voter approval of an amendment sharply limiting state tax increases (and thus compromising future state revenue collection), called the Hancock Amendment, after its chief proponent Mel Hancock. (Its wording takes up Sections 16–24 of Article X of the constitution.) Since Missouri was at that time one of the lowest tax per capita states in the Union (meaning that the legislature had been loath to raise taxes anyway), freezing taxes made little sense. However, the public's mood was interpreted as a "taxpayer revolt," similar to what had happened in other larger states with higher per capita tax burdens. To increase revenues in the face of a constitutional limitation on tax increases, new sources of state revenue had to be found. The lottery offered such a source: 45 percent of its income would flow into the state treasury, boosting state funds (another 45 percent would go for prizes, and the final 10 percent would be dedicated to administrative costs of running it). The lottery notion thus had great monetary appeal. Second, other states were setting up lotteries in this time period; they had become a popular and fashionable revenue solution for states, so Missouri was in good company when it set up its own lottery. Third, Illinois ran a lottery that attracted the gambling dollars of many Missourians, especially in the populous St. Louis area. If Missouri initiated a lottery, those dollars would potentially stay in-state; supporters contended that it would bring in $80–100 million a year.

The Missouri Baptist Convention fought tooth and nail against the proposal: it considered this kind of gambling immoral, a nefarious scheme designed to siphon money off from the public at public expense. Ira Peak, a spokesperson for the Convention's Christian Moral Concerns committee, proclaimed that the next step down the garden path to more complete immorality would be casino gambling.[38] Nonetheless the proposal was adopted with 69.8 percent approval, just slightly less than bingo's approval at 71.4 percent four years earlier.

> SECTION 39(c). **Pari-mutuel wagering may be authorized by general assembly— horse racing commission established, election procedure to adopt or reject horse racing.**—1. The general assembly may authorize on track pari-mutuel betting on horse racing in a manner provided by law. There is hereby created the Missouri Horse Racing Commission which shall consist of five members appointed by the governor with the advice and consent of the senate. Members of the commission shall be citizens and eligible voters of Missouri and shall not have been convicted of a felony. Not more than three members shall be affiliated with the same political party, and not more than one member may be a resident of any one congressional district or of any single county or of the City of St. Louis. Of the members first appointed, one shall be appointed for a one year term, one shall be appointed for a two year term, one shall be appointed for a three year term, one shall be appointed for a four year term and one shall be appointed for a five year term; and thereafter members shall be appointed for terms of five years. The governor shall designate one of the members to be chairman. The governor may remove any member of the commission from office for malfeasance or neglect of duty in office. Members of the commission shall be reimbursed and paid for the expenses which they reasonably incur in the performance of their official duties, but they shall not, however, be paid a salary or other remuneration for their services unless such be authorized by law. No person may serve as a member of the commission and his office shall be deemed vacated if:
>
> (i) The member, the member's spouse, child or parent owns any interest in a race track licensed by the Commission.
>
> (ii) The member, the member's spouse, child or parent is an officer, employee, consultant or otherwise receives any remuneration from race track licensee.

---

[38]"State Lottery Proposal: An Issue of Philosophy," *St. Louis Post-Dispatch*, November 4, 1984.

(iii) The member, the member's spouse, child or parent holds a financial interest in a management or concession contract with a race track licensee.

A member shall not, however, be disqualified because either the member or the member's spouse, child or parent is a horse owner or a horse breeder whose horse participates as other horses and wins purses or awards in a race at a licensed race track.

2. At the general election to be held in November, 1986, every officer or body in charge of the elections shall order the following question on the ballot: "Shall pari-mutuel wagering upon horse races be permitted in . . . . County (or the City of St. Louis)?" This question may also be ordered upon the ballot at the general election occurring in 1988 and every four years thereafter by the governing body of any county where pari-mutuel wagering has not been previously authorized. The general provisions of law with respect to the conduct of elections and the submission of questions to voters for determination shall apply insofar as they are applicable. No license shall be issued by the commission authorizing pari-mutuel wagering within the grounds or enclosure of a racetrack until a majority of the qualified voters of the county where the race track is proposed to be located vote to accept pari-mutuel wagering in that county at one of the elections referred to above.

Once pari-mutuel wagering on horse racing has been accepted by the voters of that county at an appropriate election, no other vote shall be held on the question of the legality of such wagering in that county. If the qualified voters of the county reject pari-mutuel wagering on horse races in that county, no elections shall be held on the question in that county except as in the manner specified above. As used in this section, the term "county" includes the City of St. Louis.

A second proposal in 1984 was put on the ballot by initiative petition; this amendment authorized pari-mutuel betting on horse races. Illinois and Nebraska had betting at tracks, and many St. Louisans and Kansas Citians patronized those attractions. As with the lottery, the thinking was that if Missouri had comparable attractions, those dollars would stay in-state. The wording package imposed a tax on wagers, and 44 percent of that tax would go into the state's coffers; 40 percent of the revenue would go toward public education (K–12 and colleges and universities), with only 5 percent going to the racing commission to be established by the amendment. In a special side payment, 10 percent would go to the veterinary school at the University of Missouri–Columbia. The tax revenue had great appeal in light of the fiscal constraints imposed by the Hancock Amendment (1980). Also offered as arguments in favor of adoption were the investments in construction of tracks and the creation of new jobs. In a concession to Missouri's strong pro-local government tradition, counties could by local election decide to prohibit horse racing within their county boundaries.

Horse owners, veterinarians, and a prominent Kansas City company (Kansas City Southern Industries) supported the proposal; the Kansas City firm strongly believed that a horse track would benefit the Kansas City metropolitan area. Opponents pointed out that the benefits weren't worth the disadvantages: they brought up the immorality of gambling, suggested that pari-mutuel betting would attract criminal elements, and also contended that adopting this small fix for the state's revenue problems would postpone and avoid grappling with the true, larger problem of increasing taxes. This proposal passed with 60 percent of the vote, showing that it was quite a bit less popular than the lottery or bingo, but still popular enough to win adoption.

But nothing happened—no tracks were developed to fulfill the promise of more jobs and economic activity. It turned out that the wording of the 1984 amendment awkwardly left a loophole open: voters in the counties could vote to approve horse racing within their county, but every four years the question of whether it should remain could be put to a public ballot in each county. No developer of horse tracks would build such a facility at an estimated cost of $70 million if they couldn't operate it into the foreseeable future.[39] So the General Assembly proposed a "patch" amendment to "clarify" the 1984 amendment: once a county voted to accept horse racing within its boundaries, it could never reverse that decision. On the other hand, if the county had previously voted to ban horse tracks, the question of changing that decision could be brought up every four years, until the county would vote to permit horse racing, a decision that would become irrevocable.[40] The actual wording is found in the last paragraph of Section 39(c): "Once pari-mutuel wagering on horse racing has been accepted by the voters of that county at an appropriate election, no other vote shall be held on the question of the legality of such wagering in that county." Voters accepted this amendment (to the earlier amendment) in August 1986 with 58 percent approval. This amendment and the necessity for it show how adding verbiage to the state constitution can beg addition of yet more verbiage, until the document begins to sink from the weight of its words.

Even with the promise of operating a track in perpetuity, no tracks were built. The existing track at the state fairgrounds in Sedalia experienced a three-year effort to set up gambling on horse races, but this effort failed when the track operator leasing the track had to file for bankruptcy, leaving many unpaid debts.[41] The Sedalia track's distance from larger population centers, particularly St. Louis, caused systemic difficulties with efforts to use that track for pari-mutuel wagering. Horse racing in Missouri remained unattractive to gamblers, and the sport failed to develop a market in the state.[42] Sampling the offerings at the Missouri State Fair in 2008, visiting

[39]Fred W. Lindecke, "Ashcroft Backer Lobbies Senate on Dog Racing Bill," *St. Louis Post-Dispatch*, February 25, 1986.
[40]The 1984 amendment had been sold to the public partially on the grounds that these elections could be held every four years and that a county that found the horse track a baleful influence and wanting to back out could rescind its permission. See "Five State Amendments," *St. Louis Post-Dispatch*, August 1, 1986.
[41]Winning horse owners were stiffed; it turned out that the racing commission created by the first (1984) amendment neglected to comply with state law requiring track operators to post bond guaranteeing payment of purses.
[42]The statute applying the 1984 and 1986 amendments authorized only limited simulcasting (where bettors wager on races at other racetracks shown on television screens) so racetrack operators could simulcast only on days live races were held. Efforts to permit simulcasting arose in the legislature in 2002 but failed narrowly.

journalists noticed that a harness racing event at the grandstand had attracted only 80 spectators—in a venue designed to accommodate 100 times as many. The state horse racing commission had met that year for the first time in a decade, a measure of how dormant the racing industry had become after all the high hopes for its contribution to the economy through construction jobs and tax revenues from the state's cut.[43]

SECTION 39(d). Gaming revenues to be appropriated to public institutions of elementary, secondary and higher education.—All state revenues derived from the conduct of all gaming activities as are now or hereafter authorized by this constitution or by law, unless otherwise provided by law on the effective date of this section, shall be appropriated beginning July 1, 1993, solely for the public institutions of elementary, secondary and higher education and shall not be included within the definition of "total state revenues" in section 17 of article X of this constitution.

After the approval of the lottery and pari-mutuel wagering on horse racing, general disappointment gradually surfaced at the legislature's way of handling the revenue from the lottery. (The income from horse racing was minimal because the industry failed to take off.) Many political leaders had "promised" that 45 percent of the money from the lottery would go for education, but education received no noticeable boost in spending. A drive for a ballot proposition to raise taxes for education brought about much grumbling. Voters asked: "What about the lottery—wasn't that supposed to go for education?" Thus, the proposed tax increase for education floundered and failed.

For eight years, proceeds from the lottery had gone into the general revenue fund, and since most state aid for education came out of the general revenue fund, state officials could claim that lottery money went for education. But they couldn't say which dollar came from the lottery and which went for education, and the public became skeptical. Complaints about this encouraged legislative leaders to concretize the promise.[44] Note that revenues from all gaming activities were to be dedicated to education. These monies would not be counted in the total state revenue in the Hancock Amendment in Article X, meaning that the state could collect and spend them without running up against the limitations imposed by that amendment. This amendment was particularly popular, getting 77.8 percent of the vote in the August 1992 primary election, a lower-turnout election.

SECTION 39(e). Riverboat gambling authorized on Missouri and Mississippi rivers—boats in moats authorized.—The general assembly is authorized to permit upon the Mississippi and Missouri Rivers only, which shall include artificial spaces that contain water and that are within 1000 feet of the closest edge of the main channel of either of those rivers, lotteries, gift enterprises and games of chance to be conducted on excursion gambling boats and floating facilities. Any license issued before or after the adoption date of this amendment for any excursion gambling boat or floating facility located in any such

---

[43]Alan Scher Zagier, "Aficionados Try to Garner Support for Harness Races at Mo. State Fair," *Southeast Missourian*, August 18, 2008.
[44]"Vote Would Guarantee More Money for Schools," *St. Louis Post-Dispatch*, August 2, 1992.

artificial space shall be deemed to be authorized by the General Assembly and to be in compliance with this Section. NOTICE: You are advised that the proposed constitutional amendment may be construed to change, repeal, or modify by implication Article III, Sections 39, 39(9), and 39(e).

The barrage of proposals legalizing and expanding gambling activities continued apace in the fall election of 1992; the General Assembly proposed via statutory referendum a law (not a constitutional amendment) that authorized riverboat casino gambling on the two main watercourses in the state. MO-Target, a committee backed by casino investors and St. Louis riverfront interests, backed the measure, selling it to the public on the basis that the riverboats would create jobs, stimulate the economies of communities in which they would operate, and generate millions in state revenue (which still badly needed growth). Opponents, particularly a religious coalition, pointed out that casinos hurt lower-income people by enticing them to gamble even though the odds favor the house, and that the amounts of state revenue projected would add only an insignificant 1.3 percent of the state's then-current education budget. Nonetheless, the proposal passed with 62.5 percent of the vote. In the next legislative session, the General Assembly repealed almost all of the statute passed in the referendum and substituted its own language, altering many provisions in the law the people had passed. (This is one of several examples of the legislature nullifying the results of a popular vote. See also Article I, Section 35, p. 37 for the story of the legislature's repeal of puppy mill regulations approved by a popular vote in 2010–11, which lead to the right to farm movement and amendment. Much earlier, consider the drastic step the legislature took in proposing to repeal the Missouri Plan for judicial selection in 1940. See commentary at Article V, Section 25, p. 144.)

But both the law passed in the popular vote and the law substituted by the legislature were legislature measures, not constitutional amendments. In January 1994 the state supreme court ruled unanimously (in *Harris v. Missouri Gaming Com'n,* 869 S.W.2d 58 [1994]) that not all gaming activities were constitutional; only those gaming activities already protected by specific constitutional wording were permitted (bingo, the lottery, and betting on horses). Other gaming activities were permitted if they were games of skill (such as poker and twenty-one) but, without constitutional permission, games of chance (such as slot machines and bingo, among others) were unacceptable. The legislature could not constitutionally vote for (nor could the people adopt) a statute that ranged beyond the constitution's grant of power to the legislature by authorizing games of chance. And furthermore, nowhere in the constitution was the legislature permitted to authorize casino gaming. Judge Duane Benton, who before his appointment to the court had argued cases opposing the legality of other forms of gambling on behalf of the Missouri Baptist Convention, wrote the opinion. The supreme court remanded the case to the trial court, directing it to figure out whether several other specific types of gaming were games of chance (and therefore lotteries) or games of skill (and therefore permissible). Effectively, the court put a stop to the startup of riverboat casinos; if restricted to offering only twenty-one and poker, these enterprises would not attract investors.

Reactions varied, but most centered on getting over this constitutional impediment thrown up by the court so that economic development and job creation could proceed. A constitutional amendment to meet the court's objections was quickly proposed in the state legislature, and both the House and Senate passed it with large majorities (70 percent in both chambers). The governor scheduled the election for April 5. Hopes ran high, but proponents were anxious to schedule the election as soon as possible; it was placed on the ballot for a low-turnout election. The amendment failed, although barely so (49.9 percent voted for it—about 1,700 more votes and it would have passed). Obviously many opponents of casino gambling were still out there, and they could be mobilized for low-turnout elections.[45]

The gaming interests, heartened by the closeness of the election, then sponsored an initiative drive for signatures to petition for a constitutional amendment with essentially the same wording to permit games of chance aboard both gambling boats and floating facilities. Once again the churches—most denominations, not just the Baptist Convention—fought hard with a low-budget campaign against the proposal. But backers of gambling amassed a treasury of more than $8 million—far more than any individual candidate or any other issue on the ballot—and used the money for a concerted campaign featuring newspaper ads, telephone banks, radio and television ads, and nearly 100,000 personal contacts with voters. In the November 1994 election the new revised amendment won 53.8 percent of the votes. Opponents suggested that the power of money had defeated them.

Yet Missouri's agonizing over gambling was still not over. In the amendment that passed in 1994, the ceiling on the distance between the river channel and the boat dock was set at 1,000 feet. Six gambling operations theoretically on the Missouri and Mississippi Rivers were actually located in off-river holding ponds: these were called, famously, "boats in moats." In 1997 the supreme court revisited the issue and decided that these casinos went beyond the intention of the voters; the boats had to be on the main channel of the river itself. Now, proponents of gambling needed another constitutional amendment to reverse this second adverse court ruling and permit the boats in moats. Under the court's new ruling, gambling operations in moats could run gambling involving games of skill but not games of chance. But since games of chance (especially slot machines) comprised two-thirds of their revenue, featuring only games of skill would be unprofitable for the gaming interests. Gambling proponents also cited a safety factor: boats actually on the river have to be equipped to move, and that requires keeping expensive sailing crews and equipment on hand. The gaming titans argued further that they had played by the rules when investing and needed consistency in public policy to protect their investments and the many jobs their industry had created. The Missouri Gaming Commission

---

[45]Terry Ganey, "High Court Delays Riverboat Gambling," *St. Louis Post-Dispatch*, January 26, 1994; see also Fred W. Lindecke, "Casino Gaming Back to Voters; Amendment Gets Last-Minute OK," *St. Louis Post-Dispatch*, February 8, 1994.

had accepted these arguments, allowing off-channel docking to protect against barge traffic, swirling currents, and lack of water rescue boats.

Arrayed against the gaming interests was another coalition of religious leaders. Opponents argued that the gaming interests had simply gambled on the future value of their investments, but lost—and as gamblers, they should accept loss. They accused the industry of bait and switch tactics, promising riverboats and delivering buildings on land. Further, they pointed to the harm done to families due to gambling addictions. Financially, the two sides were grossly unbalanced; proponents raised at least $5.5 million, while opponents had $135 thousand. The 1998 amendment that ultimately allowed these "boats in moats" carried with 52.8 percent of the votes.[46]

Another resort community not located on the two main rivers but on Lake Taneycomo in southwest Missouri sought constitutional authorization for gambling boats. Proposed via an initiative signature campaign, this proposed amendment went down to defeat, gaining only 44.2 precent of the votes cast in the primary election of 2004.

SECTION 39(f). **Raffles and sweepstakes authorized.**—Any organization recognized as charitable or religious pursuant to federal law may sponsor raffles and sweep-stakes in which a person risks something of value for a prize. The general assembly may, by law, provide standards and conditions to regulate or guarantee the awarding of prizes provided for in such raffles or sweepstakes.

SECTION 40. **Limitations on passage of local and special laws.**—The general assembly shall not pass any local or special law:

(1) authorizing the creation, extension or impairment of liens;

(2) granting divorces;

This provision is truly archaic. Legislatures used to be asked by married couples to grant divorces, but for most of the twentieth century the power to grant divorce (now referred to as dissolution) has been lodged in the courts of law.

(3) changing the venue in civil or criminal cases;

(4) regulating the practice or jurisdiction of, or changing the rules of evidence in any judicial proceeding or inquiry before courts, sheriffs, commissioners, arbitrators or other tribunals, or providing or changing methods for the collection of debts, or the enforcing of judgments, or prescribing the effect of judicial sales of real estate;

(5) summoning or empaneling grand or petit juries;

(6) for limitation of civil actions;

(7) remitting fines, penalties and forfeitures or refunding money legally paid into the treasury;

(8) extending the time for the assessment or collection of taxes, or otherwise relieving any assessor or collector of taxes from the due performance of their duties, or their securities from liability;

---

[46]Virginia Young, "Feelings Run High on Ballot Issue to OK Boats in Moats," *St. Louis Post-Dispatch*, October 25, 1998.

(9) changing the law of descent or succession;

(10) giving effect to informal or invalid wills or deeds;

(11) affecting the estates of minors or persons under disability;

(12) authorizing the adoption or legitimation of children;

(13) declaring any named person of age;

(14) changing the names of persons or places;

(15) vacating town plats, roads, streets or alleys;

(16) relating to cemeteries, graveyards or public grounds not of the state;

(17) authorizing the laying out, opening, altering or maintaining roads, highways, streets or alleys;

(18) for opening and conducting elections, or fixing or changing the place of voting;

(19) locating or changing county seats;

(20) creating new townships or changing the boundaries of townships or school districts;

(21) creating offices, prescribing the powers and duties of officers in, or regulating the affairs of counties, cities, townships, election or school districts;

(22) incorporating cities, towns, or villages or changing their charters;

(23) regulating the fees or extending the powers of aldermen, magistrates or constables;

(24) regulating the management of public schools, the building or repairing of school-houses, and the raising of money for such purposes;

(25) legalizing the unauthorized or invalid acts of any officer or agent of the state or of any county or municipality;

(26) fixing the rate of interest;

(27) regulating labor, trade, mining or manufacturing;

(28) granting to any corporation, association or individual any special or exclusive right, privilege or immunity, or to any corporation, association or individual the right to lay down a railroad track;

(29) relating to ferries or bridges, except for the erection of bridges crossing streams which form the boundary between this and any other state;

(30) where a general law can be made applicable, and whether a general law could have been made applicable is a judicial question to be judicially determined without regard to any legislative assertion on that subject.

These provisions in Section 40 are primarily hands-off rules for the legislature and reserve some powers either to local government or to the courts (for instance, courts furnish a tribune for people to change names [14] and regulate adoption in accord with statutes that have statewide application [12]).

SECTION 41. Indirect enactment of local and special laws—repeal of local and special laws.—The general assembly shall not indirectly enact a special or local law by the partial repeal of a general law; but laws repealing local or special acts may be passed.

SECTION 42. Notice of proposed local or special laws.—No local or special law shall be passed unless a notice, setting forth the intention to apply therefor and the substance of the contemplated law, shall have been published in the locality where the matter or thing to be affected is situated at least thirty days prior to the introduction of the bill into the general assembly and in the manner provided by law. Proof of publication shall be filed with the general assembly before the act shall be passed and the notice shall be recited in the act.

SECTION 43. Title and control of lands of United States—exemption from taxation—taxation of lands of nonresidents.—The general assembly shall never interfere with the primary disposal of the soil by the United States, nor with any regulation which Congress may find necessary for securing the title in such soil to bona fide purchasers. No tax shall be imposed on lands the property of the United States; nor shall lands belonging to persons residing without the state ever be taxed at a higher rate than lands belonging to persons residing within the state.

SECTION 44. Uniform interest rates.—No law shall be valid fixing rates of interest or return for the loan or use of money, or the service or other charges made or imposed in connection therewith, for any particular group or class engaged in lending money. The rates of interest fixed by law shall be applicable generally and to all lenders without regard to the type or classification of their business.

SECTION 45. Congressional apportionment.—When the number of representatives to which the state is entitled in the House of the Congress of the United States under the census of 1950 and each census thereafter is certified to the governor, the general assembly shall by law divide the state into districts corresponding with the number of representatives to which it is entitled, which districts shall be composed of contiguous territory as compact and as nearly equal in population as may be.

SECTION 45(a). Term limitations for members of U.S. Congress—effective when—voluntary observance required, when.—(1) No United States Senator from Missouri shall serve more than two terms in the United States Senate, and no United States Representative from Missouri shall serve more than four terms in the United States House of Representatives. This limitation on the number of terms shall apply to terms of office beginning on or after the effective date of this section. Any person appointed or elected to fill a vacancy in the United States Congress and who serves at least one-half of a term of office shall be considered to have served a term in that office for purposes of this subsection (1). The provisions of this subsection (1) shall become effective whenever at least one-half of the states enact term limits for their members of the United States Congress.

(2) The people of Missouri declare that the provisions of this section shall be deemed severable and that their intention is that federal officials elected from Missouri will continue voluntarily to observe the wishes of the people as stated in this section in the event any provision thereof is held invalid.

The Missouri Constitution sets out specific term limits for U.S. senators and representatives from Missouri, but these provisions are null and void because they conflict with judicial interpretation of the U.S. Constitution. After adoption of this wording in the election of 1992 (along with term limits for state legislators found in Section 8 of Article III, above), the U.S. Supreme Court struck down all state-imposed term limits on federal officeholders. In *U.S. Term Limits v. Thornton* (1995), the Court declared that no state may impose further qualifications for candidates beyond what the federal Constitution already stipulates. In anticipation of such a ruling, Clause 2 had been added, stipulating that these two- and four-term limits "shall be deemed severable" but that candidates should understand the "wishes of the people" to limit career politicians from representing the state of Missouri. However, there is no legal mechanism to enforce compliance with this provision, since the wording in Section 45(a) has no legal force and is unconstitutional in light of the supremacy of the U.S. Constitution. Another, later attempt (adopted in a 1996 amendment) to shame candidates into not running for office if they failed to support term limits is found in Article VIII, Sections 15–22. This amendment also was held unconstitutional and in violation of the U.S. Constitution and similarly has no effect.

SECTION 46. Militia.—The general assembly shall provide for the organization, equipment, regulations and functions of an adequate militia, and shall conform the same as nearly as practicable to the regulations for the government of the armed forces of the United States.

Individuals who serve in the Missouri National Guard report directly to the governor (who acts as commander in chief of the state militia) and to the president of the United States when the National Guard is called into service of the federal government. The Missouri National Guard operates under what it deems a "dual mission," supporting the needs of both the state and the nation.

SECTION 46(a). Emergency duties and powers of assembly on enemy attack.—The General Assembly, in order to ensure continuity of state and local governmental operations in periods of emergency only resulting from disasters occurring in this state caused by enemy attack on the United States, shall have the power to such extent as the General Assembly deems advisable. In the event there occurs in this state a disaster caused by enemy attack on the United States, the General Assembly shall immediately convene in the City of Jefferson or in such place as designated by joint proclamation of the highest presiding officers of each house, and shall have power

(1) To provide by legislative enactment for prompt and temporary succession to the powers and duties of public offices, of whatever nature and whether filled by election or appointment, the incumbents of which may become unavailable for carrying on the powers and duties of such offices, and

(2) To adopt by legislative enactment such other legislation as may be necessary and proper for insuring the continuity of governmental operations. Notwithstanding the power conferred by this section of the constitution, elections shall always be called as soon as possible to fill any elective vacancies in any office temporarily occupied by operation of any legislation enacted pursuant to the provisions of this section.

Adopted on November 8, 1960, Section 46(a) of Article III details what powers may be exercised by the General Assembly in the event of an emergency, such as an enemy attack. There is no corresponding "emergency powers" provision in the U.S. Constitution, and much of the debate at the federal level therefore centers on the nature and limits of the executive power vested in the president by Article II of the U.S. Constitution.

SECTION 47. State parks—appropriations for, required.—For twelve years beginning with the year 1961, the general assembly shall appropriate for each year out of the general revenue fund, an amount not less than that produced annually at a tax rate of one cent on each one hundred dollars assessed valuation of the real and tangible personal property taxable by the state, for the exclusive purpose of providing a state park fund to be expended and used by the agency authorized by law to control and supervise state parks, and historic sites of the state, for the purposes of the acquisition, supervision, operation, maintenance, development, control, regulation and restoration of state parks and state park property, as may be determined by such agency; and thereafter the general assembly shall appropriate such amounts as may be reasonably necessary for such purposes.

The amount required to be appropriated by this section may be reduced to meet budgetary demands provided said appropriation is not less than that appropriated for the prior similar appropriation period.

State and local government play a prominent role in land maintenance and conservation. In Missouri, the Department of Natural Resources is tasked with conserving the state's natural resources. The mission of the Missouri state parks rangers—housed in the Department of Natural Resources—is to protect Missouri natural resources and historic sites. Individual cities, meanwhile, often have additional departments of parks and recreation, which are individually responsible for the upkeep and maintenance of city parklands and natural resources.

SECTION 48. Historical memorials and monuments—acquisition of property.—The general assembly may enact laws and make appropriations to preserve and perpetuate memorials of the history of the state by parks, buildings, monuments, statues, paintings, documents of historical value or by other means, and to preserve places of historic or archaeological interest or scenic beauty, and for such purposes private property or the use thereof may be acquired by gift, purchase, or eminent domain or be subjected to reasonable regulation or control.

Initiative and Referendum

Initiatives and referenda allow the public (rather than members of the General Assembly) to participate directly in the proposal and approval of statutes and constitutional amendments. An initiative is placed on the ballot after receiving signatures from a certain percentage of legal voters in the state. Referenda are measures that allow voters to approve or repeal particular legislation. In Missouri, referenda may be initiated by citizen petition or by the General Assembly. Significantly, the governor's veto power does not extend to measures referred to the people.

SECTION 49. Reservation of power to enact and reject laws.—The people reserve power to propose and enact or reject laws and amendments to the constitution by the initiative, independent of the general assembly, and also reserve power to approve or reject by referendum any act of the general assembly, except as hereinafter provided.

SECTION 50. Initiative petitions—signatures required—form and procedure.— Initiative petitions proposing amendments to the constitution shall be signed by eight percent of the legal voters in each of two-thirds of the congressional districts in the state, and petitions proposing laws shall be signed by five percent of such voters. Every such petition shall be filed with the secretary of state not less than six months before the election and shall contain an enacting clause and the full text of the measure. Petitions for constitutional amendments shall not contain more than one amended and revised article of this constitution, or one new article which shall not contain more than one subject and matters properly connected therewith, and the enacting clause thereof shall be "Be it resolved by the people of the state of Missouri that the Constitution be amended:". Petitions for laws shall contain not more than one subject which shall be expressed clearly in the title, and the enacting clause thereof shall be "Be it enacted by the people of the state of Missouri:".

SECTION 51. **Appropriations by initiative—effective date of initiated laws—conflicting laws concurrently adopted.**—The initiative shall not be used for the appropriation of money other than of new revenues created and provided for thereby, or for any other purpose prohibited by this constitution. Except as provided in this constitution, any measure proposed shall take effect when approved by a majority of the votes cast thereon. When conflicting measures are approved at the same election the one receiving the largest affirmative vote shall prevail.

SECTION 52(a). **Referendum—exceptions—procedure.**—A referendum may be ordered (except as to laws necessary for the immediate preservation of the public peace, health or safety, and laws making appropriations for the current expenses of the state government, for the maintenance of state institutions and for the support of public schools) either by petitions signed by five percent of the legal voters in each of two-thirds of the congressional districts in the state, or by the general assembly, as other bills are enacted. Referendum petitions shall be filed with the secretary of state not more than ninety days after the final adjournment of the session of the general assembly which passed the bill on which the referendum is demanded.

SECTION 52(b). **Veto power—elections—effective date.**—The veto power of the governor shall not extend to measures referred to the people. All elections on measures referred to the people shall be had at the general state elections, except when the general assembly shall order a special election. Any measure referred to the people shall take effect when approved by a majority of the votes cast thereon, and not otherwise. This section shall not be construed to deprive any member of the general assembly of the right to introduce any measure.

SECTION 53. **Basis for computation of signatures required.**—The total vote for governor at the general election last preceding the filing of any initiative or referendum petition shall be used to determine the number of legal voters necessary to sign the petition. In submitting the same to the people the secretary of state and all other officers shall be governed by general laws.

ARTICLE IV
EXECUTIVE DEPARTMENT

SECTION 1. **Executive power—the governor.**—The supreme executive power shall be vested in a governor.

SECTION 2. **Duties of governor.**—The governor shall take care that the laws are distributed and faithfully executed, and shall be a conservator of the peace throughout the state.

The Missouri Constitution stipulates that the governor "shall take care that the laws are distributed and faithfully executed," language that echoes the oath of office taken by the president of the United States (see U.S. Const. Art. II, Sec. 1). The office of state governor mirrors the office of the presidency in other ways, including its concentration of executive power in one superior officer, its power to fill vacancies and appoint citizens to government jobs, and its power to command the military or state militia. Additionally, the governor and the president both have authority to pardon those convicted of crimes.

SECTION 3. **Qualifications of governor.**—The governor shall be at least thirty years old and shall have been a citizen of the United States for at least fifteen years and a resident of this state at least ten years next before election.

The requirement for a residency of 10 years is called a "durational qualification." This provision became a point of contention during the 1972 election for governor, when rising political star Christopher ("Kit") Bond first ran for the office. Bond had stunned Missouri political observers when he won a statewide election for the state auditorship in 1970, running as a Republican in a state that then leaned heavily Democratic. Attractive, young, articulate, and scion of a wealthy family, Bond then decided to run for the Republican nomination for governor in 1972. His competitor, Republican legislative leader R. J. ("Bus") King, alleged that Bond had not been a resident of the state for the 10 years required and so was ineligible to run. The Democratic Party also believed he was ineligible and did not want him winning the gubernatorial nomination because they worried he might win in the general election. The case was quickly taken to the state supreme court, which decided expeditiously so that the issue could be resolved before the August primary election. The factual record of Bond's wanderings over the years seemed to show that he was not a Missouri resident for all the time required.[47] However, the court's majority ruled that Bond met Missouri residency requirements despite the evidence to the contrary, and so he met the constitutional requirement to run for governor. Two judges of the supreme court dissented, finding that he had taken up residency in Georgia, which was incompatible with maintaining his Missouri residency (*State Ex. Rel. King v. Walsh*, 484 S.W.2d 641 [1972]).

Bond went on to win the Republican nomination for governor, then beat the Democratic candidate to win the governorship. He served one term as governor, lost for reelection in 1976, but then rebounded and was elected to a second term in 1980, serving from 1981 to 1985. He then won election as a U.S. senator in 1986 and held

[47]During the period in question, November 1962 through November 1972, Bond had lived in Virginia for law school (1960–63); in New York City for the summer of 1961; in Atlanta, Georgia, for the summer of 1962; then in Atlanta again in 1963–64, while employed as a law clerk for the U.S. Court of Appeals (Fifth Circuit); then in Washington, D.C., in 1964–67 while working for a Washington law firm. While in Virginia he applied to take the Virginia bar exam in 1963, and in that application he stated he was a Virginia resident; in Georgia he applied to take the bar exam in that state and stated he was now a Georgia resident. Nor did he file a Missouri income tax return for the years from 1962 through 1968; and, despite having interest income in the 10-year period, he did not pay the requisite intangible property tax return in any of those years. Despite these indications that Bond had out-of-state residency and had even claimed out-of-state residency during the vital period of time, he maintained that he had been a resident because he always intended to return to Missouri, arguing that residency is a question of intention. He maintained a church membership in his Missouri hometown and had other connections to his home area, such as returning annually to hunt doves.

the seat until 2010. He held office for 34 years in all (including his initial service as auditor from 1970 to 1972), a long career made possible by a split court opinion with a majority of judges who interpreted the residency requirement in the Missouri Constitution in a way that allowed Bond to run for governor.

SECTION 4. Power of appointment to fill vacancies—tenure of appointees.—The governor shall fill all vacancies in public offices unless otherwise provided by law, and his appointees shall serve until their successors are duly elected or appointed and qualified.

Note that the governor's appointees stay in office until their successors have undergone the appointment (or election) process and are ready to serve. This ensures continuity in office and prompts a new governor to make appointments early so that his or her predecessor's appointees don't run the state by default.

The power of gubernatorial appointment used to make the governorship a bonanza for both the sitting governor and his political party. Under the "spoils" system (as in "to the victor belong the spoils," using the metaphor of war for election campaigns) or the "patronage" system, people were appointed to office based on political and party loyalty instead of merit, knowledge, or expertise. The spoils system dates back to the era of Andrew Jackson,[48] when the elitism of the Founding generation gave way to more ardent democratic ideas. The idea grew that anyone could perform the functions of public office. If one agreed with the premise of equality, the conclusion that merit was equally distributed among the population followed. Therefore officeholders could appoint as subordinates any person(s) loyal to them. Loyal appointees meant obedient public servants—obedient to the political winners who appointed them. Since such winners reflect the voters' preferences, all officeholders (both those who appoint subordinates and the subordinates themselves) would theoretically be accountable to the people in a democratic fashion.

The catch is that in return for their jobs[49] and the salaries they earned, the appointees had to work to advance their political leaders' careers and their party's future success. Often, patronage appointees spent most of their time working for their party, canvassing to make sure the party organization had dependable information on the electorate and going door-to-door to promise boons such as food baskets or jobs for constituents and to do favors for supplicants, all in return for votes on Election Day.[50]

---

[48]President 1829–37. Before Jackson, presidents appointed on the basis of either qualifications or party; John Adams stuffed the federal judiciary with his co-partisans (the Federalists, a party that lost the election of 1800 and then collapsed). Jackson was the first president from a state that was not an original colony, and only two presidents before him had not hailed from Virginia. As a frontiersman, Jackson aimed to sweep away all vestiges of the "Virginia dynasty." His supporters were keen on tasting the benefits of helping him win—the benefits of jobs on the public payroll.

[49]Jackson's supporters needed the jobs for the paychecks; unlike appointees of the first six presidents, who had independent sources of income, Jackson's supporters were ordinary people without other means. The jobs they sought from Jackson and the presidents who followed him were bread-and-butter concerns for them.

[50]These activities are quite typical of city "machine" politics, and they occurred in rural areas also, where local politicos reached out to help their constituents. But many rural areas were safely

The spoils system had three disadvantages: (1) it put many incompetent people in appointive offices; (2) even if appointees were competent, they had to spend much of their time on campaign activities (for another election always loomed); and (3) office seekers begging for appointments often filled up virtually the entire schedule of the appointive authority.[51]

In the federal government, this crisis was brought to a head when a disappointed office seeker assassinated President Garfield in 1881. Congress passed the Pendleton (or Civil Service) Act in 1883, which began the process of basing federal government jobs on merit. Merit is proven by taking an open and competitive entrance examination. Gradually, more and more of the federal civil service has been placed under the merit system, until only certain high-appointed policy positions are left to open appointmet. These are listed at the time of the presidential election in the "Plum Book," formally known as "United States Government Policy and Supporting Positions." Competition is intense for these jobs, which number about 7,000, but appointment is noncompetitive—presidents can appoint favorites, for example, and no reason for favoring one person and passing over another person need be given. Presumably only the president's true loyalists have much chance.

At the state level in Missouri, the conflict between the spoils system and the merit system played out much later, and under different partisan configurations than at the federal level. The patronage system in Missouri entails the accompanying history of political parties in the state. From a political party standpoint, since the Civil War and fading from the late 1960s until 2002, the state was primarily Democratic in its citizens' voter preferences, party self-identification, and electoral outcomes. There have been isolated majority Republican places, but statewide the GOP has historically been a minority party. Republican-dominant areas have included certain mountain counties in the Ozarks of southwest Missouri, some northern counties along the Iowa line, some counties south of the Missouri River, and central and southern St. Louis County (suburban St. Louis).[52] Different historical

---

one-party-dominant, so rural politicians could count on being reelected more easily than their urban counterparts. Until the late 1880s, ballots were not secret; voters were forced to cast public ballots. Each party would provide paper sheets of a certain color, and the voters would take a ballot from the pile of paper of their party. This action was entirely visible to the party's poll watchers, so they could verify that the people who received favors, jobs, Thanksgiving turkeys, and the like from the party returned the favor by voting for the party's slated nominees for office. After the secret ballot was adopted (the first state to adopt it was Mississippi in 1891), party poll watchers found other, more clandestine ways to intimidate the voters into making the "right choice."

[51]President Lincoln particularly found this troubling; in the first several months of his first term in office, he faced the grave problem of secession by southern states, but had only a few hours each day to deal with the crisis of the Union because Republican office seekers constantly besieged him.

[52]St. Louis City is jurisdictionally separate from St. Louis County; the city has trended Democratic over the course of the twentieth century. St. Louisans seeking larger and newer housing have gushed out of the city into St. Louis County, and generally the people able to afford locating in the county have been Republican. Thus, St. Louis County became heavily Republican in voting behavior, especially in the central, western, and southern areas. Meanwhile, across the state in Kansas City,

reactions to the Civil War account for these variances. These areas contain popula-tions with a peculiar political heritage. Southwest Missouri replicates the party affiliation history of Appalachia (it was primarily peopled by migrants from that area, who never did support the Confederate cause nor secession),[53] the counties along the Iowa border are more midwestern in culture, and the counties south of the Missouri River were peopled by German settlers who supported the Union during the Civil War and emerged from that struggle with a Republican rather than a Democratic identification.

The remaining areas of the state outside metropolitan St. Louis and Kansas City have been Democratic—traditional Democratic, similar to the formerly "solid" Democratic South. For instance, a band of counties just to the north of the Missouri River is called "Little Dixie"; this area had many plantations before the Civil War and had the largest proportion of African Americans in its population. St. Louis and Kansas City are more diverse, but each supported a Democratic political machine, with political bosses corralling, buying, and selling blocs of votes at election time.

In St. Louis, the Democratic Party's "Butler" machine, led by Edward Butler, hit its peak from 1870 to 1902. The city's economic elite (nicknamed the "Big Cinch") paid it off for its help getting ordinances passed in city hall, procuring city con-struction contracts, and working around bureaucratic red tape. Boss Butler was eventually convicted for bribing city officials to sidestep awarding a garbage dis-posal contract to a new applicant. He later proclaimed that St. Louis City was really a Republican town but that he had arranged for virtually all elections to be stolen by the Democrats.

Even after the decline of the Butler machine, St. Louis City retained many fea-tures of boss politics. Candidates for party nominations in contested primary elec-tions paid ward committee members and precinct captains for their candidate endorsements, a practice that continued well into the 1980s. It should be noted that Missouri's primary election (in which party nominations for office are fought out) is set by law for the first Tuesday after the first Monday in August of even-numbered years. This date was deliberately chosen to depress voter turnout in the primary elections; urban residents were traditionally more likely to take vacations in August, and rural residents, especially farmers, were busy with the harvest. With both urban and rural voting diminished, lower turnouts would make it easier for urban machines and county courthouse crowds alike to control the outcomes of these elections. Fewer people showing up to vote translates into greater ease in identify-ing the voters who do habitually participate and contacting them to rally the vote

---

people able to afford better housing tended to move to Kansas suburbs; since these people trended Republican, their leaving Missouri drained Jackson County of Republicans, reinforcing its dominance by Democrats. Their movement also made Kansas (the state) more Republican.

[53]Far eastern Kentucky and Tennessee, and the western parts of Virginia and North Carolina, were opposed to secession but had only a minority voice during the lead-up to the Civil War. The Ozarks were populated by people heading west from this mountain area; they stopped in Missouri because the scenery and land were so similar to their original home.

for party-supported candidates. In St. Louis and Kansas City, ward leaders and precinct captains knew whom to contact to assure votes for candidates "slated" (supported) by the party organization.

As the Butler machine's star set in the east, the Kansas City Pendergast machine's star rose in the west (1900–64). Tom Pendergast only briefly held office but attained immense power as chair of the Jackson County Democratic Party. He didn't mind using voter fraud and intimidation by "goons" to induce, force, and coerce the electorate into electing his candidates. The Pendergast machine was a source of patronage jobs and government contracts,[54] but Pendergast himself, although personally wealthy, was always supportive of equality for the "common" people and undertook many visionary policies. He got Harry Truman elected as a U.S. senator, where Truman's work attracted the attention of FDR himself and led to Truman's selection as FDR's running mate in 1944.

Patronage politics remained central to local Missouri politics until the late 1960s and early 1970s. County government provides multiple elective positions (county clerk, treasurer, assessor, collector, auditor, recorder, sheriff, circuit clerk, prosecuting attorney, county counselor, and public administrator), and the offices of these elective officials need appointive employees to round out the workforce. The dominant local party wins the elective positions and with them the right to the spoils—to fill out the bureaucracy with appointees. In the minority of counties dominated by the Republican Party, plenty of jobs as elective county officers or as appointive assistants in the offices of the elective officers helped boost the employment rate of loyal Republican partisans and election workers. In the majority of counties with Democratic voter leanings, only Democrats needed to apply. Selection for appointive office has been primarily on the basis of loyalty and political compatibility.

When the Republicans won national elections, the appointive power of the presidency would kick in and federal patronage appointments for the state would be channeled through the state Republican committee. New federal appointive officials such as the U.S. attorneys (the federal prosecutors) or federal judges would be selected in conjunction with advice from the state's Republicans.

But in state government, with only one Republican governor from 1933 through 1973,[55] the Democratic Party was able to indulge its appetite for patronage, and even take the practice of it to a new art form.

---

[54]Many beautiful boulevards and parks were established during Pendergast's peak years of power (1925–39). Their appeal to the Boss, however, lay less in their beauty or in their demonstration of good urban planning but rather in their worth as sources of income for the machine through contractors' kickback payments. He developed a gambling addiction, especially on horse racing, and eventually was convicted of income tax evasion in 1939. The Kansas City machine outshone the one in St. Louis, getting involved in gangland slayings and threats of violence, while the St. Louis machine stuck to voter fraud and simple bribery.

[55]The intervening Republican governor was Forrest Donnell, 1941–45; the era of Democratic dominance of the governorship is bookended by Governor Caulfield, the last Republican (1929–33), and by Governor Bond (1973–77).

Patronage had many facets. To imagine how it works, let's say that you are looking for a job in government during this time period. If you aspire to a position in state government, the first consideration is whether you are a faithful Democrat. If you are, and you have performed party duties rounding up voters, helping the party organization keep up its lists of voters, canvassing for the party, and obediently casting votes in party committees as you were directed, you will most likely be able to get a sponsorship from your county chair. If you don't know him or her, probably your ward chair or your precinct committee representative can put in a good word for you. Someone with "pull" in the party organization needs to vouch for you before you can possibly be appointed to a position. If you consider yourself a Republican, you are limited to looking for employment at the county level in one of the Republican dominant counties, but if you are not "from" there (i.e., not a "native"), you probably have no chance whatsoever, because however well you might have performed the job, your competitors for the position have much better contacts in the local party than you do, and "pull" is what counts. And, if you are a Republican, your prospects for state employment are virtually nil. If you are an Independent, forget about it—you have no chance.[56]

To keep your job, you needed to contribute to the party's coffers. This was done through the practice of the "lug." To understand how the lug was handled, it's important to understand that in the days before direct deposit, or even in the days before cutting checks for paychecks, workers were given a pay envelope that contained their take-home pay in cash. On payday, workers would line up at the cashier's window, give their name, show some identification, and collect their pay. State employees in the patronage agencies would have to pay the lug, which was 2 percent of their take-home pay, by handing that amount of cash over to the cashier. (The envelope contained a separate piece of paper with the amount of the lug, and the cashier would make change if necessary.) Anyone unwilling to do this was fired on the spot.[57] The lug was, essentially, a private tax for having a job furnished by the party organization.

Another practice that enriched the party organization at the expense of patronage employees was forced purchase of tickets to picnics and barbeques sponsored by the party organizations. Employees of patronage-based agencies in Jefferson City were on the line to purchase tickets—and to attend these events, because not

---

[56]Missouri does not have party registration, so voters cannot be "officially" tagged with a party membership. In fact, voter registration was not statewide until the mid-1970s; in cities, voters were required to register to qualify to vote, but in non-incorporated areas voters just showed up and election judges decided if they were qualified to vote or not. In the rural areas everyone knew everyone else, so the system worked.

[57]One of the authors has heard accounts of how this process worked directly from people waiting in line for their pay envelope; a new naïve employee unaware of how the lug worked declined to pay it, which delayed the line a short time while the cashier made clear to the recalcitrant employee that his employment was over.

participating was a sign of disloyalty. This custom was yet another tax—on both a person's money and time—for being employed by the state.

Manifold rewards were possible for the governor's allies. For instance, the Department of Revenue runs two types of motor vehicle registration offices. "License offices" are run by employees of the Department of Revenue in premises leased by the state. Renewing your automobile license or your driver's license means paying the state. But another type of office is possible: the "fee offices." The governor used to award these to his key supporters, and individuals so favored would collect an extra "fee" on each transaction. Although low, these fees add up, and for some locations on busy roads they mount up fast and make fortunes for the holder of the fee office. For the citizen, the tradeoff is waiting in long lines at a state license office or going to a convenient fee office and paying a little more.[58] The awardee of the office has to select the location, pay rent and utilities, and hire personnel, but (depending on the location) he or she stands to benefit greatly from alliance with the sitting governor.

Another odd benefit for the governor's allies and supporters has been low-number automobile license plates. The benefits of these are both the prestige of letting other drivers on the road know that you have found favor with the governor and the subdued reaction of highway patrol officers more inclined to give special treatment to drivers of such cars.

These patronage practices have faded, and the chokehold they had on state government eased as the Democratic Party lost control over the nominations process. A political party can remain tightly organized as long as it can control who governs in its name, and the Missouri Democratic Party organization, both statewide and in the counties it dominated, was able to choose its candidates despite having to carry the primary election before they become the "official" Democratic Party nominees. The party was strong enough organizationally to be able to "slate" its choices for the various offices and then reach and line up behind its endorsed candidates the small number of voters who participated in the primaries. The party was too strong to oppose; it could fend off ambitious office seekers because it always won, so what was the point of going up against one of the organization's choices in the primary?

The first crack in the party's armor appeared in 1952. The party organization, including the Pendergast machine and incumbent president Harry Truman, endorsed the state attorney general, "Buck" Taylor, for the Democratic nomination for U.S. senator. But a competitor emerged: Stuart Symington had been a troubleshooter for the besieged Truman administration, serving in numerous capacities, among them as the first secretary of the air force. He was the scion of an aristocratic Eastern family, grandson of a U.S. senator, but a newcomer in the state. Observers contended that he

---

[58]There are other possibilities of special treatment with the fee offices. One author was acquainted with an elderly matron who neglected to renew her driver's license. To get it back, she had to pass a written test. Unfortunately, she had only gone to school through the sixth grade, and not in English. She tried the written test several times at the license office but to no avail. Finally she called a friend who worked at a fee office; she went there, the fee office employee filled out the test for her, and she was relicensed. Many people like the informality, neighborliness, and "chumminess" of the fee offices.

didn't personally know more than 100 people in Missouri. Could such a political amateur, who had never run for office before, successfully parachute in and challenge the party organization by taking his fight to the voters? Symington put high energy into his campaign for the nomination; he appeared in outstate areas that were unaccustomed to seeing candidates for statewide office, shook hands, and asked for and got the support of disparate elements of the party, including county courthouse crowds in rural Missouri and the remnants of the old machine in St. Louis City. Symington racked up large pluralities previously unknown in the city and benefited from numerous Republicans taking the Democratic ballot to vote for him. He was the wave of the future—one of the first super-qualified, attractive candidates to hit the Missouri political scene.[59] He won the nomination and then in the general election prevailed over the Republican incumbent. The St. Louis machine, meanwhile, was defeated on its own turf; its candidate for sheriff lost badly, and the Kansas City machine was humiliated too. Symington's victory signaled a new political era— the old style party organizations would have to adapt to survive.

But the Missouri Democratic Party took this upset in stride, looking on it as an aberration. The party went back to its habits of deciding who among its elected officials should proceed to which higher office next. Since any one person was term limited to only two terms as governor, and the terms could not be consecutive, the notion of having the person who the party slated as lieutenant governor be the next nominee for governor had substantial appeal. People could prepare for being governor by establishing a sharper profile in the lower statewide office. Lesser statewide elective offices could offer bush league training for the governorship or the U.S. Senate seats. In 1960, Democrats Warren Hearnes (a state representative) and Hilary Bush won the offices of secretary of state and lieutenant governor respectively. To follow the custom, Bush's turn to run for the Democratic nomination for governor would come in 1964, while Hearnes would run for the Democratic nomination for lieutenant governor. It was assumed by one and all that whoever got the Democratic nomination was going to win in the general election, so sure was the Democratic Party organization of victory over the Republicans.

But Hearnes didn't want to wait his turn; he wanted to have the governorship early. So he challenged Bush in the 1964 primary election. He fought the organization. Bush proved less than fully engaged as a campaigner, and Hearnes was able to tie him to the Pendergast machine and thus come across as a fresh face uncorrupted by dealings with boss politics. Hearnes beat the organization and won the primary, then went on to beat the Republican candidate to ascend to the governorship in November. This time the party organization was hurt badly; the outgoing governor, John Dalton, had thrown his support and the support of the party organization behind Bush. Virtually all the patronage employees of state government actively backed Bush, and soon they heard the bell tolling for their jobs.

---

[59]Edward F. Woods, "How Symington Won in Primary Election—Political Novice Got Good Advice, Worked Hard," *St. Louis Post-Dispatch*, August 10, 1952.

Hearnes took over as governor and soon rallied his party in the legislature to vote up a proposed constitutional amendment to remove the limitation on the governor serving consecutive terms (the wording is in Section 17 of Article IV). Approved by 72.9 percent of the electorate, the measure marked Hearnes's popularity and removed a large barrier to powerful executive leadership. A governor who might be around for eight years is a much more formidable force, more able to push forward an agenda, than a governor who has only four years to accomplish a legacy.

As for the Democratic Party organization, it floundered. In 1968 three Democrats competed for its nomination for U.S. Senate, and by 1972 five major and five minor candidates were competing for the party's gubernatorial nomination. The party organization was no longer able to manage, referee, or head off the ambitions of its increasing pool of aspiring candidates. By the early 1970s the weakness of the Democrats had spread to the Republicans: in 1972 the new-wave candidate Kit Bond challenged and beat party regular Bus King (recall the earlier discussion on p. 76). Missouri political party organizations had clearly lost their punch. Hearnes was able to rebuild the party organization's strength and organize his insurgent supporters, and he was especially capable at captivating legislators of his party with his leadership chops, but in 1970 an initiative taking a tax increase to the voters went awry, and Hearnes stood weakened from that point onward until the end of his term in January 1973.

The patronage system started collapsing along with party rule. Although Hearnes was able to supply supporters with positions in the state bureaucracy and satisfy their needs for gainful employment, losing control over primary election outcomes meant that even the governor had no way to ensure the future continuity of his appointments. Who would win which nomination next? Would another insurgent take the governorship? Could the Democratic Party remain impregnable? More personally, each patronage employee had to ask, "How long can I keep this job?" Doubts grew.

In the meantime, pressures were mounting for reorganization of state government. Eighty-seven separate entities reported directly to the governor, and amid this mishmash of agencies, bureaus, offices, boards, and other administrative bodies, the governor, who was technically the superior and therefore responsible to the electorate for the performance of every administrative unit, had a hard time keeping an eye on all of them at once. Few units were delineated by function, and they were mostly staffed through patronage. Reorganization brought merit personnel systems to some new departments, such as social services and mental health, although some departments kept the patronage system[60] (the customs of the "lug" and enforced attendance at political party picnics, however, did fade out). The Department of Highways already used bipartisan hiring practices. Everywhere that patronage waned, the governor faced greater odds in accomplishing his or her agenda through the bureaucracy because under reorganization, instead of appointing all employees, the governor was restricted

---

[60]The former Department of Consumer Affairs, Regulation, and Licensing (CARL), now the Department of Economic Development, still used patronage considerations in hiring as late as the 1980s.

to appointing the department head and a small number of sub-cabinet positions. And to complete many of these appointments post-reorganization the governor needed Senate confirmation, whereas for the patronage appointments, the governor did not have to run his or her personnel choices past the Senate.

With these three shifts—(1) reorganization, (2) the expansion of the governor's time in office to two successive terms, and (3) the decline of patronage—all hitting at the same time, where does the governor's power now stand?

Certainly having two successive terms seems to have turned into a plus for the governor's power. Since Hearnes, three governors have succeeded themselves,[61] and each of the first two has been a formidable advocate for his agenda (we withhold judgment on the outgoing incumbent because it would be premature to classify him yet). In this period, "Kit" Bond served two terms (1973–77 and 1981–85), but non-sequential due to the intervening victory of the one-term Democrat Joe Teasdale (1977–81), and there have been two other one-term governors, Bob Holden (2001–05) and Matt Blunt (2005–09). The one-term governors have generally had only one term due to faltering popularity; Holden ran for reelection but was successfully challenged in the Democratic primary by then state auditor (now U.S. senator) Claire McCaskill;[62] Blunt faced low numbers in performance polls. These results are inconclusive but offer some basis to assert that governors who lose (or never achieve) popularity will only hold the office for one term,[63] and that governors who are reelected for a second term have a better chance at policy breakthroughs.[64]

The streamlining of state government helps the governor focus more effectively on his or her agenda, but there is a potential price to pay in having to share appointment power with the Senate. The Senate has not wielded its power to check the governor excessively, but power tussles have taken place. In 2002–03, Governor Holden appointed on an interim basis as chair of the Labor and Industrial Relations Commission Renee Slusher, who had been a board member of the trial lawyers association (MATA). The Republicans thought she was biased in favor of unions. Holden defended the appointee's record as balanced (she had a record because she had already been voting on the commission since her interim appointment). But the Republicans were feeling empowered, having just taken over as majority party in the assembly, and Slusher suffered for it. Still, the Senate confirmed 200 other interim

[61]These were John Ashcroft (1985–93), Mel Carnahan (1993–2000), and Jay Nixon (2009–present). Carnahan died in an airplane crash while campaigning for a U.S. Senate seat but had been reelected to the governorship and only missed the last three months of his second term.

[62]Holden lost popularity almost immediately on taking up the reins of the governorship by throwing the costliest inauguration ceremony in state history; he had to spend the rest of his term in office raising money to pay off the debts so incurred. The Republicans took over the General Assembly during his tenure (election of 2002), and having the opposition party in control (for the first time in 48 years) made for difficulties in getting his agenda accomplished.

[63]They may step down, like Blunt in 2008, or lose in their bid for reelection, like Bond in 1976, Teasdale in 1980, or Holden in 2004.

[64]Writing in 1978, Larry Sabato, in his classic study of the office of American governor, *Goodbye to Good-Time Charlie* (D. C. Heath & Company), rates Hearnes and Bond as particularly good leaders.

appointments,[65] so refusal to confirm is atypical and may not present as much of an impediment to gubernatorial power as one might think. Governors do need, however, to take note of the possibility that the Senate might deny confirmation, even if that is quite unlikely. In June 2016, Governor Nixon appointed three new members to the nine-member University of Missouri Board of Curators, despite Republican party leadership warnings that they would not confirm any of his appointments because he was a "lame duck" governor. One of Nixon's nominees, Mary Nelson, an African American lawyer from St. Louis, was nominated in 2015 but did not receive Senate approval then. One Senate leader protested that Nixon was stacking the university's board with his "lawyer buddies" so that when he left the governorship he could be appointed to the vacant presidency of the university.[66]

Probably the streamlining of the state agencies is of most help to governors with an activist or a reform agenda. The snag is that few recent Missouri governors have had such an agenda. Hearnes was once acclaimed as an insurgent with new ideas, and he did try to increase state revenues but was beaten back on that issue (Senator Blackwell's initiative to repeal the new tax measure is discussed in Article X, p. 212). Hearnes set the stage for administrative reorganization by helping usher through the constitutional amendments that facilitated this modernization of the face of state government. Bond embraced administrative reorganization and was a driver in its accomplishment, but was otherwise conservative in his approach. Ashcroft pursued term limits, but, except for getting this notion accepted for the General Assembly, was played the fool by the federal courts that snagged the provision requiring that candidates for office be shame-labeled on the ballot as to whether or not they supported term limits. Ashcroft's agenda was otherwise quite conservative—his reforms were conservative reforms such as making the criminal justice system harsher and lowering taxes. Carnahan had success in school finance reform, enjoying as he did Democratic majorities. Holden and Blunt, the two most recent one-termers, had little success in the legislature. The lesson to pull from their experience is that personal popularity is key to getting legislative cooperation—Carnahan had it, Holden lost it, and Blunt never had it. As for Nixon, he faced strong Republican majorities in both chambers his entire governorship in a time of high partisan polarization. It can't be held against him that he was unable to achieve much of an agenda.

SECTION 5. Commissions of state officers.—The governor shall commission all officers unless otherwise provided by law. All commissions shall be issued in the name of

[65]Julian Pecquet, "Senate Republicans Reject Gov. Holden's Labor Commission Appointee," Missouri Digital News, www.mdn.org (accessed 1/9/17).
[66]Koran Addo, "Nixon Names 3 New UM Curators, Ignoring Republican Threat to Reject Them," *St. Louis Post-Dispatch*, June 8, 2016. It should be noted that the argument against Nixon's naming of these officials was essentially the same argument used against President Obama's nomination of Merrick Garland to the U.S. Supreme Court. Both Nixon and Obama were considered "lame ducks," even though that term is ordinarily used only for incumbents who have lost their bid for reelection and not applied to incumbents serving out the last year of their last permissible term.

the state, signed by the governor, sealed with the great seal of the state and attested by the secretary of state.

SECTION 6. Commander in chief of militia—authority.—The governor shall be the commander in chief of the militia, except when it is called into the service of the United States, and may call out the militia to execute the laws, suppress actual and prevent threatened insurrection, and repel invasion.

Militias in Great Britain and colonial America included all able-bodied males, usually from 18 through 45 or 50 years of age. These men were supposed to equip themselves with a musket or other arm and stay prepared to serve on short deployments in case of emergency. In 1903, Congress acted to reorganize and modernize state militias by creating a professional "organized" militia, dubbed the (state) National Guard, as distinguished from the colonial-era "unorganized" militia. Congress has since created various other organized units, such as the Air National Guard. Some states have also organized their own defense units. The term *militia* was still in use in 1875 when Missouri's third constitution was adopted, and the wording was retained in the 1945 Constitution even though the militia had been redefined.

The governor can use the militia for the purposes mentioned above, but the president can also, under the U.S. Constitution, "federalize" the state military units to enforce federal law (which might run counter to state law). A notable example of this was President Eisenhower's handling of the Little Rock, Arkansas, school desegregation crisis of 1957. The Supreme Court had ordered the desegregation of Central High School in Little Rock, but Governor Orval Faubus called out the Arkansas National Guard and ordered it to prevent the black students from entering the school. President Eisenhower then took charge of the situation by federalizing the Arkansas National Guard and ordering them back to their barracks and armories; he then brought in the 101st Airborne Division to protect the black students while rioting mobs tried to prevent integration. Later, after Eisenhower could be confident that they would follow orders, he returned the Arkansas National Guard to duty.[67] A notable example of use of the Missouri state National Guard unfolded in Ferguson, Missouri, in the summer of 2014, when Governor Nixon called out the Guard in response to unrest over the police killing of Michael Brown, an unarmed young black man.

SECTION 7. Reprieves, commutations and pardons—limitations on power.—The governor shall have power to grant reprieves, commutations and pardons, after conviction,

---

[67]Another well-known example was Alabama Governor George Wallace's "stand in the schoolhouse door" in 1963; the University of Alabama at Tuscaloosa was to begin summer school, and two black students were going to register. Governor Wallace stood in the doorway of the building in which the new students would register for classes, aiming to symbolically interpose himself as a barrier between the federal government and the people of the state of Alabama. But President Kennedy federalized 100 troops from the Alabama National Guard to enforce desegregation, and Wallace backed down almost immediately since he did not want violence.

for all offenses except treason and cases of impeachment, upon such conditions and with such restrictions and limitations as he may deem proper, subject to provisions of law as to the manner of applying for pardons. The power to pardon shall not include the power to parole.

Like the president of the United States (see U.S. Const. Art. II, Sec. 2), the governor of the state of Missouri has the power to grant reprieves, commutations, and pardons for criminal offenses. In effect, a pardon commutes the sentence of a convicted criminal and allows him or her to leave jail or prison. In Missouri, the governor can issue either a full pardon or a partial pardon.

SECTION 8. Concurrent resolutions—duty of governor—exceptions—limitation of effect.—Every resolution to which the concurrence of the senate and house of representatives may be necessary, except on questions of adjournment, going into joint session, and of amending this constitution, shall be presented to the governor, and before the same shall take effect, shall be proceeded upon in the same manner as in the case of a bill; provided, that no resolution shall have the effect to repeal, extend, or amend any law.

SECTION 9. Governor's messages and recommendations to assembly—call of extra sessions.—The governor shall, at the commencement of each session of the general assembly, at the close of his term of office, and at such other times as he may deem necessary, give to the general assembly information as to the state of the government, and shall recommend to its consideration such measures as he shall deem necessary and expedient. On extraordinary occasions he may convene the general assembly by proclamation, wherein he shall state specifically each matter on which action is deemed necessary.

Both the U.S. Constitution (see U.S. Const. Art. II, Sec. 3) and the Missouri Constitution require the executive to address the legislature annually and give a report on the state of the government and to recommend measures he or she deems "necessary and expedient." Typically, both the governor's and the president's address are given in the form of a speech in front of the gathered legislature in January of each year. President Woodrow Wilson in 1913 began the modern tradition of delivering the State of the Union on the floor of the House of Representatives.

SECTION 10. Lieutenant governor—qualifications, powers and duties.—There shall be a lieutenant governor who shall have the same qualifications as the governor and shall be ex officio president of the senate. In committee of the whole he may debate all questions, and shall cast the deciding vote on equal division in the senate and on joint vote of both houses.

Modeled after the U.S. vice president (see U.S. Const. Art. II, Sec. 1), the lieutenant governor of Missouri serves as the second-in-command of the executive behind the governor. As the Missouri Constitution stipulates, the lieutenant governor must qualify for the position in the same way as the governor and also presides over the state Senate (just as the vice president presides over the U.S. Senate). In *State v. Cason*, 507 S.W.2d 405 (Mo. 1974), the supreme court of Missouri held that the lieutenant governor has the explicit right to preside over the Senate but is also subject to the same procedural rules as the senators when he or she acts as the presiding officer. But the Senate, which had voted before this ruling to give the power to assign bills (to committee) and to rule on points of order to the president pro tempore of the Senate, could oblige the lieutenant governor to abide by these same rules. Thus the lieutenant governor cannot assign bills to committee nor rule on points of order, but has the power to preside and can vote in case of a tie vote.

Interestingly, since the offices of the governor and the lieutenant governor are elected separately, the lieutenant governor may end up being from a different political party than the governor. For example, in the 2012–16 office term cycle, Jay Nixon, a Democrat, was the governor while Peter Kinder, a Republican, was the lieutenant governor. Originally, it was possible under the U.S. Constitution for the president and vice president to be from different political parties—as was the case when Thomas Jefferson (a Democratic-Republican) served as vice president to John Adams (a Federalist)—but the passage of the Twelfth Amendment has made this unlikely in modern times.

SECTION 11(a). **Order of succession to governorship, when.**—If the governor-elect dies before taking office, the lieutenant governor-elect shall take the term of the governor-elect. On the death, conviction or impeachment, or resignation of the governor, the lieutenant governor shall become governor for the remainder of the term. If there be no lieutenant governor the president pro tempore of the senate, the speaker of the house, the secretary of state, the state auditor, the state treasurer or the attorney general in succession shall become governor. On the failure to qualify, absence from the state or other disability of the governor, the powers, duties and emoluments of the governor shall devolve upon the lieutenant governor for the remainder of the term or until the disability is removed. If there be no lieutenant governor, or for any of said causes the lieutenant governor is incapable of acting, the president pro tempore of the senate, the speaker of the house, the secretary of state, the state auditor, the state treasurer, and the attorney general in succession shall act as governor until the disability is removed.

The most recent succession in office took place in 2000, when Lieutenant Governor Roger Wilson became governor for the short remaining term of office after Governor Mel Carnahan was killed in an airplane accident. Carnahan had about two months left in his second term.

SECTION 11(b). **Governor's declaration of disability, effect of—disability board, membership, duties—governor to resume office, when—disputed illness, supreme court to decide.**—Whenever the governor transmits to the president pro tempore of the senate and the speaker of the house of representatives his written declaration that he is unable to discharge the powers and duties of his office, and until he transmits to them a written declaration to the contrary, such powers and duties shall be discharged by the lieutenant governor, or if there be no lieutenant governor, by the president pro tempore of the senate, the speaker of the house, secretary of state, the state auditor, the state treasurer, or the attorney general in succession, as acting governor. Whenever a majority of a disability board comprised of the lieutenant governor, the secretary of state, the state auditor, the state treasurer, the attorney general, president pro tempore of the senate, the speaker of the house of representatives, the majority floor leader of the senate, and majority floor leader of the house, transmits to the president pro tempore of the senate and the speaker of the house of representatives their written declaration that the governor is unable to discharge the powers and duties of his office, the lieutenant governor, or if there be no lieutenant governor, the president pro tempore of the senate, the speaker of the house, the secretary of state, the state auditor, the state treasurer or the attorney general in succession, shall immediately assume the powers and duties of the office as acting governor. Thereafter when the governor transmits to the disability board his written declaration that no inability exists, he shall resume the powers and duties of his office on the fourth day after he transmits such declaration unless a majority of the disability board transmits their written declaration that the governor is unable to discharge the powers and duties of his office to the supreme court within that four day period, and the supreme court shall then convene to decide the issue. If the supreme court within twenty-one days after receipt of such declaration, determines by a majority vote of all members thereof that the governor is unable to discharge the powers and duties of his office, the acting governor shall continue to discharge the same as acting governor; otherwise, the governor shall resume the powers and duties of his office.

SECTION 11(c). **Acting as governor not to vacate regular office.**—If any state officer other than the lieutenant governor is acting as governor, his regular elective office shall not be deemed vacant and all duties of that office shall be performed by his chief administrative assistant.

SECTION 12. **Executive department, composition of—elective officials—departments and offices enumerated.**—The executive department shall consist of all state elective and appointive officials and employees except officials and employees of the legislative and judicial departments. In addition to the governor and lieutenant governor there shall be a state auditor, secretary of state, attorney general, a state treasurer, an office of administration, a department of agriculture, a department of conservation, a department of natural resources, a department of elementary and secondary education, a department of higher education, a department of highways and transportation, a department of insurance, a department of labor and industrial relations, a department of economic development, a department of public safety, a department of revenue, a department of social services, and a department of mental health. In addition to the elected officers, there shall not be more than fifteen departments and the office of administration. The general assembly may create by law two departments, in addition to those named, provided that the departments shall be headed by a director or commission appointed by the governor on the advice and consent of the senate. The director or commission shall have administrative responsibility and authority for the department created by law. Unless discontinued all present or future boards, bureaus, commissions and other agencies of the state exercising administrative or executive authority shall be assigned by law or by the governor as provided by law to the office of administration or to one of the fifteen administrative departments to which their respective powers and duties are germane.

SECTION 13. **State auditor—qualifications and duties—limitations on duties.**—The state auditor shall have the same qualifications as the governor. He shall establish appropriate systems of accounting for all public officials of the state, post-audit the accounts of all state agencies and audit the treasury at least once annually. He shall make all other audits and investigations required by law, and shall make an annual report to the governor and general assembly. He shall establish appropriate systems of accounting for the political subdivisions of the state, supervise their budgeting systems, and audit their accounts as provided by law. No duty shall be imposed on him by law which is not related to the supervising and auditing of the receipt and expenditure of public funds.

SECTION 14. Secretary of state—duties—state seal—official register—limitation on duties.—The secretary of state shall be custodian of the seal of the state, and authenticate therewith all official acts of the governor except the approval of laws. The seal shall be called the "Great Seal of the State of Missouri," and its present emblems and devices shall not be subject to change. He shall keep a register of the official acts of the governor, attest them when necessary, and when required shall lay copies thereof, and of all papers relative thereto, before either house of the general assembly. He shall be custodian of such records, and documents and perform such duties in relation thereto, and in relation to elections and corporations, as provided by law, but no duty shall be imposed on him by law which is not related to his duties as prescribed in this constitution.

SECTION 15. State treasurer—duties—custody, investment and deposit of state funds—duties limited—nonstate funds to be in custody and invested by department of revenue—nonstate funds defined.—The state treasurer shall be custodian of all state funds and funds received from the United States government. The department of revenue shall take custody of and invest nonstate funds as defined herein, and other moneys authorized to be held by the department of revenue. All revenue collected and moneys received by the state which are state funds or funds received from the United States government shall go promptly into the state treasury. All revenue collected and moneys received by the department of revenue which are nonstate funds as defined herein shall be promptly credited to the fund provided by law for that type of money. Immediately upon receipt of state or United States funds the state treasurer shall deposit all moneys in the state treasury in banking institutions selected by him and approved by the governor and state auditor, and he shall hold them for the benefit of the respective funds to which they belong and disburse them as provided by law. Unless otherwise provided by law, all interest received on nonstate funds shall be credited to such funds. The state treasurer shall determine by the exercise of his best judgment the amount of moneys in his custody that are not needed for current expenses and shall place all such moneys on time deposit, bearing interest, in banking institutions in this state selected by the state treasurer and approved by the governor and state auditor or in obligations of the United States government or any agency or instrumentality thereof maturing and becoming payable not more than five years from the date of purchase. In addition the treasurer may enter into repurchase agreements maturing and becoming payable within ninety days secured by United States Treasury obligations or obligations of United States government agencies or instrumentalities of any maturity, as provided by law. The treasurer may also invest in banker's acceptances issued by domestic commercial banks possessing the highest rating issued by a nationally recognized rating agency and in commercial paper issued by domestic corporations which has received the highest rating issued by a nationally recognized rating agency. Investments in banker's acceptances and commercial paper shall mature and become payable not more than one hundred eighty days from the date of purchase, maintain the highest rating throughout the duration of the investment and meet any other requirements provided by law. The state treasurer shall prepare, maintain and adhere to a written investment policy which shall include an asset allocation plan limiting the total amount of state money which may be invested in each investment category authorized by this section. The investment and deposit of state, United States and nonstate funds shall be subject to such restrictions and requirements as may be prescribed by law. Banking institutions in which state and United States funds are deposited by the state treasurer shall give security satisfactory to the governor, state auditor and state treasurer for the safekeeping and payment of the deposits and interest thereon pursuant to deposit agreements made with the state treasurer pursuant to law. No duty shall be imposed on the state treasurer by law which is not related to the receipt, investment, custody and disbursement of state funds and funds received from the United States government. As used in the section, the term "banking institutions" shall include banks, trust companies, savings and loan associations, credit unions, production credit associations authorized by act of the United States Congress, and other financial institutions which are authorized by law to accept funds for deposit or which in the case of production credit associations, issues securities. As used in this section, the term "nonstate funds" shall include all taxes and fees imposed by political subdivisions and collected by the department of revenue; all taxes which are imposed by the state, collected by the department of revenue and distributed by the department of revenue to political subdivisions; and all other moneys which are hereafter designated as "nonstate funds" to be administered by the department of revenue.

Besides determining the order of succession in office, Sections 10–15 and Section 17 set up what we call the "collective elective executive." As in most states, Missouri has multiple executive officers who win their offices not by gubernatorial appointment but by being elected independently of the governor. This is another upshot of the Jacksonian heritage: elections lend greater legitimacy to officials' actions and policy decisions, so having decision making in government dosed out to more elected leaders can make the task of governing easier. Such officeholders owe their offices to the electorate, which can therefore hold them accountable; if they displease the electorate, the mechanism of voter reprisals in the next election can punish them for erring. Five positions besides the governor are established in these sections: the lieutenant governor, the state treasurer, the secretary of state, the attorney general, and the state auditor. All except the auditor are elected in the fall of each leap year, putting them on the ballot in the same election as the candidates for president (and vice president), U.S. representatives, and U.S. senator (if one of the state's U.S. senator's terms is at an end).[68]

We need to make two comparisons to the national slate of officeholders to grasp how the governors face greater difficulty in governing their states than does the president in effectively exercising the reins of executive power. First, we will draw comparisons of the president's cabinet to the governor's cabinet, and then we will turn to comparing the governor's immediate successor (the lieutenant governor) to the president's immediate successor (the vice president).

---

[68]Ordinarily, each state has a U.S. senatorial election in two out of three even-numbered general elections, and no senatorial election at the other third national general election.

First, the president chooses all members of his Cabinet with senatorial consent. Ordinarily senatorial consent is easily achieved, although occasionally a presidential choice is turned down.[69] The federal Cabinet members (and their Missouri counterparts) are the vice president (lieutenant governor), secretary of state (same title in Missouri but different duties), secretary of the Treasury (state treasurer), attorney general (same title in Missouri), and comptroller general (state auditor, with somewhat different duties). The president chooses all these national Cabinet members and others (such as the secretaries of Agriculture, Commerce, Labor, and so on) and can fire them for any reason. For instance, President George W. Bush fired his first secretary of the Treasury, Paul O'Neill, for publicly disagreeing with the administration line that tax increases were undesirable. Bush also let go Secretary of Defense Donald Rumsfeld immediately after the election of 2006 resulted in the return of the opposition Democrats to majority control of both chambers of Congress, but Rumsfeld went through the ritual of resigning rather than being terminated. The president is in complete control over these key staffers; if they don't conform to his expectations, he can terminate their appointment. As subordinates, they are obliged to follow their boss's agenda—or else!

Let's look at the Missouri counterparts. The national secretary of state handles foreign affairs, but the Missouri secretary of state has no role in foreign affairs. Missouri's secretary of state's role bears on supervising elections, reporting election results, publishing the state manual ("Blue Book"), and maintaining the state's database.

Nationally, the secretary of the Treasury has an important role in financial policy. In Missouri, the treasurer is in charge of investing state funds, which implies deciding the soundest investments. Until 1972 the state didn't earn interest on its deposits in bank accounts.[70] Since 1972, in a reformed practice, the treasurer deposits funds where they will earn the most interest, and may even make deposits out of state. The treasurer is, like the governor, limited to two terms of office, which can be consecutive.

The national attorney general heads the Department of Justice, in charge of enforcing federal law, with a presence in each "district" of federal trial court in the form of the U.S. attorney, who serves as prosecutor of violations of federal law in that district. Missouri has two districts of federal trial court.[71] The U.S. attorney is

[69]The last contemporary refusal by the Senate to confirm a cabinet appointee was George H. W. Bush's appointment of Senator John Tower as secretary of defense (1989). Tower is the only former senator turned down by the Senate. For a while it looked like the Senate might reject Loretta Lynch, President Obama's nominee for attorney general, but the Senate eventually mustered a bare majority vote for her (56–43). However, she was nominated on November 8, 2014, and her appointment only came up for a Senate vote on April 16, 2015; her wait involved a longer delay than the combined wait of the previous seven nominees for that post.

[70]Thus, attracting these deposits was a bonanza for banks; the decision as to which bank to favor was patronage-based, so the treasurer could oblige the banks in which he made deposits to return the favor to him personally, giving treasurers good possibilities for runs for higher office.

[71]The two districts are Missouri East, with headquarters in St. Louis, in which court is held ordinarily in either St. Louis, Hannibal, or Cape Girardeau; and Missouri West, with headquarters in

charged with carrying forward the policy objectives of the Department of Justice by indicting (using federal grand juries) probable violators of federal law and trying the cases against those indicted in federal court. If a trial jury is empaneled, it will be composed of people from all counties within the division. Each U.S. attorney has a staff composed of lawyers who are appointed as assistant U.S. attorneys, as well as backup personnel for assistance. The federal attorney general's policy role includes determining which crimes to enforce tightly and which to let go. Under President Obama, for example, the attorney general has been in charge of DAPA and DACA. Under these policies, the laws against illegal immigration have not been pursued against noncitizen parents of minor American citizens or minors who are not citizens but have spent most of their life in the United States. The numerous districts of the Department of Justice have been following suit by not enforcing the full rigor of the law. The future of DAPA and DACA is now unsure; as this book goes to press, not only does the Supreme Court, in a tie vote on the merits of this policy, find itself upholding an adverse ruling by the Fifth Circuit U.S. Court of Appeals, but President Trump sounds committed to reversing these executive orders.

The state attorney general is the state's attorney. He or she defends the state against all legal claims, including felony criminal convictions at risk of being overturned on appeal to the Missouri Court of Appeals or the state supreme court. He or she is also required to represent the state in all civil claims necessary to protect the state's interests, rights, or powers. If the constitutionality of any state law is challenged, the attorney general (or a lawyer from the AG office) appears and answers for the state in any proceedings. The attorney general also has the power to issue official opinions that the executive or legislative branches or the county prosecuting attorneys may pose relating to their legal duties. Unlike the federal attorney general, the Missouri attorney general does not control prosecution policy.[72]

Kansas City, in which court is ordinarily held in Jefferson City, Springfield, Kansas City, St. Joseph, or Joplin. Court can be held elsewhere within these districts, but dedicated courtrooms are available in the places noted, and these cities are considered the headquarters of geographically designated "divisions." For instance, the central division of U.S. District Court in the Western District of Missouri ordinarily sits in Jefferson City.

[72]Decisions on whether or not to prosecute particular persons of interest (i.e., the process of indictment or filing an information to formally charge that person, and then proceeding to prepare to take that case to trial, even if the case ends up plea bargained so no trial is ultimately held) lie in the hands of the locally elected county prosecutors (called prosecuting attorneys in all counties of Missouri save in the county of St. Louis City, where the office title is circuit attorney). Prosecution policy is not determined centrally as it is at the federal level, where the U.S. attorneys implement policies laid out by the Department of Justice; instead, local prosecuting attorneys are elected by the county electorate, and the prosecutors choose which criminal laws they will enforce, which they will tread lightly upon, and which they will disregard altogether. Determining these priorities is called *prosecutorial discretion*. The state attorney general has little or no control over how the county prosecutors prioritize crimes, so law enforcement is highly localized in Missouri, as it is in most states.

The state auditorship is less comparable to its federal counterpart, the comptroller general. The comptroller audits accounts of spending agencies of the federal government to ensure that the monies are being spent for the correct purpose (i.e., the intention of the appropriations legislation) and validates payments for services, supplies, and the like. The auditor has roughly similar tasks: he or she and the office audit all state agencies, boards, commissions, the state court system, and counties that don't have a county auditor. The auditor can also be asked to audit local governmental entities by citizen petition. Both the federal and state offices constitute a check on the bureaucracy at their level of government. The big difference is that the state auditor is elected on a statewide basis, thus engaging the Jacksonian mechanism whereby elected officials are considered superior to appointed officials because they have a direct connection to, and direct approval from, the people. In contrast the comptroller general is appointed by the president and confirmed by the Senate[73] for a 15-year term, whereas the Missouri state auditor must seek reelection every four years.

The occupants of these four elective offices enjoy an accomplished staff that can perform the tasks of each office quite routinely, freeing up the elected head to use the office as a steppingstone for publicizing his or her activities and increasing his or her profile in preparation to run for higher office. Winning an election statewide to public office can whet the appetite for yet higher office.

The auditorship can particularly be parlayed into a more prominent and powerful elective office; examples include Kit Bond, who used only a two-year stint in the auditorship (1970–72) to propel himself successfully into the governorship (election of 1972), and Claire McCaskill, whose rise has been more deliberate: she was a state legislator (1983–89), then prosecuting attorney of Jackson County (1989–98), before ascending to statewide office as auditor in 1998. While auditor, she took on and beat the sitting governor in the Democratic primary election (2004) but lost narrowly in the general election; in 2006 she defeated the incumbent Republican U.S. senator and started in 2007 to serve the first of what has become two terms (possibly with more to follow) in the U.S. Senate.

The secretary of state can also rise within the ranks of statewide officeholders; Warren Hearnes, the insurgent Democrat who took on the party organization and the Pendergast machine in 1964, got the Democratic nomination for governor and took the governorship for two terms. Roy Blunt spent two terms as secretary of state (1985–93) before becoming a congressman (something of a step down) but eventually a U.S. senator (from 2011). Blunt's challenger for his senatorial seat in 2016 was then Secretary of State Jason Kander. Roy Blunt's son, Matt Blunt, won the office of secretary of state in the 2000 election, and then four years later became governor.

---

[73]Additionally, the comptroller general is removable by impeachment or joint resolution of Congress, so the Supreme Court has ruled that he or she and the General Accountability Office (GAO) are part of the legislative branch, and not of the executive branch (*Bowsher v. Synar,* 478 U.S. 714 [1986]). By way of comparison, the Missouri state auditor is part of the executive branch and not part of the legislative branch.

Robin Carnahan[74] replaced him in the office in the election of 2004 and held the office for two terms, during which she ran (unsuccessfully) for the U.S. Senate (2010), being thwarted by former secretary of state Roy Blunt. Needless to say, this office is a good launching pad for rising in the ranks of office.

Holding the office of state treasurer can also boost one's political career prospects. Jim Spainhower was treasurer from 1973 to 1981, and then unsuccessfully challenged Governor Joe Teasdale for the Democratic nomination for governor.[75] Mel Carnahan served as treasurer for one term (1981–85) and then after one term out returned as lieutenant governor, before being elected as governor in the 1992 cycle. Bob Holden served two terms as treasurer before successfully winning the governorship in the election of 2000.

The office of attorney general has in like manner served as a steppingstone for many political figures on their way up. Tom Eagleton was attorney general (1961–65), then lieutenant governor (1965–69), before running successfully in a competitive primary election in 1968 for the U.S. Senate seat.[76] The office of attorney general was also a big draw for Republicans as they labored in the 1960s and 1970s to become more than a minority party that habitually lost statewide elections. A great breakthrough was the election of John ("Jack") Danforth as attorney general in 1968; his victory ended a drought for Republicans in state politics. He hired Kit Bond and Clarence Thomas (later a Supreme Court justice) onto the staff of the attorney general's office; Bond, of course, soon demonstrated his electability when he ran successfully for state auditor in 1970, then for the Republican nod for governor, and finally took the governorship in the general election of 1972. Danforth tried for the U.S. Senate in 1970 but Stuart Symington, the incumbent Democrat, prevailed over him. In 1976, Danforth took the Senate seat in an election season that saw many upsets.[77] He served for 18 years in the U.S. Senate.[78]

[74]She is the daughter of Mel Carnahan, governor from 1993 to 2000, and Jean Carnahan, who was appointed U.S. senator in 2001 to serve out the first two years of the term to which Mel Carnahan was elected despite having passed away in an airplane crash during his campaign for that U.S. Senate seat. Jean Carnahan served those two years before losing her bid for reelection in the fall general election of 2002.

[75]Teasdale went on to lose to the Republican contender, Kit Bond, who was making a bid to return to the governor's mansion after four years in the political wilderness.

[76]Eagleton was briefly the 1972 Democratic vice presidential nominee (with George McGovern) but despite being removed and replaced on the national ticket he was able to serve from 1969 to 1987—18 years!—as U.S. senator.

[77]In 1976 the Democratic Party had three main candidates for the Senate seat nomination: the incumbent's son, James Symington; former governor Warren Hearnes; and Jerry Litton, a congressman with great charisma whom many were also betting on to become a future presidential contender. Litton won the primary but he and his entire family were killed when the airplane they were taking to a victory party in Kansas City crashed. The party committee had to choose whom to substitute on the ballot and selected Hearnes, but Danforth was a fresher face and won fairly easily.

[78]Danforth's career is notable for his many accomplishments, but one particularly memorable feat was his strategically valuable supporting orchestration on behalf of Clarence Thomas in 1991 during Senate Judiciary Committee hearings on Anita Hill's accusations of sexual harassment against Thomas.

Danforth was followed in the attorney general's office by John Ashcroft, who had first held office when Governor Kit Bond appointed him to serve out his (Bond's) term as auditor (1973–75). But Ashcroft lost his bid for reelection; the Democratic candidate was a CPA and successfully made an issue of Ashcroft's lack of that essential qualification for the office. So Attorney General Danforth provided employment for Ashcroft as an assistant attorney general. (Danforth's hires were a form of sponsorship verging on patronage.) When Danforth went for the Senate in 1976, Ashcroft won election as attorney general. Ashcroft served two terms in this office (1977–85), then ran for and took the governorship (1985–93). When Danforth stepped down as U.S. senator after three terms, Ashcroft replaced him (1994 election) but did not win a second term running against Mel Carnahan. Governor Carnahan had died in an airplane crash two weeks before the election, but his name remained on the ballot and the lieutenant governor, Roger Wilson (who became governor), promised to appoint Mrs. Jean Carnahan, the governor's widow, as U.S. senator if Carnahan's name drew a majority of the votes. Carnahan's name got 51 percent of the vote, marking the first time anyone ever won a Senate seat posthumously. Wilson appointed Mrs. Carnahan, and George W. Bush, winning the presidency, appointed Ashcroft as national attorney general, a post he held for the first term of the Bush administration.

All four of these offices of the "collective elective executive" permit ample flexibility for their occupants to heighten their public profiles, work out their standing on a set of issues that suits their emergent political designs, and pursue wider political contacts. Their functions in office are uncomplicated, and they can achieve kudos for simply allowing their professional staff to perform professionally.[79] In policy, they have less territory than the governor, but within that territory they can threaten the governor if he or she trespasses on their realm. The governor may have been elected, but so have they. They are potential trouble for the governor; they can breathe down his or her back if he or she turns hostile in any way, and without much media glare, while the governor will bear the brunt of any bad publicity. For all these reasons, the collective elective executive positions are thorns in the governor's side.

---

[79]The authors can identify only one of these officeholders in the last 40 years whose actions were said to impede the smooth functioning of employees. Also, one secretary of state, Judith Moriarty, was impeached and removed from office. Moriarty was awarded the fee office in Sedalia upon the electoral victory of Joseph Teasdale, later became county clerk of Pettis County (1982–90), and then won the election of 1992 to become Missouri's first woman secretary of state. Moriarty made waves when she changed the binding of the State Manual, the Blue Book, to mauve in celebration of women's role in the state's history. She also had copies of the state constitution bound in mauve. Unfortunately, in 1994, she was accused of using her position to help her son file for political office after the deadline for filing had passed; she had her office back-date a form. The Missouri House of Representatives impeached her and the state supreme court removed her from office. Governor Carnahan appointed Rebecca Cook as her replacement. But it should be noted that Moriarty was never accused of impeding the functioning of her professional staff in general, just of interfering in this one particular case involving her son.

It weakens the governor to have these independent and potentially ambitious power-holders nipping at his or her heels.

The lieutenant governor, in particular, poses special problems for the governor. Some states with lieutenant governors (not all states have this office) have decision rules that force the gubernatorial candidate to choose a lieutenant governor candidate and run as a team, with the voters casting one vote for the team; this way, compatibility is assured. If the governor leaves the state, he or she can rest assured that the lieutenant governor will not start reversing key executive orders and repudiating the governor's commitments. But Missouri has separate elections for the two offices, so the governor does not pick the lieutenant governor. This system leaves open the possibility of a clash between them. In Missouri, we have witnessed Democratic governors who have to govern with Republican lieutenant governors looking over their shoulders, and vice versa. Since the first election of Kit Bond in 1972, the governor and lieutenant governor have been of the same party for four terms, or 16 years, but these two offices have been held by candidates of different parties for seven terms, or 28 years.

The lieutenant governorship has not been as favorable to political career development as the four other elective executive positions. Bond's first lieutenant governor, William Phelps, won a second term under a Democratic governor, but then went nowhere. Kenneth Rothman, Bond's second lieutenant governor, ran against John Ashcroft in 1984 but received a drubbing in a campaign in which Ashcroft pitted rural Missouri against urban Missouri; Ashcroft ended up carrying 106 counties and 57 percent of the vote—then the largest Republican victory for a gubernatorial candidate in state history. Harriett Woods was the first woman to hold statewide office when she won the lieutenant governorship in 1984, but she retired after one term (1985–89). Mel Carnahan was the second lieutenant governor in Ashcroft's second term as governor (1989–93), and he did succeed in moving on up to the governorship. Carnahan's lieutenant governor, Roger Wilson, inherited the office when Carnahan died, and then stepped down. Joe Maxwell was Holden's lieutenant governor but only served one term (2000–05), leaving public life due to an illness in his family. In 2004, Peter Kinder, a Republican, won the lieutenant governorship, and held the position through early 2017. He was succeeded by current lieutenant governor Republican Mike Parson.

SECTION 16. Filing of administrative rules and regulations.—All rules and regulations of any board or other administrative agency of the executive department, except those relating to its organization and internal management, shall take effect not less than ten days after the filing thereof in the office of the secretary of state.

SECTION 17. Elective state officers—time of election and terms—limitation on reelection—selection of department heads—removal and qualifications of appointive officers.—The governor, lieutenant governor, secretary of state, state treasurer and attorney general shall be elected at the presidential elections for terms of four years each. The state auditor shall be elected for a term of two years at the general election in the year 1948, and his successors shall be elected for terms of four years. No person shall be elected governor or treasurer more than twice, and no person who has held the office of governor or treasurer, or acted as governor or treasurer, for more than two years of a term to which some other person was elected to the office of governor or treasurer shall be elected to the office of governor or treasurer more than once. The heads of all the executive departments shall be appointed by the governor, by and with the advice and consent of the senate. All appointive officers may be removed by the governor and shall possess the qualifications required by this constitution or by law.

SECTION 18. Election returns—board of state canvassers—time of meeting and duties—requirement for election—tie votes.—The returns of every election for governor, lieutenant governor, secretary of state, state auditor, state treasurer and attorney general shall be sealed and transmitted by the returning officers to the secretary of state, who shall appoint two disinterested judges of a court of record of the state, and the three shall constitute a board of state canvassers. The board shall meet at the state capitol on, or at the call of the secretary of state before, the second Tuesday of December next after the election and forthwith open and canvass the returns of the votes cast and from the face thereof ascertain and proclaim the result of the election. The persons having the highest number of votes for the respective offices shall be declared elected, and if two or more persons have an equal and the highest number of votes for the same office, at its next regular session the general assembly, by joint vote and without delay, shall choose one of such persons for the office.

SECTION 19. Department personnel—selection and removal—merit system— veterans' preference.—The head of each department may select and remove all appointees in the department except as otherwise provided in this constitution, or by law. All employees in the state eleemosynary and penal institutions, and other state employees as provided by law, shall be selected on the basis of merit, ascertained as nearly as practicable by competitive examinations; provided that any honorably discharged member of the armed services of the United States who is a citizen of this state shall have preference in examination and appointment as prescribed by law.

Section 19 positions the merit system as an ideal toward which the state should strive; it was inserted in the constitution with the expectation that the General Assembly would over time provide for merit selection of employees by law. Some employees are under merit systems (notably, employees in state eleemosynary [charitable] and penal institutions; the state's hospitals, including mental hospitals; and its prison system), but the use of merit considerations is still not universal. Even where used, there is flexibility within this provision; competitive exams should be used "as nearly as practicable," so they are not absolutely required even for the specified subset of employees. It must be said that state jobs do not pay well; Missouri state employees are near the bottom in comparison to state employees nationwide. The state has ended up with "lite" merit systems where it has them because its pay scales are unattractive to new hires. This section was amended in October 1971, under the leadership of Warren Hearnes, to include preference for all veterans, rather than only veterans who were Missouri residents when they entered military service. The amendment was quite popular, passing with 65.5 percent of the ballots cast.

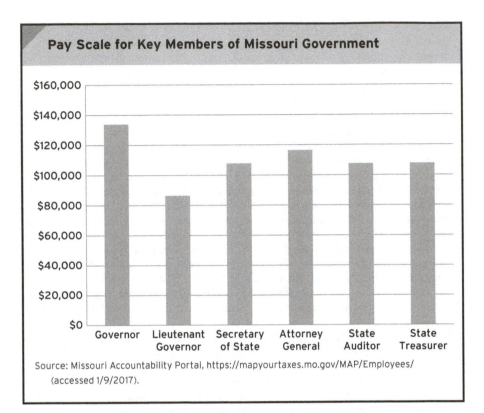

Pay Scale for Key Members of Missouri Government

Source: Missouri Accountability Portal, https://mapyourtaxes.mo.gov/MAP/Employees/ (accessed 1/9/2017).

SECTION 20. Location of executive and administrative offices.—The executive and administrative officials and departments herein provided for shall establish their principal offices and keep all necessary public records, books and papers at the City of Jefferson.

SECTION 21. Limitation on changes of salaries—fees, costs.—The officers named in this article shall receive for their services salaries fixed by law, which shall not be increased or diminished during their terms. After the expiration of the terms of those now in office the officers named shall not receive to their own use any fees, costs, perquisites of office or other compensation, and all fees provided by law for any service performed by them shall be paid in advance into the state treasury.

Revenue

SECTION 22. Department of revenue, duties of—director, appointment of.—The department of revenue shall be in charge of a director of revenue appointed by the governor, by and with the advice and consent of the senate. The department shall have divisions as provided by law. The department shall collect all taxes and fees payable to the state as provided by law.

SECTION 23. Fiscal year—limitations on appropriations—specification of amount and purpose.—The fiscal year of the state and all its agencies shall be the twelve months beginning on the first day of July in each year. The general assembly shall make appropriations for one or two fiscal years, and the sixty-third general assembly shall also make appropriations for the six months ending June 30, 1945. Every appropriation law shall distinctly specify the amount and purpose of the appropriation without reference to any other law to fix the amount or purpose.

Sections 22–28 provide rules for the appropriation and expenditure of state monies. The fiscal year is constitutionally defined (at the federal level it is defined statutorily) in Section 23, which was carried forward in the proposed and accepted constitution of 1945. The 1945 date was included to cover the fiscal half-year gap created by the changeover in constitutions.

SECTION 24. Governor's budget and recommendations as to revenue.—The governor shall, within thirty days after it convenes in each regular session, submit to the general assembly a budget for the ensuing appropriation period, containing the estimated available revenues of the state and a complete and itemized plan of proposed expenditures of the state and all its agencies. The Governor shall not determine estimated available revenues of the state using any projection of new revenues to be created from proposed legislation that has not been passed into law by the general assembly. Estimates of any unspent fund balances, without regard to actual or estimated revenues but accounting for all existing appropriations, that will constitute a surplus during the fiscal year immediately preceding the fiscal year or years for which the governor is recommending a budget, may be included in the estimated revenue available for expenditure during the fiscal year or years for which the governor is recommending a budget. As used in this section, new revenues shall not include existing provisions of law subject to expiration during the ensuing appropriation period.

This is the executive budget, which gives the governor the power to play first. Here, the executive branch proposes, and the legislative branch disposes. But proposing is the first step, and it permits seizing the initiative. The governor's office (the Division of Budget and Planning in the Office of Administration) determines an estimate of state revenue based on economic projections, which gives some idea of the money that will be available for state programs. While the governor's office works on this estimate, each entity in the state government prepares a report on how it spent the money appropriated to it in the previous cycle, what is happening in the present cycle, and what it proposes to meet its needs in the upcoming cycle. The Division of Budget and Planning then assembles this information and works with the governor's staff to match estimated state income to proposed state spending in the executive budget. This is a line-item budget: it displays every item, whether it be a "service" item (i.e., salaries, wages, and staff benefits) or an equipment item (i.e., copy machines, trucks, fuel, utilities, and the like). The governor then decides the level of spending to propose for each separate item. If the governor disfavors particular programs, his or her executive budget can allocate less money to the agency for that program; if he or she favors particular programs or entities of government, his or her budget can reflect those priorities. This budget then goes to the legislature. It is generally considered that by acting first, the governor has much more influence than the legislature does over the eventual outcome(s); the governor acts, and the legislature reacts.

In 2014 the wording of this section was altered. The governor could previously include potentially collectible tax monies in the budget estimate of revenue, on the supposition that new tax measures would pass the legislature. The second sentence of the section targets this situation: it stems from the suspicion that the governor might manipulate the budget by including taxes proposed but not actually adopted in the total estimated revenues. The next two sentences are murky but do seem to allow inclusion of unspent funds as estimated revenue. Yet if a tax expires, the revenue it produces shall not be included in the estimated revenue in the budget. Dropping the last provision is ominously anti-tax: before the adoption of the changed and expanded wording, the constitution urged the governor to propose new revenue measures to meet budgetary needs; now this is suppressed.

The addition of this new wording (and the dropping of the old wording) doesn't have fixed meaning until the courts react; we must await lawsuits to determine how this will fall out. The major metropolitan dailies (both the *St. Louis Post-Dispatch* and the *Kansas City Star*) took editorial stands against adoption of this amendment, arguing that it reflected a grudge match between the Republicans dominant in the legislature and Governor Nixon. Governor Nixon had used his constitutional powers to reduce spending for certain budgeted programs (to see how he could do this, look

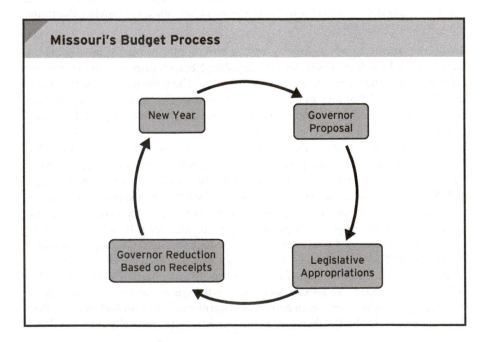

Missouri's Budget Process

New Year → Governor Proposal → Legislative Appropriations → Governor Reduction Based on Receipts → New Year

to Section 26 of this article). But the Republican majority complained that he was doing this even when revenues were meeting expectations, policy moves that Nixon defended as both within his power and prudently advisable to maintain a balanced budget. The *St. Louis Post-Dispatch* commented that this measure could potentially weaken the state's ability to adjust expenditures to revenue prospects, which could inspire the credit rating agencies to lower Missouri's AAA score, making the interest rate that the state pays go up.

SECTION 25. Limitation of governor's budget on power of appropriations.—Until it acts on all the appropriations recommended in the budget, neither house of the general assembly shall pass any appropriation other than emergency appropriations recommended by the governor.

SECTION 26. Power of partial veto of appropriation bills—procedure—limitations.— The governor may object to one or more items or portions of items of appropriation of money in any bill presented to him, while approving other portions of the bill. On signing it he shall append to the bill a statement of the items or portions of items to which he objects and such items or portions shall not take effect. If the general assembly be in session he shall transmit to the house in which the bill originated a copy of the statement, and the items or portions objected to shall be reconsidered separately. If it be not in session he shall transmit the bill within forty-five days to the office of the secretary of state with his approval or reasons for disapproval. The governor shall not reduce any appropriation for free public schools, or for the payment of principal and interest on the public debt.

This section gives the governor the power of the item veto, a major power that the president of the United States lacks.[80] The Missouri governor may reduce, even reduce to zero, any appropriation (except for the public schools and for payment of interest or repayment of principle on public debt). Even with these exceptions, the line-item veto gives the governor immense power; the legislature may alter the priorities in the executive budget proposed by raising spending for a particular program, but the governor can reduce the amounts right back down to what he or she proposed (or lower).

SECTION 27. Power of governor to control rate of and reduce expenditures.—The governor may control the rate at which any appropriation is expended during the period of the appropriation by allotment or other means, and may reduce the expenditures of the state or any of its agencies below their appropriations whenever the actual revenues are less than the revenue estimates upon which the appropriations were based.

Even if the governor does not exercise the item veto, he or she can control and lower the rate of the release of funds. Again, vis-à-vis the General Assembly, this is

---

[80]There was a move to give the line-item veto to the president; Congress passed the Line Item Veto Act in 1996. But the U.S. Supreme Court found it unconstitutional in the case of *Clinton v. City of New York* (1998).

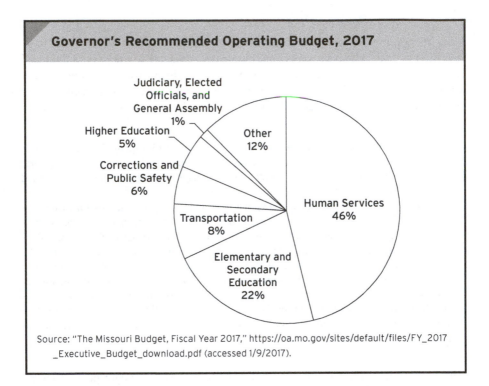

Governor's Recommended Operating Budget, 2017

Source: "The Missouri Budget, Fiscal Year 2017," https://oa.mo.gov/sites/default/files/FY_2017 _Executive_Budget_download.pdf (accessed 1/9/2017).

a formidable power, and its exercise seems to be what has provoked the legislature into passing and promoting the changes noted above in Section 24.[81]

SECTION 27(a). Budget Reserve Fund established—investment—excess transfer to general revenue, when.—1. There is hereby established within the state treasury a fund to be known as the "Budget Reserve Fund". The balances in the cash operating reserve fund and the budget stabilization fund shall be transferred to the budget reserve fund.

2. The commissioner of administration may, throughout any fiscal year, transfer amounts from the budget reserve fund to the general revenue fund or any other state fund without

---

[81]The president also lacks this power, as President Richard Nixon found out when he tried to reduce appropriations due to local governments under the Federal Water Pollution Control Act (FWPCA) by impounding some of the money. Congress had passed amendments to the FWPCA, over Nixon's veto, which made federal money grants available to local governments for sewers and clean water projects. Nixon directed the head of the Environmental Protection Agency (EPA) to withhold some of the money available to the recipients of the program. New York City sued Russell E. Train, head of the EPA, to force the administration to release the impounded funds. The U.S. Supreme Court found no authorization in the legislation establishing the EPA for such impoundments, and no constitutional authority for an impoundment either (*Train v. City of New York*, 420 U.S. 35 [1975]). Even if the president opposes the law, he or she is required to faithfully execute it. The Missouri governor faces no such barrier to the exercise of budgetary power.

other legislative action if he determines that such amounts are necessary for the cash requirements of this state. Such transfers shall be deemed "cash operating transfers".

3. The commissioner of administration shall transfer from the general revenue fund or other recipient fund to the budget reserve fund an amount equal to the cash operating transfer received by such fund pursuant to subsection 2 of this section, together with the interest that would have been earned on such amount, prior to May sixteenth of the fiscal year in which the transfer was made. No cash operating transfers out of the budget reserve fund may be made after May fifteenth of any fiscal year.

4. Funds in the budget reserve fund shall be invested by the treasurer in the same manner as other state funds are invested. Interest earned on such investments shall be credited to the budget reserve fund. Subject to the provisions of subsection 7 of this section, the unexpended balance in the budget reserve fund at the close of any fiscal year shall remain in the fund.

5. In any fiscal year in which the governor reduces the expenditures of the state or any of its agencies below their appropriations in accordance with section 27 of this article, or in which there is a budget need due to a disaster, as proclaimed by the governor to be an emergency, the general assembly, upon a request by the governor for an emergency appropriation and by a two-thirds vote of the members elected to each house, may appropriate funds from the budget reserve fund to fulfill the expenditures authorized by any of the existing appropriations which were affected by the governor's decision to reduce expenditures pursuant to section 27 of this article or to meet budget needs due to the disaster. Such expenditures shall be deemed to be for "budget stabilization purposes". The maximum amount which may be appropriated at any one time for such budget stabilization purposes shall be one-half of the sum of the balance in the fund and any amounts appropriated or otherwise owed to the fund, less all amounts owed to the fund for budget stabilization purposes but not yet appropriated for repayment to the fund.

6. One-third of the amount transferred or expended from the budget reserve fund for budget stabilization purposes during any fiscal year, together with interest that would otherwise have been earned on such amount, shall stand appropriated to the budget reserve fund during each of the next three fiscal years, and such amount, and any additional amounts which may be appropriated for that purpose, shall be transferred from the fund which received such transfer to the budget reserve fund by the fifteenth day of the fiscal year for each of the next three fiscal years or until the full amount, plus interest, has been returned to the budget reserve fund. The maximum amount, which may be outstanding at any one time and subject to repayment to the budget reserve fund for budget stabilization purposes shall be one-half of the sum of the balance in the fund and all outstanding amounts appropriated or otherwise owed to the fund.

7. If the balance in the budget reserve fund at the close of any fiscal year exceeds seven and one-half percent of the net general revenue collections for the previous fiscal year, the commissioner of administration shall transfer that excess amount to the general revenue fund unless such excess balance is as a result of direct appropriations made by the general assembly for the purpose of increasing the balance of the fund; provided, however, that if the balance in the fund at the close of any fiscal year exceeds ten percent of the net general revenue collections for the previous fiscal year, the commissioner of administration shall transfer the excess amount to the general revenue fund notwithstanding any specific appropriations made to the fund. For purposes of this section, "net general revenue collections" means all revenue deposited into the general revenue fund less

refunds and revenues originally deposited into the general revenue fund but designated by law for a specific distribution or transfer to another state fund.

8. If the sum of the ending balance of the budget reserve fund in any fiscal year and any amounts owed to the fund pursuant to subsection 6 of this section is less than seven and one-half percent of the net general revenue collections for the same year, the difference shall stand appropriated and shall be transferred from the general revenue fund to the budget reserve fund by the fifteenth day of the succeeding fiscal year.

SECTION 27(b). **Facilities maintenance and review fund created, purpose—state facilities, defined—transfer of monies into fund, reduction or elimination of transfer by governor.**—1. The "Facilities Maintenance Reserve Fund" is hereby created in the state treasury for use in maintaining, repairing and renovating state facilities. "State facilities" shall include all improvements to real property owned by the state except real property owned or possessed by the conservation and highways and transportation commissions, including bridges and highways constructed pursuant to article IV, section 29.

2. Beginning July 1, 1997, moneys shall be transferred from the general revenue fund to the facilities maintenance reserve fund. The amount transferred in fiscal year 1998 shall be equal to one-tenth of one percent of net general revenue collections of fiscal year 1997. During each succeeding fiscal year the percentage of the immediately preceding fiscal year's net general revenue collections to be transferred to the facilities maintenance reserve fund shall be increased by one-tenth of one percent, until the total percentage transferred equals one percent of the net general revenue collections for the immediately preceding fiscal year. Each year thereafter one percent of the net general revenue collections for the immediately preceding fiscal year shall be transferred to the facilities maintenance reserve fund; provided, however, that the governor may reduce or eliminate the amount of this transfer during any fiscal year in which he exercised his right to reduce expenditures pursuant to article IV, section 27, or during the next succeeding fiscal year after he exercised such power. The general assembly may also appropriate other moneys to the fund.

3. Moneys in the facilities maintenance reserve fund shall be invested by the state treasurer in the same manner as other state funds are invested. Interest earned on such investments shall be credited to the facilities reserve maintenance fund.

4. The general assembly may appropriate moneys from the fund to be used for maintenance, repair or renovation of state facilities.

SECTION 28. **Treasury withdrawals, how made, certified how—appropriation, period of.**—No money shall be withdrawn from the state treasury except by warrant drawn in accordance with an appropriation made by law, nor shall any obligation for that payment of money be incurred unless the commissioner of administration certifies it for payment and certifies that the expenditure is within the purpose as directed by the general assembly of the appropriation and that there is in the appropriation an unencumbered balance sufficient to pay it. At the time of issuance each such certification shall be entered on the general accounting books as an encumbrance on the appropriation. No appropriation shall confer authority to incur an obligation after the termination of the fiscal period to which it relates, and every appropriation shall expire six months after the end of the period for which made.

Most of the remaining sections of this article have to do with state government reorganization. The quest for more efficient administration in state government dates back more than 100 years. President Taft headed up the Commission on Economy and Efficiency in the national government from 1910 to 1912, and the issue of administrative organization for maximum efficiency also took root at the state level at that time.[82]

Missouri's state bureaucracy became bloated and misshapen over the years, and in 1955 a commission on reorganization was established; about 30 percent of this commission's recommendations were accepted. A second commission in 1965 made 105 recommendations and repeated about one-third of the unadopted recommendations from 1955. Only 18 were made into law; 13 more administrative changes were made, and 13 more recommendations for administrative change were partially applied. A third commission reported its recommendations in 1971, and in that year the legislature created the Office of Administration, an important step forward. The Office of Administration is a tool the governor can use to supervise the bureaucracy; its Division of Budget and Planning is particularly valuable in holding the many administrative units of state bureaucracy accountable. The 1971 commission faced a complicated schema of agencies, bureaus, entities, boards, commissions, and offices, many of which had some tenuous relationship to the governor through patronage appointment of administrators. In most instances, the governor did not share appointment authority with the state Senate. Overall, there were 87 separate units in charge of 440 separate programs.[83] Then-governor Hearnes supported the concept of executive branch reorganization tepidly but cooperated by putting the measure on the ballot in August 1972 (the primary election), helping it to pass.

The commission's recommendation was for 14 departments, with all the many existing units each to be assigned to a department. Most departments were to be headed by a cabinet member with some appointive authority over subordinates. The constitutional wording provides most of the departmental names, and amendments have changed a few of these over time; for instance, the Department of Highways and the separate Department of Transportation (with only 20 employees) were eventually merged.

However, the reorganization is in some ways incomplete. The Department of Conservation, which has existed since a highly successful initiative petition drive put it into the constitution in 1936, is held separate from the new Department of Natural Resources, which has a similar mission. The reason? The Department of Conservation is a bureaucratic "sacred cow"; when it was set up it replaced a corrupt patronage agency that had earned the enmity of hunters, fishermen, and wildlife enthusiasts across the state. Many species of wildlife had become extinct in the state; there were even very few deer left. It has a dedicated permanent one-eighth percent sales tax

[82]The first reorganization at the state level in Illinois in 1917 under the aegis of Governor Lowden consolidated 54 independent agencies into 14 units. The heads of most of these departments were made subject to gubernatorial appointment. This tightened the lines of accountability and increased efficiency.
[83]Fred W. Lindecke, "State Revision Success for Both Sides," *St. Louis Post-Dispatch*, February 3, 1974.

and a commission runs it; the governor appoints the four members of the commission for staggered terms of six years, and no more than two commissioners may be of the same political party (see Section 40). Senate approval is necessary for appointment, which helps remove this entity from political back and forth. In contrast, the Department of Natural Resources has a one-tenth percent sales tax that needs renewal every 10 years (in a public vote), so it has less of a revenue base (and a less secure revenue base) than the Conservation Department does. While these two entities have largely overlapping concerns and missions and it would be more rational to merge them, the Conservation Department has a separate legacy and keys into revenue in a way that is impossible for the Department of Natural Resources to match.

The amendments that make up this part of Article IV form the skeletal outline of the ideal of administrative reshuffling. Once they were passed, the legislature still had to accomplish the actual placement of existing units within the departments that it would create—some constitutionally designated, others with a simple statutory basis. This was attempted starting in January 1973. Governor Bond had been elected and taken office and Democrats, enjoying majority strength in the legislature, were not highly motivated to accommodate the changes. Their first plan reduced the 87

Departments of the Executive Branch
Administration
Agriculture
Conservation
Corrections
Economic Development
Elementary and Secondary Education
Health and Senior Services
Higher Education
Insurance, Financial Institutions, and Professional Registration (DIFP)
Labor and Industrial Relations (DOLR)
Mental Health
Natural Resources
Public Safety
Revenue
Social Services
Transportation

separate units of bureaucracy only to 80, and Bond complained that the bill had other major failings. Bond said that the plan the legislature approved would have set up "lines of authority spewing out of the Governor's office like spaghetti."[84] The young new governor then showed considerable ingenuity; in a gutsy move, he called a special session, to run concurrently with the first segment of the 1974 regular session, to produce a reorganization bill he could accept. If the legislature were to do nothing, there was the risk that the deadline would come without stuffing the hulls of the new constitutional units of bureaucracy while leaving intact the old administrative entities. But the old entities would no longer have either constitutional or legal authority, which could lead to the regulations any one of these entities issued coming under legal attack as having no authority, leading to a general breakdown of state government authority as litigation tied up the bureaucracy in knots. Facing the threat of such a free-for-all, the Democrats had to abandon their hopes for preserving patronage and go along with Bond, who played a strong hand. Bond threatened the General Assembly that he could use his executive authority to categorize the agencies thematically into the new departments, which acted as a spur for the legislators. Several compromises were made, but a satisfactory reorganization bill was accomplished.

Highways and Transportation

SECTION 29. **Highways and transportation commission—qualifications of members and employees—authority over state highways and other transportation programs.—** The highways and transportation commission shall be in charge of the department of transportation. The number, qualifications, compensation and terms of the members of the highways and transportation commission shall be fixed by law, and not more than one-half of its members shall be of the same political party. The selection and removal of all employees shall be without regard to political affiliation. The highways and transportation commission (i) shall have authority over the state highway system; (ii) shall have authority over all other transportation programs and facilities as provided by law, including, but not limited to, aviation, railroads, mass transportation, ports, and waterborne commerce; and (iii) shall have authority to limit access to, from and across state highways and other transportation facilities where the public interests and safety may require. All references to the highway commission and the department of highways in this constitution and in the statutes shall mean the highways and transportation commission and the department of transportation.

SECTION 30(a). **Apportionment of motor vehicle fuel tax—director of revenue responsible for apportionment—limitation on local fuel taxes—fuel taxes not part of total state revenues or expenses of state government.—**1. A tax upon or measured by fuel used for propelling highway motor vehicles shall be levied and collected as provided by law. Any amount of the tax collected with respect to fuel not used for propelling highway motor vehicles shall be refunded by the state in the manner provided by law. The remaining net proceeds of the tax, after deducting actual costs of collection of the department of revenue (but after June 30, 2005, not more than three percent of the amount collected) and refunds for overpayments and erroneous payments of such tax as permit-

---

[84]Jerry W. Venters, "Reorganization Bill Veto Criticized," *St. Louis Post-Dispatch*, August 1, 1973.

ted by law, shall be apportioned and distributed between the counties, cities and the state highways and transportation commission as hereinafter provided and shall stand appropriated without legislative action for the following purposes:

(1) Ten percent of the remaining net proceeds shall be deposited in a special trust fund known as the "County Aid Road Trust Fund". In addition, beginning July 1, 1994, an additional five percent of the remaining net proceeds which is derived from the difference between the amount received from a tax rate equal to the tax rate in effect on March 31, 1992, and the tax rate in effect on and after July 1, 1994, shall also be deposited in the county aid road trust fund, and of such moneys generated by this additional five percent, five percent shall be apportioned and distributed solely to cities not within any county in this state. After such distribution to cities not within any county, the remaining proceeds in the county aid road trust fund shall be apportioned and distributed to the various counties of the state on the following basis: One-half on the ratio that the county road mileage of each county bears to the county road mileage of the entire state as determined by the last available report of the state highways and transportation commission and one-half on the ratio that the rural land valuation of each county bears to the rural land valuation of the entire state as determined by the last available report of the state tax commission, except that county road mileage in incorporated villages, towns or cities and the land valuation in incorporated villages, towns or cities shall be excluded in such determination, except that, if the assessed valuation of rural lands in any county is less than five million dollars, the county shall be treated as having an assessed valuation of five million dollars. The funds apportioned and distributed to each county shall be dedicated, used and expended by the county solely for the construction, reconstruction, maintenance and repairs of roads, bridges and highways, and subject to such other provisions and restrictions as provided by law. The moneys generated by the additional five percent of the remaining net proceeds which is derived from the difference between the amount received from a tax rate equal to the tax rate in effect on March 31, 1992, and the tax rate in effect on and after July 1, 1994, shall not be used or expended for equipment, machinery, salaries, fringe benefits or capital improvements, other than roads and bridges. In counties having the township form of county organization, the funds distributed to such counties shall be expended solely under the control and supervision of the county commission, and shall not be expended by the various townships located within such counties. "Rural land" as used in this section shall mean all land located within any county, except land in incorporated villages, towns, or cities.

(2) Fifteen percent of the remaining net proceeds shall be apportioned and distributed to the various incorporated cities, towns and villages within the state solely for construction, reconstruction, maintenance, repair, policing, signing, lighting and cleaning roads and streets and for the payment of principal and interest on indebtedness on account of road and street purposes, and the use thereof being subject to such other provisions and restrictions as provided by law. The amount apportioned and distributed to each city, town or village shall be based on the ratio that the population of the city, town or village bears to the population of all incorporated cities, towns or villages in the state having a like population, as shown by the last federal decennial census, provided that any city, town or village which had a motor fuel tax prior to the adoption of this section shall annually receive not less than an amount equal to the net revenue derived therefrom in the year 1960; and

(3) All the remaining net proceeds in excess of the distributions to counties, and to cities, towns and villages under this section shall be apportioned, distributed and deposited

in the state road fund and shall be expended and used solely as provided in subsection 1 of section 30(b) of Article IV of this Constitution.

2. The director of revenue of the state shall make the apportionment, distribution and deposit of the funds monthly in the manner required hereby.

3. Except for taxes or licenses which may be imposed uniformly on all merchants or manufacturers based upon sales, or which uniformly apply ad valorem to the stocks of merchants or manufacturers, no political subdivision in this state shall collect any tax, excise, license or fee upon, measured by or with respect to the importation, receipt, manufacture, storage, transportation, sale or use, on or after the first day of the month next following the adoption of this section of fuel used for propelling motor vehicles, unless the tax, excise, license or fee is approved by a vote of the people of any city, town or village subsequent to the adoption of this section, by a two-thirds majority. All funds collected shall be used solely for construction, reconstruction, maintenance, repair, policing, signing, lighting, and cleaning roads and streets and for the payment and interest on indebtedness incurred on account of road and street purposes.

4. The net proceeds of fuel taxes apportioned, distributed and deposited under this section to the state road fund, counties, cities, towns and villages shall not be included within the definition of "total state revenues" in section 17 of article X of this constitution nor be considered as an "expense of state government" as that term is used in section 20 of article X of this constitution.

Missouri has implemented a fuel tax of 17 cents per gallon on motor fuels from gasoline to diesel. To effectively charge this tax, the cost is passed on to the consumer purchasing gasoline at the pump. The revenue from the tax is then given to the Missouri Department of Transportation, as well as the individual Missouri cities and counties for projects such as construction and highway upkeep. But it is noteworthy that these provisions allocate not a cent toward mass transit. Many critics find this to be a gaping lack of concern for the metro areas choking on traffic congestion. Individuals may apply for a fuel tax exemption and receive a reimbursement of the tax if the fuel is used for city construction or agricultural functions.

SECTION 30(b). **Source and application of state road fund—sales tax imposed on sale of motor vehicles, apportionment, how, use of revenue—distribution of increases—sales taxes not part of total state revenues or expenses of state government.**—1. For the purpose of constructing and maintaining an adequate system of connected state highways all state revenue derived from highway users as an incident to their use or right to use the highways of the state, including all state license fees and taxes upon motor vehicles, trailers and motor vehicle fuels, and upon, with respect to, or on the privilege of the manufacture, receipt, storage, distribution, sale or use thereof (excepting those portions of the sales tax on motor vehicles and trailers which are not distributed to the state road fund pursuant to subsection 2 of this section 30(b) and further excepting all property taxes), less the (1) actual cost of collection of the department of revenue (but not to exceed three percent of the particular tax or fee collected), (2) actual cost of refunds for overpayments and erroneous payments of such taxes and fees and maintaining retirement programs as permitted by law and (3) actual cost of the state highway patrol in administering and enforcing any state motor vehicle laws and traffic regulations, shall be deposited in the state road fund which is hereby created within the state treasury and stand appropriated without legislative action to be used and expended by the highways and transportation commission for the following purposes, and no other:

First, to the payment of the principal and interest on any outstanding state road bonds. The term state road bonds in this section 30(b) means any bonds or refunding bonds issued by the highways and transportation commission to finance or refinance the construction or reconstruction of the state highway system.

Second, to maintain a balance in the state road fund in the amount deemed necessary to meet the payment of the principal and interest of any state road bonds for the next succeeding twelve months.

The remaining balance in the state road fund shall be used and expended in the sole discretion of and under the supervision and direction of the highways and transportation commission for the following state highway system uses and purposes and no other:

(1) To complete and widen or otherwise improve and maintain the state highway system heretofore designated and laid out under existing laws;

(2) To reimburse the various counties and other political subdivisions of the state, except incorporated cities and towns, for money expended by them in the construction or acquisition of roads and bridges now or hereafter taken over by the highways and transportation commission as permanent parts of the state highway system, to the extent of the value to the state of such roads and bridges at the time taken over, not exceeding in any case the amount expended by such counties and subdivisions in the construction or acquisition of such roads and bridges, except that the highways and transportation commission may, in its discretion, repay, or agree to repay, any cash advanced by a county or subdivision to expedite state road construction or improvement;

(3) In the discretion of the commission to plan, locate, relocate, establish, acquire, construct and maintain the following:

(a) interstate and primary highways within the state;

(b) supplementary state highways and bridges in each county of the state;

(c) state highways and bridges in, to and through state parks, public areas and reservations, and state institutions now or hereafter established to connect the same with the state highways, and also national, state or local parkways, travelways, tourways, with coordinated facilities;

(d) any tunnel or interstate bridge or part thereof, where necessary to connect the state highways of this state with those of other states;

(e) any highway within the state when necessary to comply with any federal law or requirement which is or shall become a condition to the receipt of federal funds;

(f) any highway in any city or town which is found necessary as a continuation of any state or federal highway, or any connection therewith, into and through such city or town; and

(g) additional state highways, bridges and tunnels, either in congested traffic areas of the state or where needed to facilitate and expedite the movement of through traffic.

(4) To acquire materials, equipment and buildings and to employ such personnel as necessary for the purposes described in this subsection 1; and

(5) For such other purposes and contingencies relating and appertaining to the construction and maintenance of such state highway system as the highways and transportation commission may deem necessary and proper.

2. (1) The state sales tax upon the sale of motor vehicles, trailers, motorcycles, mopeds and motortricycles at the rate provided by law on November 2, 2004, is levied and imposed by this section until the rate is changed by law or constitutional amendment.

(2) One-half of the proceeds from the state sales tax on all motor vehicles, trailers, motorcycles, mopeds and motortricycles shall be dedicated for highway and transportation use and shall be apportioned and distributed as follows: ten percent to the counties, fifteen percent to the cities, two percent to be deposited in the state transportation fund, which is hereby created within the state treasury to be used in a manner provided by law and seventy-three percent to be deposited in the state road fund. The amounts apportioned and distributed to the counties and cities shall be further allocated and used as provided in section 30(a) of this article. The amounts allocated and distributed to the highways and transportation commission for the state road fund shall be used as provided in subsection 1 of this section 30(b). The sales taxes which are apportioned and distributed pursuant to this subdivision (2) shall not include those taxes levied and imposed pursuant to sections 43(a) or 47(a) of this article. The term "proceeds from the state sales tax" as used in this subdivision (2) shall mean and include all revenues received by the department of revenue from the said sales tax, reduced only by refunds for overpayments and erroneous payments of such tax as permitted by law and actual costs of collection by the department of revenue (but not to exceed three percent of the amount collected).

(3) (i) From and after July 1, 2005, through June 30, 2006, twenty-five percent of the remaining one-half of the proceeds of the state sales tax on all motor vehicles, trailers, motorcycles, mopeds and motortricycles which is not distributed by subdivision (2) of subsection 2 of this section 30(b) shall be deposited in the state road bond fund which is hereby created within the state treasury; (ii) from and after July 1, 2006, through June 30, 2007, fifty percent of the aforesaid one-half of the proceeds of the state sales tax on all motor vehicles, trailers, motorcycles, mopeds and motortricycles which is not distributed by subdivision (2) of subsection 2 of this section 30(b) shall be deposited in the state road bond fund; (iii) from and after July 1, 2007, through June 30, 2008, seventy-five percent of the aforesaid one-half of the proceeds of the state sales tax on all motor vehicles, trailers, motorcycles, mopeds and motortricycles which is not distributed by subdivision (2) of subsection 2 of this section 30(b) shall be deposited in the state road bond fund; and (iv) from and after July 1, 2008, one hundred percent of the aforesaid one-half of the proceeds of the state sales tax on all motor vehicles, trailers, motorcycles, mopeds and motortricycles which is not distributed by subdivision (2) of subsection 2 of this section 30(b) shall be deposited in the state road bond fund. Moneys deposited in the state road bond fund are hereby dedicated to and shall only be used to fund the repayment of bonds issued by the highways and transportation commission to fund the construction and reconstruction of the state highway system or to fund refunding bonds, except that after January 1, 2009, that portion of the moneys in the state road bond fund which the commissioner of administration and the highways and transportation commission each certify is not needed to make payments upon said bonds or to maintain an adequate reserve for making future payments upon said bonds may be appropriated to the state road fund. The highways and transportation commission shall have authority to issue state road bonds for the uses set forth in this subdivision (3). The net proceeds received from the issuance of such bonds shall be paid into the state road fund and shall only be used to fund construction or reconstruction of specific projects for parts of the state

highway system as determined by the highways and transportation commission. The moneys deposited in the state road bond fund shall only be withdrawn by appropriation pursuant to this constitution. No obligation for the payment of moneys so appropriated shall be paid unless the commissioner of administration certifies it for payment and further certifies that the expenditure is for a use which is specifically authorized by the provisions of this subdivision (3). The proceeds of the sales tax which are subject to allocation and deposit into the state road bond fund pursuant to this subdivision (3) shall not include the proceeds of the sales tax levied and imposed pursuant to sections 43(a) or 47(a) of this article nor shall they include the proceeds of that portion of the sales tax apportioned, distributed and dedicated to the school district trust fund on November 2, 2004. The term "proceeds from the state sales tax" as used in this subdivision (3) shall mean and include all revenues received by the department of revenue from the said sales tax, reduced only by refunds for overpayments and erroneous payments of such tax as permitted by law and actual costs of collection by the department of revenue (but not to exceed three percent of the amount collected).

3. After January 1, 1980, any increase in state license fees and taxes on motor vehicles, trailers, motorcycles, mopeds and motortricycles other than those taxes distributed pursuant to subsection 2 of this section 30(b) shall be distributed as follows: ten percent to the counties, fifteen percent to the cities and seventy-five percent to be deposited in the state road fund. The amounts distributed shall be apportioned and distributed to the counties and cities as provided in section 30(a) of this article, to be used for highway purposes.

4. The moneys apportioned or distributed under this section to the state road fund, the state transportation fund, the state road bond fund, counties, cities, towns or villages shall not be included within the definition of "total state revenues" as that term is used in section 17 of article X of this constitution nor be considered as an "expense of state government" as that term is used in section 20 of article X of this constitution.

When purchasing a new car in Missouri, the buyer must pay a motor vehicle sales tax. This tax applies to all motor vehicles, trailers, ATVs, and watercrafts, and, before purchasing, can be calculated online at the Missouri Department of Revenue's website.[85]

SECTION 30(c). Transportation programs and facilities, administration of by commission, use of moneys.—The highways and transportation commission shall have authority to plan, locate, relocate, establish, acquire, construct, maintain, control, and as provided by law to operate, develop and fund public transportation facilities as part of any state transportation system or program such as but not limited to aviation, mass transportation, transportation of elderly and handicapped, railroads, ports, waterborne commerce and intermodal connections, provided that funds other than those designated or dedicated for highway purposes in or deposited in the state road fund or the state road bond fund pursuant to sections 30(a) or 30(b) of this constitution are made available for such purposes. No moneys which are distributed to the state transportation fund pursuant to section 30(b) shall be used for any purpose other than for transportation purposes as provided in this section.

[85]Missouri Department of Revenue, http://dor.mo.gov.

SECTION 30(d). Prohibition against diverting revenue for non-highway purposes—severability of provisions—effective date.—1. No state revenues derived from highway users which are to be allocated, distributed or deposited in the state road fund pursuant to either section 30(a) or section 30(b) shall be diverted from the highway purposes and uses specified in subsection 1 of section 30(b). No state revenues derived from highway users which are to be allocated, distributed or deposited in the state road bond fund pursuant to subdivision (3) of subsection 2 of section 30(b) shall be diverted from the highway purposes and uses specified in said subdivision (3).

2. All of the provisions of sections 29, 30(a), 30(b), 30(c) and 30(d) shall be self executing. All of the provisions of sections 29, 30(a), 30(b), 30(c) and 30(d) are severable. If any provision of sections 29, 30(a), 30(b), 30(c) and 30(d) is found by a court of competent jurisdiction to be unconstitutional or unconstitutionally enacted, the remaining provisions of these sections shall be and remain valid.

3. The provisions of sections 29, 30(a), 30(b), 30(c) and 30(d) shall become effective on July 1, 2005.

SECTION 31. State highways in municipalities.—Any state highway authorized herein to be located in any municipality may be constructed without limitations concerning the distance between houses or other buildings abutting such highway or concerning the width or type of construction. The commission may enter into contracts with cities, counties or other political subdivisions for and concerning the maintenance of, and regulation of traffic on any state highway within such cities, counties or subdivision.

SECTION 32. Apportionment of funds for supplementary state highways.—The funds which are allotted by the commission to the construction or acquisition of supplementary state highways and bridges in each of the counties of the state shall be apportioned to the several counties as follows: One-fourth in the ratio that the area of each county bears to the area of the state, one-fourth in the ratio of the population, and two-fourths on such basis as the commission may deem to be for the best interest of highway users; provided the areas and population of cities having a population of 150,000 or more shall not be considered in making such apportionment, and the latest available United States decennial census shall be used; provided further, that if traffic on any supplementary state highway becomes such that a higher type than ordinary supplementary highway construction shall be required, then the commission may construct such higher type and charge such extra cost to unallotted state highway funds. Supplementary state highways shall be selected by mutual agreement of the commission and the local officials having charge of or jurisdiction over roads in the territory through which such supplementary state highways are to be constructed.

SECTION 32(a).—(Repealed November 6, 1979, L. 1979 1st Reg. Sess. SS HCS HJR 39, 40, 44 and 48 Sec. 1)

SECTION 33. Retirement benefits not changed.—Any transfer of employees made pursuant to the provisions of this article shall not affect or abridge any rights or benefits accrued under any retirement system in which such employees are members on the effective date of this article, and the employees may continue coverage under such retirement system until otherwise provided by law.

SECTION 34. Recognition of outstanding bonds—determination, certification and collection of annual state highway bond tax.—All bonds issued under or recognized by section 44a of article IV of the previous constitution, which remain unpaid shall be valid obligations of the state and shall be paid according to the tenor thereof. On or before the first day of July of each year the state auditor shall determine the rate of taxation for that year necessary to raise the amount of money needed to pay the principal and interest maturing in the next succeeding year, taking into consideration available funds, delinquencies and the cost of collection. The auditor shall annually certify the rate of taxation so determined to the officer in each county whose duty it is to make up and certify the tax books wherein are extended the state taxes. Said officers shall extend upon the tax books the taxes to be collected and certify the same to the collector of revenue of their respective counties, who shall collect such taxes at the same time and in the same manner and by the same means as are provided by law for the collection of state and county taxes, and pay the same into the state treasury.

Agriculture

SECTION 35. Agriculture, department of—director, how appointed—funds to be provided, how.—The department of agriculture shall be in charge of a director appointed by the governor by and with the advice and consent of the senate. The general assembly shall provide the department of agriculture with funds adequate for administration of its functions; and shall enact such laws and provide such other appropriations as may be required to protect, foster and develop the agricultural resources of the state.

SECTION 36. Forestry and forest fires.—The general assembly may enact laws to encourage forestry, and prevent and suppress forest fires on private lands.

Economic Development

SECTION 36(a). Economic development, department of—duties of department—director, how appointed.—The department of economic development shall be in charge of a director appointed by the governor, by and with the advice and consent of the senate. The department shall administer all programs provided by law relating to the promotion of the economy of the state, the economic development of the state, trade and business, and other activities and programs impacting on the economy of the state.

Insurance

SECTION 36(b). Department of insurance, established—director, appointment—office of consumer affairs to be established within department, duties.—The department of insurance shall be headed by a director of the department of insurance who shall be appointed by the governor with the advice and consent of the senate. The organization and duties of the department of insurance shall be determined by law. All references to the division of insurance and the insurance division in this constitution and in the statutes shall mean the department of insurance. There shall be an office of consumer affairs within the department of insurance to investigate in conjunction with other personnel of the department all allegations of unfair or unlawful acts by any person or entity whose activities are regulated by the department of insurance.

Social Services

SECTION 37. **Social services, department of—duties of department—director, how appointed.**—The health and general welfare of the people are matters of primary public concern; and to secure them there shall be established a department of social services in charge of a director appointed by the governor, by and with the advice and consent of the senate, charged with promoting improved health and other social services to the citizens of the state as provided by law, and the general assembly may grant power with respect thereto to counties, cities or other political subdivisions of the state.

Mental Health

SECTION 37(a). **Mental health, department of—duties of department—director, how appointed.**—The department of mental health shall be in charge of a director who shall be appointed by the commission, as provided by law, and by and with the advice and consent of the senate. The department shall provide treatment, care, education and training for persons suffering from mental illness or retardation, shall have administrative control of the state hospitals and other institutions and centers established for these purposes and shall administer such other programs as provided by law.

SECTION 38.—**(Repealed August 8, 1972, L. 1971 2nd Reg. Sess. HJR 65 Sec. 1)**

SECTION 39. **Cooperation with federal and other state governments.**—In all matters of public welfare the general assembly may provide by law for cooperation with the United States, or other states.

Conservation

SECTION 40(a). **Conservation commission, members, qualifications, terms, how appointed—duties of commission—expenses of members.**—The control, management, restoration, conservation and regulation of the bird, fish, game, forestry and all wildlife resources of the state, including hatcheries, sanctuaries, refuges, reservations and all other property owned, acquired or used for such purposes and the acquisition and establishment thereof, and the administration of all laws pertaining thereto, shall be vested in a conservation commission consisting of four members appointed by the governor, by and with the advice and consent of the senate, not more than two of whom shall be of the same political party. The members shall have knowledge of and interest in wildlife conservation. The members shall hold office for terms of six years beginning on the first day of July of consecutive odd years. Two of the terms shall be concurrent; one shall begin two years before and one two years after the concurrent terms. If the governor fails to fill a vacancy within thirty days, the remaining members shall fill the vacancy for the unexpired term. The members shall receive no salary or other compensation for their services as members, but shall receive their necessary traveling and other expenses incurred while actually engaged in the discharge of their official duties.

SECTION 40(b). **Incumbent members.**—The members of the present conservation commission shall serve out the terms for which they were appointed, with all their powers and duties.

SECTION 41. Acquisition of property—eminent domain.—The commission may acquire by purchase, gift, eminent domain, or otherwise, all property necessary, useful or convenient for its purposes, and shall exercise the right of eminent domain as provided by law for the highway commission.

SECTION 42. Director of conservation and personnel of commission.—The commission shall appoint a director of conservation who, with its approval, shall appoint the assistants and other employees deemed necessary by the commission. The commission shall fix the qualifications and salaries of the director and all appointees and employees, and none of its members shall be an appointee or employee.

SECTION 43(a). Sales tax, use for conservation purposes.—For the purpose of providing additional moneys to be expended and used by the conservation commission, department of conservation, for the control, management, restoration, conservation and regulation of the bird, fish, game, forestry and wildlife resources of the state, including the purchase or other acquisition of property for said purposes, and for the administration of the laws pertaining thereto, an additional sales tax of one-eighth of one percent is hereby levied and imposed upon all sellers for the privilege of selling tangible personal property or rendering taxable services at retail in this state upon the sales and services which now are or hereafter are listed and set forth in, and, except as to the amount of tax, subject to the provisions of and to be collected as provided in the "Sales Tax Law" and subject to the rules and regulations promulgated in connection therewith; and an additional use tax of one-eighth of one percent is levied and imposed for the privilege of storing, using or consuming within this state any article of tangible personal property as set forth and provided in the "Compensating Use Tax Law" and, except as to the amount of the tax, subject to the provisions of and to be collected as provided in the "Compensating Use Tax Law" and subject to the rules and regulations promulgated in connection therewith.

SECTION 43(b). Use of revenue and funds of conservation commission.—The moneys arising from the additional sales and use taxes provided for in section 43(a) hereof and all fees, moneys or funds arising from the operation and transactions of the conservation commission, department of conservation, and from the application and the administration of the laws and regulations pertaining to the bird, fish, game, forestry and wildlife resources of the state and from the sale of property used for said purposes, shall be expended and used by the conservation commission, department of conservation, for the control, management, restoration, conservation and regulation of the bird, fish, game, forestry and wildlife resources of the state, including the purchase or other acquisition of property for said purposes, and for the administration of the laws pertaining thereto, and for no other purpose. The moneys and funds of the conservation commission arising from the additional sales and use taxes provided for in 43(a) hereof shall also be used by the conservation commission, department of conservation, to make payments to counties for the unimproved value of land for distribution to the appropriate political subdivisions as payment in lieu of real property taxes for privately owned land acquired by the commission after July 1, 1977 and for land classified as forest cropland in the forest cropland program administered by the department of conservation in such amounts as may be determined by the conservation commission, but in no event shall the amount determined be less than the property tax being paid at the time of purchase of acquired lands.

SECTION 43(c). Effective date—self-enforceability.—The effective date of this amendment shall be July 1, 1977. All laws inconsistent with this amendment shall no longer remain in full force and effect after July 1, 1977. All of the provisions of sections 43(a)–(c) shall be self-enforcing except that the general assembly shall adjust brackets for the collection of the sales and use taxes.

SECTION 44. Self-enforceability—enabling clause—repealing clause.—Sections 40–43, inclusive, of this article shall be self-enforcing, and laws not inconsistent therewith may be enacted in aid thereof. All existing laws inconsistent with this article shall no longer remain in force or effect.

SECTION 45. Rules and regulations—filing—review.—The rules and regulations of the commission not relating to its organization and internal management shall become effective not less than ten days after being filed with the secretary of state as provided in section 16 of this article, and such final rules and regulations affecting private rights as are judicial or quasi-judicial in nature shall be subject to the judicial review provided in section 22 of article V.

SECTION 46. Distribution of rules and regulations.—The commission shall supply to all persons on request, printed copies of its rules and regulations not relating to organization or internal management.

Natural Resources

SECTION 47. Natural resources, department of—duties of department—director, how appointed.—The department of natural resources shall be in charge of a director appointed by the governor, by and with the advice and consent of the senate. The department shall administer the programs of the state as provided by law relating to environmental control and the conservation and management of natural resources.

SECTION 47(a). Sales and use tax levied for soil and water conservation and for state parks—distribution of parks sales tax fund to counties, purpose, limitation.—For the purpose of providing additional monies to be expended and used by the department of natural resources through the state soil and water districts commission as defined in Section 278.070, RSMo, for the saving of the soil and water of this state for the conservation of the productive power of Missouri agricultural land, and by the department of natural resources through the division responsible for the State park system for the acquisition, development, maintenance and operation of state parks and state historic sites in accordance with Chapter 253, RSMo, and for the administration of the laws pertaining thereto, an additional sales tax of one-tenth of one percent is hereby levied and imposed upon all sellers for the privilege of selling tangible personal property or rendering taxable services at retail in this state upon the sales and services which now are or hereafter are listed and set forth in, and, except as to the amount of tax, subject to the provisions of and to be collected as provided in the "Sales Tax Law" and subject to the rules and regulations promulgated in connection therewith; and an additional use tax of one-tenth of one percent is levied and imposed for the privilege of storing, using or consuming within this state any article of tangible personal property as set forth and provided in the "Compensating Use Tax Law" and, except as to the amount of the tax, subject to the provisions of and to be collected as provided in the "Compensating Use Tax Law" and subject to the rules and regulations promulgated in connection therewith. In addition, monies deposited in the state parks sales tax fund pursuant to the provisions of section 47(b) of this article shall also be appropriated to make payments to counties for a period of five years for the unimproved value of land for distribution to the appropriate political subdivisions as payment in lieu of real property taxes for privately owned land acquired by the department of natural resources for park purposes after July 1, 1985, in such amounts as determined by appropriation, but in no event shall such amounts be more than the amount of property tax imposed by political subdivisions at the time the department acquired or acquires such land.

SECTION 47(b). Disbursement of revenue, purposes.—Fifty percent of the monies arising from the additional sales and use taxes provided for in Section 47(a) hereof shall be deposited in the Soil and Water Sales Tax Fund and fifty percent shall be deposited in the State Park Sales Tax Fund, and the monies in both funds shall be expended pursuant to appropriation by the General Assembly and used by the state soil and water districts commission and the department of natural resources for the purposes set forth in Section 47(a), and for no other purpose.

SECTION 47(c). Provisions self-enforcing, exception—not part of general revenue or expense of state—effective and expiration dates.—All laws inconsistent with this amendment shall no longer remain in full force and effect after the effective date of this section. All of the provisions of Sections 47(a), 47(b) and 47(c) shall be self-enforcing except that the General Assembly shall adjust brackets for the collection of the sales and use taxes. The additional revenue provided by Sections 47(a), 47(b) and 47(c) shall not be part of the "total state revenue" within the meaning of Sections 17 and 18 of Article X of this Constitution. The expenditure of this additional revenue shall not be an "expense of state government" under Section 20 of Article X of this Constitution. Upon voter approval of this measure in a general election held in 2006, or at a special election to be called by the governor for that purpose, the provisions of this section, 47(b), and 47(a) shall be reauthorized and continue until a general election is held in 2016 or at a special election to be called by the governor for that purpose. Every ten years thereafter, the issue of whether to continue to impose the sales and use tax described in this section shall be resubmitted to the voters for approval. If a majority of the voters fail to approve the continuance of such sales and use tax, Section 47(a), 47(b), and 47(c) shall terminate at the end of the second fiscal year after the last election was held.

The wording in the last nine lines of Section 47(c) provides for the decennial ballot on whether or not to retain the one-tenth of a cent sales tax for the Department of Natural Resources, which is put toward soil and water conservation and maintenance of state parks and historic sites. In 2016 voters approved reauthorization of this tax for another 10 years.

Public Safety

SECTION 48. Public safety, department of—duties of department—director, how appointed.—The department of public safety shall be in charge of a director to be appointed by the governor by and with the advice and consent of the senate, and shall administer the programs provided by law to protect and safeguard the lives and property of the people of the state.

Labor and Industrial Relations

SECTION 49. Labor and industrial relations, department of—duties—commission members, how appointed, terms, qualifications.—The department of labor and industrial relations shall be in charge of a "Labor and Industrial Relations Commission" consisting of three members appointed by the governor by and with the advice and consent of the senate. One member of the commission shall be a person who, on account of his previous vocation, employment, affiliation or interests shall be classified as a representative of employers, and one member who, on account of his previous vocation, employment, affiliation or interests shall be classified as a representative of employees, and one member, who, by reason of his previous activities and interests shall be classified as a representative of the public and who is licensed to practice law in the state of Missouri; except that not more than two members of the commission shall be of the same political party. A member of the commission shall be designated by the governor as the chairman. The labor and industrial commission shall be the successor to the industrial commission and the terms of members shall be as provided by law for the industrial commission. The department shall also administer the programs of the state relating to the protection and improvement of human rights.

Office of Administration

SECTION 50. Administration, office of—commissioner, how appointed.—The office of administration shall be in charge of a commissioner of administration. The commissioner shall be appointed by the governor by and with the advice and consent of the senate.

Appointment of Administrative Heads

SECTION 51. Appointments, how made—failure to confirm, effect of.—The appointment of all members of administrative boards and commissions and of all department and division heads, as provided by law, shall be made by the governor. All members of administrative boards and commissions, all department and division heads and all other officials appointed by the governor shall be made only by and with the advice and consent of the senate. The authority to act of any person whose appointment requires the advice and consent of the senate shall commence, if the senate is in session, upon receiving the advice and consent of the senate. If the senate is not in session, the authority to act shall commence immediately upon appointment by the governor but shall terminate if the advice and consent of the senate is not given within thirty days after the senate has convened in regular or special session. If the senate fails to give its advice and consent to any appointee, that person shall not be reappointed by the governor to the same office or position.

This wording results in the governor's patronage appointments without senatorial confirmation yielding to his or her having to get senatorial consent for appointments.

Higher Education

SECTION 52. Higher education, department of established—coordinating board for higher education established, members, terms, qualifications.—There shall be established a department of higher education. A "Coordinating Board for Higher Education" which shall consist of nine members appointed by the governor by and with the advice and consent of the senate shall be established within the department. The qualifications and terms of the members of the board shall be fixed by law, but not more than five of its members shall be of the same political party. The coordinating board shall succeed the commission on higher education with all its powers and duties and shall have such other powers and duties as may be prescribed by law.

Nondiscrimination in Appointments

SECTION 53. Discrimination as to race, creed, color or national origin prohibited.— The appointment of all members of administrative boards and commissions and of all departments and division heads and all the employees thereof shall be made without regard to race, creed, color or national origin.

ARTICLE V
JUDICIAL DEPARTMENT

Perhaps one of the starkest contrasts between the U.S. Constitution and the Missouri Constitution is the length and content of the articles establishing the judiciary. Article III of the U.S. Constitution consists of six paragraphs outlining the general role of a "Supreme Court" and other inferior courts, and the jurisdiction of the federal courts. The Missouri Constitution's discussion of the judicial department, found in Article V below, includes 27 sections, ranging from details on judicial term restrictions (Section 19) to the prohibition of political campaigning by judicial officials (Section 25f). The wording is young; except for Section 25, which dates from 1940, all the rest of the provisions date back to 1970, 1976, and 1982. Many of the framers of the major part of this Article are still alive and could be consulted as to their intent in choosing the wording. This introductory section serves as a backdrop for understanding the first of the two main sets of provisions in Article V (Sections 1–24), which primarily concern court organization. Sections 25–27 deal with how judges are selected, which we will discuss later.

Understanding courts first entails understanding the notion of "jurisdiction," which comes from the Latin words *ius, iuris* (meaning "law") and *dicere* (meaning "to say"). Thus, jurisdiction is the authority to say what the law is. Courts have the power to apply the law to individual cases that arise within their jurisdiction. In the United States, courts' powers are based on explicitly granted jurisdiction, which is accomplished formally either in the U.S. Constitution (for the federal courts) or in the appropriate state constitution (in each state for its own system of state courts). Jurisdiction is also granted by statute—that is, not a constitutional provision but a law passed by the legislature of the appropriate governmental level (federal or state). Certain court rulings interpreting the appropriate constitutional and/or statutory provision(s) are also important for defining a particular court's jurisdiction.

Jurisdiction has several facets, and working out the proper jurisdiction of Missouri's courts has been the aim of many amendments to Article V. We can consider courts' jurisdiction along two key dimensions: horizontal (distinguishing courts across the entire spectrum of courts at the same level of authority) or vertical (distinguishing courts by their level of authority in a hierarchy). When we look at courts' jurisdictions horizontally, two key comparisons can be made. First, we can look at courts in different geographical venues. Second, we can consider courts in terms of any limitations on their jurisdiction in terms of the type of case they can handle—their specialization.

In Missouri, separate geographical districts are called "circuits."[86] For example, we can compare Missouri state trial courts in St. Louis City[87] with those in St. Louis County. At present, they have somewhat symmetrical structures. Each set of courts has the same title, "circuit court," and each is a full circuit (district) unto itself. Each circuit is geographically limited in jurisdiction to its respective county/city boundaries. Missouri's judicial districts, or more properly, its judicial "circuits," are numbered rather than being named geographically. The circuit court of St. Louis County is the 21st Circuit and the circuit court of St. Louis City is the 22nd Circuit. Although the number of judges of each type varies from circuit to circuit, in this case and as of this writing, each circuit has 36 judgeships (not all filled).

Each circuit contains municipal courts established by municipalities; these are an organizational division of their circuit court and subject to its control. The 22nd Circuit has one municipal court, because the City of St. Louis is a single municipality, but the 21st Circuit has many municipal courts, because many small municipalities are contained within St. Louis County. These courts are only lightly controlled by the 21st Circuit court and the state supreme court, which has allowed municipal courts to develop exploitive procedures. For example, the municipal courts' practice of issuing escalating fines and arrest warrants for minor violations contributed to the racial problems that Ferguson, Missouri, and the St. Louis area faced in 2014 and 2015 (see Article I, Section 11).

The most important way in which these two circuits differ is in where the conflict that engenders the case or lawsuit happens: if in St. Louis County, the legal action should arise in the 21st Circuit Court; if in the City of St. Louis, the legal action should arise in the 22nd Circuit Court. A serious crime committed in St. Louis County is prosecuted by the prosecuting attorney's office in St. Louis County and the charges are filed (via either information or indictment; see Article I, Section 16) in the circuit court (one of its several criminal divisions) of St. Louis County. If the

---

[86]In federal court, the term "district" is used. Some states use the term "district" for their geographical divisions also.

[87]Recall that the City of St. Louis is a separate county, that is, an independent city. It is often referred to as the "County of the City of St. Louis," although that moniker is so awkward that not even the constitution, nor laws, uses it consistently.

trouble is a traffic violation, or other minor offense, the case is prosecuted by the police officer making the stop, who refers the ticket as an information to the city prosecutor, who prosecutes the case in that town's municipal court as a functioning subunit of the appropriate circuit court.

Civil cases are different from criminal cases and are usually pursued by private parties.[88] A civil case arising from a troubled relationship (whether a marriage, business relationship, or something else) in St. Louis City, or of which a key transaction took place within the city limits, would be deemed properly brought before the 22nd Circuit Court. If the conflict happened in the county, the St. Louis County circuit court would have jurisdiction and the case would properly begin in that court system.

The legislature has divided Missouri into 45 judicial circuits. Many contain only one county, especially in the populous metropolitan areas. In rural areas, the law establishing the current circuits often consolidates two or more counties into one circuit. Each circuit has at least one circuit judge (with a six-year term of office) and the state provides also at least one associate circuit judge (considered a lower-ranking judge with a four-year term of office) per county in the circuit. In this way all counties are equipped with a resident judge so that the courts can function conveniently and without undue delay. Each of these 45 separate circuit courts, if swamped with litigation, can now ask for judges from other circuits to be assigned on a temporary basis to help clear the dockets (see this Article, Section 6).

Boone County, where the University of Missouri is located, is an example of a county that shares its judicial circuit with another county, Callaway County, immediately to the east. The number of judgeships allocated to any circuit or county is in proportion to its tax base and population; Boone County has a larger population, so it has four associate circuit judges, while Callaway County has two associate circuit judges. The two counties share four circuit judges. These 10 judges together hire two commissioners, judges performing specialized deputized functions under the guidance and control of the circuit court bench; one commissioner presides over "family court," and the other presides over "drug court."[89]

The example of Boone County introduces another horizontal distinction on venue in addition to geography: specialized jurisdiction. Courts in the same circuit (geographical area) may be differentiated on the basis of the kinds of cases/lawsuits that they are empowered to handle (by the constitution, statutes, or judicial rulings). The

---

[88]Governments can engage in civil litigation, either suing or being sued; such cases are not criminal cases and involve not a verdict of either guilty or not guilty (acquittal) but rather a finding of liability or nonliability for damages. Another type of civil case is a case in equity; here the litigants seek a court order to remedy a situation where an actual or potential injury threatens. Much of the litigation involving desegregation of schools in Kansas City and in and around St. Louis was equity litigation. In cases seeking a finding of liability, such a finding may result in damages being awarded to the successful plaintiff; in cases invoking a court's equity jurisdiction, the goal for the successful plaintiff may be court orders, such as court orders that a school district take certain steps to desegregate its schools.

[89]Family court hears cases involving dissolution (divorce) and child custody; drug court handles cases involving drug addiction and rehabilitation for first-time offenders.

upshot of several court reforms has been to consolidate courts of various types of specialized jurisdiction into a unified court structure, that is, the circuit court structure, which is now fairly uniform throughout the state's 45 geographical circuits.[90]

Vertical jurisdiction has to do with the distinctions among trial courts and courts that hear appeals from trial courts. Trial courts, sometimes called courts of first instance, are courts of original jurisdiction—they hear cases for the first time. Trial courts issue findings of fact and come to conclusions of law based on the application of the law to those facts. If the plaintiff or defendant in a case is dissatisfied with the court's decision, he or she can appeal to a court that has appellate jurisdiction over the trial court in which the case was initially heard. With one major exception,[91] the appellate court (also called an appeals court) will not retry the facts of the case but will review and audit the application of the law to those facts.[92]

One more distinction between and among court systems will be useful in approaching the evolution of Missouri's court system. Appellate courts are "higher" courts, while trial courts are "lower" courts, which implies at least two levels of

[90]The reader may have heard of "change of venue." This is a motion filed in court claiming that the local judiciary cannot provide a defendant with a fair trial due to intense local media coverage about the crime. The motion asks the court to find that the local citizenry's opinions have been so polluted by the publicity that a fair and impartial trial jury of local residents cannot be composed. Trying the defendant with such local jurors would undermine the requirements for a fair and impartial jury in the Sixth Amendment to the U.S. Constitution and Article I, Section 18(a) of the Missouri Constitution. "Change of venue" was how this used to be handled; the case would be transferred to another jurisdiction in a different media market, where the alleged crime and defendant are unheard of, and potential jurors' attitudes are uncorrupted. But under current practice Missouri courts empanel the jury in the circuit unaffected by the publicity and then import that impartial jury to the circuit where the trial is to take place, usually keeping the jury sequestered so that it remains unaffected by local gossip and opinions.

[91]The exception is appeal from a court that doesn't keep records of how it applies the law. We call this a "court not of record." Such a court would be fairly low on the totem pole; it might be a police court, a municipal court, or a small claims court. The old justice of the peace courts would also be a good example of a court not of record. Such courts make an entry of their decision but there is no record of the arguments, no trace of the legal reasoning, no transcript of the proceedings, nor any record of the testimony. Thus the facts and the way the law is applied are indiscernible to a court with appellate jurisdiction over the court not of record—the appeals court cannot review and audit the case decision if it cannot know it. The appeals court for such a court not of record is usually a more important trial court, which has to start from scratch to determine the facts and how to apply the law to those facts. This kind of case is given a trial *de novo*, or a new trial that serves as an appeal to check the decision of the lower court and also establishes a record of the case that would be needed if the case is appealed again to a yet higher appeals court.

[92]If it is the first appeals court to review the case, it would be a court of second instance; if it is the second appeals court to review the case, having taken the case from the first appeals court, it would be a court of third instance, and so on. It is possible for a case to wend its way up through a tri-level state court system, and then be appealed to the U.S. Supreme Court, which would then be acting as the court of fourth instance. And it used to be possible for certain cases to filter through a tri-level court system and then start at the lower federal district court again and then work their way up through the tri-level federal court system, with the Supreme Court serving as the court of sixth instance.

court. If only two levels are present in the court system, we say it is a "two-tier" or "dual level system." But most states' court organization features three levels: trial courts at the bottom of the system, an intermediate level of appellate courts, and the state court of last resort (called the state supreme court in 45 states) at the top. A typical three-tier system organizationally resembles the federal court system, which has U.S. district courts as courts of first instance, the U.S. Courts of Appeals as appellate courts, and finally, at the apex of the system, the U.S. Supreme Court.[93] In deciding cases, trial courts use one judge, whereas appellate courts have multiple judges. Intermediate level courts usually sit in "panels" of three judges unless a case is especially important, in which case all members of that bench may sit *en banc* to hear and decide the case. But most state courts of last resort, like the U.S. Supreme Court, sit on cases *en banc*, with as close to full membership of the bench as possible.

Missouri now has a three-tier system of courts. Its court of last resort, the Missouri Supreme Court, sits at the top of the system, and the Missouri Court of Appeals (with three geographic districts, Eastern in St. Louis, Western in Kansas City, and Southern in Springfield and Poplar Bluff) holds the intermediate tier between the supreme court and the trial courts. How the current system evolved and the thinking behind its design are addressed in the commentaries that follow on Article V, Sections 1–24 and 26–27, which establish the design of the state court system.

Every provision in Article V flows from the creativity and hard work of judicial reformers, both independent non-lawyer citizens and the organized bar association (The Missouri Bar), of which all lawyers practicing in the state are members. Sections 1–24 and 26–27 came about through the efforts of The Missouri Bar and a Citizens' Committee, which pushed for adoption statewide of a far-sweeping reform that corrals all courts in the state into a single and unified nonpartisan organization. More than 30 years earlier, in the 1930s, a separate reform on how to choose judges, the so-called nonpartisan judicial selection system, had the same proponents. Their plan met resistance in the legislature, and they then started up a constitutional initiative petition to put it on the ballot, resulting in adoption of the Missouri Plan for selecting state judges, embodied in Section 25 (discussed below).

SECTION 1. Judicial Power—constitutional courts.—The judicial power of the state shall be vested in a Supreme Court, a court of appeals consisting of districts as prescribed by law, and circuit courts.

[93]The federal trial courts are split into 94 districts, and these districts hear cases arising in their geographical areas. The U.S. Courts of Appeals are organized in 12 geographical districts. Missouri has two districts of U.S. district court: Missouri East, centered in St. Louis, and Missouri West, centered in Kansas City. Together with six other states (Arkansas, Iowa, Minnesota, Nebraska, North Dakota, and South Dakota), Missouri is clustered by federal law into the Eighth Circuit of the U.S. Court of Appeals. This court is headquartered in St. Louis but also convenes in other cities throughout the "circuit," particularly St. Paul. Together with the other numbered circuits of the U.S. Court of Appeals (1st through 11th) and the named U.S. Court of Appeals for the District of Columbia, this court makes up the intermediate tier of the federal court system.

Section 1 constitutionally dictates the architecture of a three-tier system of courts, names the courts in the new system, and consigns the judicial power to these courts. Naming the appeals courts this way changed their names from the old-fashioned terms using city names: before the adoption of this amendment in 1970, the three district appeals courts were called, respectively, the St. Louis Court of Appeals, the Kansas City Court of Appeals, and the Springfield Court of Appeals. The Constitution of 1875 established the St. Louis Court of Appeals as the first and only intermediate tiered court in the state, with appellate jurisdiction over the circuit courts in only four counties in the St. Louis area. Remaining counties had no intermediate appellate court, so appeals from courts in those circuits went straight to the Missouri Supreme Court. (This was a typical oddity of court structure in the nineteenth century.) Because the supreme court was having to accept too many cases on direct appeal under this system, in 1884 the constitution was amended to extend the jurisdiction of the St. Louis Court of Appeals to about half the state's counties, and to create the Kansas City Court of Appeals to handle the appeals in the western half of the state's counties. The constitutional amendment also authorized the legislature to create one more court of appeals and to retrofit boundaries of all three districts, so in 1909 it created the Springfield Court of Appeals to cover circuits across the southern area of the state. At present, the legislature has the power under Section 1 to reorganize the districts of the court of appeals but the number of districts cannot go below three (as specified in Section 13 of Article V).

SECTION 2. Supreme Court—controlling decisions—number of judges—sessions. The supreme court shall be the highest court in the state. Its jurisdiction shall be co-extensive with the state. Its decisions shall be controlling in all other courts. It shall be composed of seven judges, who shall hold their sessions in Jefferson City at times fixed by the court.

Note that judges of the supreme court are referred to as "judges"; such is their proper title. Only the chief justice is called by the term "justice." The number of judges on the Missouri Supreme Court is constitutionally ordained, in contrast with the U.S. Supreme Court, whose judgeships are determined by statute. While the U.S. Supreme Court currently has 9 justices as set by statute, it has had between 6 and 10 justices in the past (Congress is allowed under wording of the federal constitution to choose the number).[94] From 1820 to 1872 the Missouri Supreme Court had three judges; from 1872 to 1890 it had five, and finally in 1890 it acquired the present number (seven) of constitutional judgeships.

Until this amended section of the constitution took effect, the Missouri Supreme Court had 13 judges—7 constitutional judges plus 6 "commissioners" (a commissioner is a "helper" judge). The legislature created these positions to relieve the court's burden in handling the many cases appealed to it; until 1970 and the adoption of this amendment, the supreme court was handling a docket of about 1,000 cases per year. The constitutional judges (i.e., the six judges and the chief justice) hired the six com-

[94]The number of Supreme Court justices has been set at nine since 1869.

missioners for four-year terms. Commissioners earned the same salary as the regular judges, their votes on the court counted the same, and the constitutional judges had to appoint an equal number of Republicans and Democrats. At first there were four commissioners, two of each party; then the legislature added two more, so that there would be three commissioners of each party. These commissioners had other functions; for instance, they served as backstop decision makers in case the redistricting commissions couldn't come to a conclusive plan for the state legislative districts based on census results (see Article III, Section 2, paragraph 10, for House of Representatives districting, and Section 7, paragraph 8, for Senate seat redistricting).[95]

Commissioners also were deputized to decide many of the more routine cases on their own (under the tutelage of the constitutional judges of the court), and many commissioners spent long careers on the court, being rehired every four years because the constitutional judges had confidence in their prudent judgment and legal writing skills.

> SECTION 3. **Jurisdiction of the supreme court.**—The supreme court shall have exclusive appellate jurisdiction in all cases involving the validity of a treaty or statute of the United States, or of a statute or provision of the constitution of this state, the construction of the revenue laws of this state, the title to any state office and in all cases where the punishment imposed is death. The court of appeals shall have general appellate jurisdiction in all cases except those within the exclusive jurisdiction of the supreme court.

This section outlines the types of cases over which the supreme court of Missouri has exclusive appellate jurisdiction, meaning these cases skip the state court of appeals completely and are immediately filed for review by the supreme court. These cases fall under the supreme court's mandatory jurisdiction; that is, the court is commanded by the constitution to take such cases and apply the law to them. The first type of case, one involving the validity of a federal treaty or statute, probably wouldn't arise in state court in Missouri; most lawyers would file such lawsuits in federal court. But state courts can litigate the meaning of U.S. statutes and treaties, even the meaning of U.S. constitutional provisions, and all state judges throughout the country are by oath obliged to support the U.S. Constitution, laws, and treaties if they clash with state laws or constitutional provisions (see U.S. Const. Art. VI, para. 2).[96]

The second category is fairly self-evident: the meaning of state law and constitutional provisions should be litigated in state court; if no federal issue is involved, the federal courts will decline to take any such case under the doctrine of *Murdoch v. City of Memphis,* 20 Wall. 590 (1875). Most cases challenging a state law as

---

[95]Another way of coping with the supreme court's high workload was to split into divisions. Originally there were two divisions, one with three judges and one with four. That there were 13 judges on the supreme court (including the commissioners) wasn't unwieldy because the judges would hear cases in divisions, with some commissioners serving on one division and the others serving on the other. The supreme court building still has two courtrooms, one for Division I and one for Division II.

[96]Federal law permits the case to be reviewed by the federal courts if federal issues are truly involved.

unconstitutional on state grounds will begin in the 19th Circuit, the location of the capital city of Jefferson.

State laws concerning revenue are a third category of cases that go directly from trial (circuit) courts to the state supreme court. A fourth category is any case involving a disputed election for a state office, and finally, the fifth category is any criminal case in which the death penalty has been imposed. These five categories of cases are appealed directly to the state supreme court because they are considered important enough to be fast-tracked to the ultimate authority. All other cases go to the Missouri Court of Appeals, that is, to one of its geographic divisions (Eastern, Western, or Southern), depending on the circuit in which the case was originally tried.

The wording of this provision, adjusted in 1982, slims down the types of cases immediately appealable to the state supreme court by subtracting from its direct appellate jurisdiction cases involving terms of life imprisonment; these are now reviewed by the state court of appeals, and the supreme court can accept them on appeal from there if its intervention is warranted (i.e., as an exercise of discretionary appellate jurisdiction).

SECTION 4. Superior courts to control inferior courts—courts administrator, salary—reapportionment commission, appointment.—1. The supreme court shall have general superintending control over all courts and tribunals. Each district of the court of appeals shall have general superintending control over all courts and tribunals in its jurisdiction. The supreme court and districts of the court of appeals may issue and determine original remedial writs. Supervisory authority over all courts is vested in the supreme court which may make appropriate delegations of this power.

2. The supreme court may appoint a state courts administrator and other staff to aid in the administration of the courts, and it shall appoint a clerk of the supreme court and may appoint other staff to aid in the administration of the business of the supreme court. Each such appointee shall serve at the pleasure of the court. The clerk's and administrator's salary shall be fixed by law. All other appointees shall have salaries fixed by the court within the legislative limits of the appropriation made for that purpose.

3. In the event that six commissioners of the supreme court are not available to sit as a reapportionment commission as provided in sections 2, 3 and 7 of article III of the constitution of this state, a commission composed of six members appointed by the supreme court from among the judges of the court of appeals, shall serve in lieu of the commissioners of the supreme court. No more than two members of any division of the court of appeals shall be appointed to the commission.

Section 4 importantly grants the supreme court supervisory power over all courts in the system. Before the adoption of this provision, the supreme court had to wait for a case in which a judge made a mistake to come up on appeal before it could correct the error in application of the law. Under this wording (paragraph 1 of Section 4) and under the wording of Section 5, the supreme court may make rules that preemptively control the lower courts' decision making, thereby nipping error in the bud. The supreme court may also delegate this rule-making power; the wording anticipates that one entity to which the supreme court might delegate its power to make rules is the court of appeals.

Section 4, paragraph 2 authorizes the supreme court to appoint a state courts administrator and a clerk of the supreme court, with salaries to be set by the legislature. The salaries of other appointees in the offices of the clerk and of the state courts administrator are to be set by the court (although the legislature controls the appropriation of funds for their salaries).

Paragraph 3 anticipates the phasing out of the commissioners. Time lapse wording no longer included in the constitution provided that no new commissioners would be appointed to replace those who retired or resigned,[97] so if the supreme court could not appoint the full number of supreme court commissioners to a reapportionment commission, it should instead appoint two court of appeals judges from each district of the court of appeals. While the redistricting of 1971 involved the six commissioners, the commissioners were gone by the time of the next redistricting in 1981. In their place, the supreme court had to appoint court of appeals judges in accordance with Section 4.[98]

SECTION 5. Rules of practice and procedure—duty of supreme court—power of legislature.—The supreme court may establish rules relating to practice, procedure and pleading for all courts and administrative tribunals, which shall have the force and effect of law. The rules shall not change substantive rights, or the law relating to evidence, the oral examination of witnesses, juries, the right of trial by jury, or the right of appeal. The court shall publish the rules and fix the day on which they take effect, but no rule shall take effect before six months after its publication. Any rule may be annulled or amended in whole or in part by a law limited to the purpose.

Section 5 allows the supreme court to make rules for the entire judiciary, but notably also allows the legislature to reverse or amend these rules by simple majority vote, thereby putting in place a potential check on the judiciary.

SECTION 6. Assignment of judges—authority of supreme court—eligible judges.— The supreme court may make temporary transfers of judicial personnel from one court or district to another as the administration of justice requires, and may establish rules with respect thereto. Any judge shall be eligible to sit temporarily on any court upon assignment by the supreme court or pursuant to supreme court rule.

Section 6 shows the newfound flexibility of the corps of judges; they can now be reassigned to help out in jurisdictions suffering from an overload of cases. Any judge may be reassigned temporarily. It should be noted that the supreme court itself has the authority to bring up trial judges or retired jurists to fill out its ranks in cases

[97]Absence of this wording in today's document shows that it is possible to "clean up" the constitution by omitting obsolete wording. The last commissioner, Andrew Jackson Higgins, was appointed to full membership as a constitutional judge in 1979, a move that reduced the population of commissioners on the court to zero.

[98]The language in Article III was changed subsequently (1982) to accept the substitution of selected courts of appeals judges for commissions as the backup decision maker in redistricting.

where one or more supreme court judges is absent for any reason. This contrasts with practice on the U.S. Supreme Court where justices are not replaced if they are sick or recuse themselves; the U.S. Supreme Court has a quorum rule of six justices. Missouri's supreme court would still be able to function if it had vacancies by "bringing up" judges from lower courts as "senior" judges or "special" judges.

SECTION 7. Supreme court and court of appeals may sit in divisions.—The supreme court may sit en banc or in divisions as the court may determine. Any district of the court of appeals may sit at such places within the district and in divisions as the judges of such district may determine. Each division of the supreme court or of the court of appeals shall be composed of not less than three judges, at least one of whom shall be a regular judge of the court. A majority of a division shall constitute a quorum thereof, and all orders, judgments, and decrees of a division, as to causes and matters pending before it, shall have the force and effect of those of the court.

Section 7 pertains to the divisions of the supreme court and the court of appeals. Before adoption of this wording, the supreme court operated in set "divisions." Division 1 had four (constitutional) judges, and Division 2 had three. When they were elected (before 1942; see discussion at Article V, Sections 25–27), judges ran for designated divisions; after adoption of the Missouri Plan (discussed later at Section 25), they were appointed or retained in office for positions designated as belonging to either division. Division 2 handled criminal cases while other cases went to Division 1. This distinction was inflexible; while it empowered the court to function effectively as two courts, thereby doubling its ability to handle the docket, its rigidity also made for inefficiencies in handling the docket. If Division 1 was overloaded and Division 2's business was slow, the judges from Division 2 could not help out temporarily, and vice versa. The court had some flexibility in being able to assign cases to the commissioners, but overall it was locked in by constitutional strictures.

The new wording of Section 7 allows the court to decide how to use the divisions itself in accordance with need and docket burdens—that is, with full flexibility. If the court's judges so decide, they can handle cases *en banc*, that is, with full membership of seven judges sitting on the case. Alternatively, they can split into divisions that do not have to follow the lines of the previous constitutionally designated divisions. The court actually experimented with a new division, Division 3, for a while in the early 1970s, but eventually did away with the divisions entirely as its docket shrank. Whether or not to have divisions, and how to set them up, are decisional powers given by the constitution entirely to the supreme court. With the newly expanded numbers of judgeships on the court of appeals taking up the workload, the supreme court was freed of much of its burden, except for the cases that it was obliged to take directly from the circuit courts. Meanwhile, the court of appeals was also freed from the burden of constitutionally dictated divisions.

SECTION 8. Chief justice and chief judges, election, terms—authority of chief justice.—The judges of the supreme court shall elect from their number a chief justice to preside over the court en banc, and the judges of the court of appeals in each district shall elect from their number a chief judge of the district. The terms of the chief justice and chief judges shall be fixed by the courts over which they preside. The chief justice of the supreme court shall be the chief administrative officer of the judicial system and, subject to the supervisory authority of the supreme court, shall supervise the administration of the courts of this state.

Section 8 delineates the procedure for choosing the chief justice on the supreme court and similarly for selecting the chief judge on the court of appeals benches. The chief justice is elected for a two-year term and by custom the choice is always the senior-most judge who has not yet served as chief.[99] We can describe the chief justiceship on the Missouri Supreme Court as rotational, in contrast to the chief justiceship on the national Supreme Court, which is a designated position.

SECTION 9. **Transfer of causes to supreme court en banc.**—A cause in the supreme court shall be transferred to the court en banc when the members of a division are equally divided in opinion, or when the division shall so order, or on application of the losing party when a member of the division dissents from the opinion therein, or pursuant to supreme court rule.

Section 9 provides a means of reconciling differences of opinion within a division of the supreme court by having the full membership of the court take up the case. Note that provision is made for a division with an even number of judges (because the wording anticipates an equally divided vote on the case). Since the court no longer uses divisions, this wording could be considered no longer necessary, but it was necessary during the transitional phase when the court was still using commissioners and divisions to manage its caseload.

SECTION 10. **Transfer of cases from court of appeals to supreme court—scope of review.**—Cases pending in the court of appeals shall be transferred to the supreme court when any participating judge dissents from the majority opinion and certifies that he deems said opinion to be contrary to any previous decision of the supreme court or of the court of appeals, or any district of the court of appeals. Cases pending in the court of appeals may be transferred to the supreme court by order of the majority of the judges of the participating district of the court of appeals, after opinion, or by order of the supreme court before or after opinion because of the general interest or importance of a question involved in the case, or for the purpose of reexamining the existing law, or pursuant to supreme court rule. The supreme court may finally determine all causes coming to it from the court of appeals, whether by certification, transfer or certiorari, the same as on original appeal.

---

[99]Only once in modern times did the court not follow this rule: in 1985, when Judge Albert Rendlen stepped down after his term as chief, he conspired with three other judges to bypass Judge Warren Welliver, whose turn was next up to be chief. Welliver complained publicly about this, which, together with other complaints from Judge Robert Donnelly, created a public scandal. Ever since, the court has observed its custom of taking turns at the chief justiceship. See Greg Casey, "Public Perceptions of Judicial Scandal: The Missouri Supreme Court 1982–88," *The Justice System Journal* 13 (1988–89), 284–307; and Kenyon D. Bunch and Gregory Casey, "Political Controversy on Missouri's Supreme Court: The Case of Merit vs. Politics," *State and Local Government Review* 22.1 (Winter 1990), 5–16.

Section 10 provides a way to signal when a case is significant enough to merit review by the supreme court sitting as the court of third instance. If a court of appeals judge dissents in a case, and is willing to certify that the case was or is being decided wrongly, that disagreement labels the case as "juicy" enough to merit consideration by the supreme court. The court of appeals can also transfer cases to the supreme court if it needs guidance. All these provisions are intended to funnel the most important cases to the supreme court, either before or after a decision is reached by the intermediate court.

> **SECTION 11. Want of jurisdiction, effect—transfers.**—In all proceedings reviewable on appeal by the supreme court or the court of appeals, appeals shall go directly to the court or district having jurisdiction, but want of jurisdiction shall not be ground for dismissal, and the proceeding shall be transferred to the appellate court having jurisdiction. An original action filed in a court lacking jurisdiction or venue shall be transferred to the appropriate court.

Section 11 provides that lawyers cannot argue want of jurisdiction to keep their cases from being litigated; if the case is in the wrong court, it should be taken by the right court, based on correct interpretations of the jurisdiction.

> **SECTION 12. Judicial opinions—filing and publication—memorandum decisions and orders.**—The opinions of the supreme court and court of appeals and all divisions or districts of said courts shall be in writing and filed in the respective causes, and shall become a part of the records of the court, be available for publication, and shall be public records. The supreme court and the court of appeals may issue memorandum decisions or dispose of a cause by order pursuant to and as authorized by supreme court rule.

Section 12 is a guarantee that the courts, especially the appellate courts, should make public their reasoning for their decisions. However, the supreme court is authorized to make rules that would permit memorandum decisions, brief summaries of the court's order(s) that do not reveal its full rationale (*ratio decidendi*). Trial courts' bases for decision are ordinarily found in the trial courts' records, may be quite perfunctory, and are seldom published. Appellate courts often furnish a longer justification for their decisions. Missouri no longer publishes its appellate court decisions in its own print shop; its opinions are instead published officially in the *South Western Reporter* by West Law Publishing Company, and in LexisNexis.

> **SECTION 13. Court of appeals, districts, judges.**—The court of appeals shall be organized into separate districts, the number, not less than three, geographical boundaries, and territorial jurisdiction of which shall be prescribed by law. Each district of the court of appeals shall be composed of such number of judges, not less than three, as may be provided by law.

Section 13 gives the architecture of the court of appeals and reaffirms the restriction in Section 1 directing there to be districts of the court of appeals (rather than just one district). Here the number of such districts is specifically set at a minimum of three, carrying forward the tradition begun when the legislature created the third district intermediate court of appeals in 1909 with the establishment of the Springfield Court of Appeals.

SECTION 14. Circuit courts—jurisdiction—sessions.—(a) The circuit courts shall have original jurisdiction over all cases and matters, civil and criminal. Such courts may issue and determine original remedial writs and shall sit at times and places within the circuit as determined by the circuit court. (b) Procedures for the adjudication of small claims shall be as provided by law.

Section 14 consigns original jurisdiction to the circuit courts and allows the General Assembly to provide for small claims courts, which under law are a division of circuit courts.

SECTION 15. Judicial circuits—establishment and changes—general terms and divisions—judges—presiding judge—court personnel.—1. The state shall be divided into convenient circuits of contiguous counties. In each circuit there shall be at least one circuit judge. The circuits may be changed or abolished by law as public convenience and the administration of justice may require, but no judge shall be removed from office during his term by reason of alteration of the geographical boundaries of a circuit. Any circuit or associate circuit judge may temporarily sit in any other circuit at the request of a judge thereof. In circuits having more than one judge, the court may sit in general term or in divisions. The circuit judges of the circuit may make rules for the circuit not inconsistent with the rules of the supreme court.

2. Each circuit shall have such number of circuit judges as provided by law.

3. The circuit and associate circuit judges in each circuit shall select by secret ballot a circuit judge from their number to serve as presiding judge. The presiding judge shall have general administrative authority over the court and its divisions.

4. Personnel to aid in the business of the circuit court shall be selected as provided by law or in accordance with a governmental charter of a political subdivision of this state. Where there is a separate probate division of the circuit court, the judge of the probate division shall, until otherwise provided by law, appoint a clerk and other non-judicial personnel for the probate division.

Section 15 steps up the number of judges constitutionally mandated for the trial courts. Instead of only one judge per circuit, as was the case before the amendment's effective date of January 1979, this section now calls for one judge per county within the circuit (recall that many counties are grouped into multi-county circuits). This follows through on the provision of more judges for the court of appeals and presumes growth in the trial judiciary to accommodate increased litigation. The fourth sentence reaffirms the new system's flexibility in assigning judges to help with docket overloads when necessary.

The fifth sentence permits judges of circuit courts to break up into one-judge divisions as the members of the circuit court decide.[100] Typical divisions would be

[100]Such divisions of trial courts are unlike the "divisions" that once dominated the state supreme court and court of appeals. Instead of "panels" of three judges (or four, in the case of the old Division 1 of the supreme court), these divisions are one-judge benches with specialized dockets. However, the

criminal, juvenile, family (dissolutions of marriage, custody of children), small claims, probate (administering estates of decedents), and drug court. Each circuit may now arrange its total workload as it sees fit; it can deal out particular types of cases to divisions that it creates, giving them to particular judges who may have more talent for handling some types of strife. This is a huge contrast to the *status quo ante* (pre-1976), when circuit judges, magistrate judges, and probate judges functioned in separate silos, and could not pitch in and help out their colleagues in the next silo over.[101]

The last sentence of the first provision allows circuit judges to make local rules for their circuit. Associate circuit judges are not included in this rule-making authority. This led to a dispute in the St. Louis County (21st) circuit when the 20 circuit judges created a rule that had the effect of excluding the associate circuit judges from the election of the presiding judge. The local rule specified that the election would be by a nomination seconded by a majority of the circuit judges, excluding the associate judges from effective involvement in the election because they had no say in the seconding. This local rule contradicted the third provision, above, ordaining that election of the presiding judge should be by vote of both circuit and associate circuit judges. The local rule also went against the "secret ballot" part of the provision; a motion to second is by definition public and therefore cannot be kept secret. In a case pitting one judge against another judge on the same court, the supreme court resolved this contradiction by throwing out the local rule; the state constitution took priority over a local judge-made rule.[102]

The second provision authorizes the legislature to create the judgeships, and the third provision tells how the circuit court benches are to be governed.

The bickering over governance that kept arising in the circuit court of St. Louis County (21st Circuit), the state's largest bench, in the early and mid-1980s owed primarily to the court consolidation mandated by Sections 1–15 and 22–24. On January 1, 1979, all these courts were amalgamated together in one circuit court with the magistrate judges becoming associate circuit judges, the probate judges becoming circuit judges, and some special adjustments in St. Louis City to phase out the judges of the court of criminal corrections (its two judges became circuit judges) and fit the municipal court into the circuit court structure. Court employees and judges became apprehensive and uncomfortable as measures to centralize the

---

assignments of the specialized dockets are not constitutionally dictated nor are they frozen by statute; the circuit court is authorized to carve up its workload as suits it, and this power enables it to make maximum use of its judicial personnel.

[101] It was even worse in the city of St. Louis, where a municipal court and a court of criminal corrections constituted separate judicial empires (and fonts of patronage). By the time of the reform, most "courts of common pleas" had shut down, but two remained (in Hannibal and Cape Girardeau), confusing lines of jurisdiction in those areas.

[102] *Gregory v. Corrigan*, 685 S.W.2d 840 (1985). The court ruled that since the "amended local rule in its present form effectively circumvents this constitutional directive and is tantamount to a disenfranchisement, it is hereby declared invalid."

court staff advanced. For the court employees, promotions in grade and salary were at stake. They feared demotions and salary losses, and the judges feared losing their loyal staffers. Signatory authority over bank accounts was also at stake in tightening the financial strings; a centralized fiscal officer posed the risk that expenditures would be questioned. The associate circuit judges' staffs (formerly the magistrate judges' separate staffs) had not yet been merged with the office of the chief clerk of the circuit, and the associate circuit judges resisted changes away from a decentralized form of administrative organization that would enable them to continue operating autonomously in their courtrooms with their own staffers. Their resistance was incompatible with the spirit of reform embodied in the passage of the 1976 judicial reform—reform meant rational bureaucracy, avoidance of duplicative and overlapping tasks, and a clear chain of command up to the top. These associate judges' devotion to decentralization also reflected a continuing devotion to the patronage that had existed before court re-organization. Court employees "gamed" the associate judges, cementing alliances with their judicial patrons and egging them on into bickering with the corps of circuit judges. Presiding Judge Corrigan pushed centralization of circuit authority over all judges and court employees, but resistance gelled.

In the early 1985 election of a new Presiding Judge, the 13 associate circuit judges made common cause with a minority of the 20 circuit judges to prevail numerically and elect Judge Campbell as Presiding. Campbell tried to bring the court together. In a meeting of all judges, the circuit judges adopted new rules, and authorized an administrative planning committee with the authority to set aside orders of the Presiding Judge (Campbell). Then, the minority group of circuit judges met with the associate circuit judges and voted to table these new rules. But were these actions valid, in light of the constitutional wording? Another lawsuit involving judges of the 21st Circuit as party litigants rose to the state supreme court. This time the court decided that the rules in whose adoption the associate circuit judges had played a role were unconstitutional in setting limits on the administrative authority of the presiding judge. Also, the authority of the presiding judge could not be delegated to or shared with a planning committee: the constitution states plainly that the "Presiding Judge shall have general administrative authority over the court and its divisions" (Section 15, paragraph 3, second sentence).[103]

Now Presiding Judge Campbell declined to call a meeting of the circuit judges to adopt new rules. (He did appoint a committee to propose new rules.) At this point, the majority of circuit judges met and adopted rules, but Campbell refused to accept and certify the rules, so the judge group asked the supreme court to certify the rules. In response, in the new case arising from this ongoing struggle, the supreme court dressed down the 21st Circuit Court,[104] and went the further step of declaring unconstitutional the constitutional wording allowing the associate judges to participate in

[103]*Nolan v. Stussie*, 695 S.W.2d 869 (1985).
[104]*In re Rules of Circuit Court*, 702 S.W.2d 457 (Mo. 1985).

the election of the presiding judge. The court determined that this provision, despite being nestled within the constitution, conflicted with the electorate's overall general purpose in establishing a consolidated court system. When conflicts between two constitutional provisions arise (in this case between the provision in Section 15, paragraph 3, first sentence, on the one hand, and the spirit behind Article V, Sections 1–15, 17, and 20–24, on the other hand) the supreme court has to use its powers of judicial review to determine which provision takes priority. In this case the overall intent behind the judicial reform held sway. Finally, the high court threatened the 21st Circuit Court with takeover by a neutral judge from another circuit whom the supreme court would appoint as presiding, but through whom the supreme court would work to ensure that the dysfunctionality would end.

But this warning was insufficient; the mischief of the 21st Circuit continued to play out. See the commentary at Section 24 of this article for further details.

The fourth provision provides that the probate division, if there is such, should appoint its own clerk and other personnel (patronage appointments). This is a bow to the heavily specialized work of probate law. Hires for the circuit court should be in accordance with either state law or the county's personnel policies.

SECTION 16. Associate circuit judges, selection.—Each county shall have such number of associate circuit judges as provided by law. There shall be at least one resident associate circuit judge in each county. Associate circuit judges shall be selected or elected in each county. In those circuits where the circuit judge is selected under section 25 of article 5 of the constitution the associate circuit judge shall be selected in the same manner. All other associate circuit judges shall be elected in the county in which they are to serve.

Section 16 places the associate circuit judges under the merit selection system (see the description of the three stages of merit appointment in the commentary on Section 25 of this Article) if their county has opted for that system; otherwise, they are elected on party ballots. Although circuit judges are selected on a circuitwide basis (i.e., if they are in a multicounty system, all counties in the circuit are involved in selecting them), associate circuit judges are selected by the electorate in only one county.[105]

SECTION 17. Associate circuit judges, jurisdiction.—Associate circuit judges may hear and determine all cases, civil or criminal and all other matters as now provided by law for magistrate or probate judges and may be assigned such additional cases or classes of cases as may be provided by law. In probate matters the associate circuit judge shall have general equitable jurisdiction.

Section 17 extends the jurisdiction of associate circuit judges to everything that the circuit court can do. They can be deployed as their court sees fit.

SECTION 18. Judicial review of action of administrative agencies—scope of review.—All final decisions, findings, rules and orders on any administrative officer or body existing under the constitution or by law, which are judicial or quasi-judicial and affect private

---

[105]Note that no multicounty circuit has opted for the merit selection plan, so all judges in multicounty circuits are elected on a party ballot.

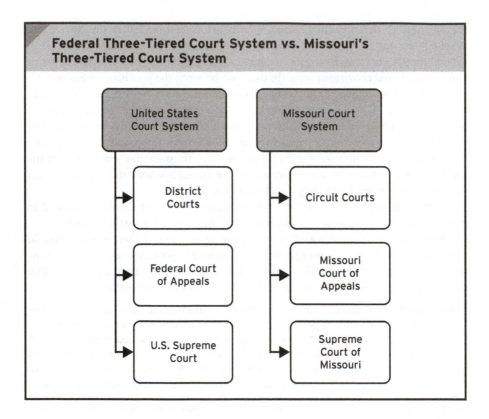

Federal Three-Tiered Court System vs. Missouri's Three-Tiered Court System

rights, shall be subject to direct review by the courts as provided by law; and such review shall include the determination whether the same are authorized by law, and in cases in which a hearing is required by law, whether the same are supported by competent and substantial evidence upon the whole record. Unless otherwise provided by law, administrative decisions, findings, rules and orders subject to review under this section or which are otherwise subject to direct judicial review, shall be reviewed in such manner and by such court as the supreme court by rule shall direct and the court so designated shall, in addition to its other jurisdiction, have jurisdiction to hear and determine any such review proceeding.

Section 18 provides for judicial review of administrative decisions and grants state courts jurisdiction as superintended by the supreme court. The doctrine of judicial review refers to the court's power to review the lawfulness and constitutionality of statutes passed by the legislature or actions taken by the executive. Such a power is not explicitly granted to the federal judiciary in the U.S. Constitution but rather stems from *Marbury v. Madison* (1803). In *Marbury*, Chief Justice John Marshall argued that the power of judicial review could be inferred from the structure and logic of the Constitution. Judicial review is now a common and accepted power of

U.S. courts, both at the state and federal levels. Section 18 above focuses on judicial review of administrative agencies.

> **SECTION 19. Terms of judges.**—Judges of the supreme court and of the court of appeals shall be selected for terms of twelve years, judges of the circuit courts for terms of six years, and associate circuit judges for terms of four years.

Section 19 is quite plain in indicating the length of judicial terms. The 1945 Constitution extended the terms of appellate judges from 10 years to 12 years. Federal judges enjoy life terms, while Missouri judges have fixed terms of office. Judges in some states, such as Massachusetts and New Jersey, also have life terms.

> **SECTION 20. Salaries and compensation of judges—provision against other special compensation and practice of law—travel and other expenses.**—All judges shall receive as salary the total amount of their present compensation until otherwise provided by law, but no judge's salary shall be diminished during his term of office. No judge shall receive any other or additional compensation for any public service. No supreme, appellate, circuit or associate circuit judge shall practice law or do law business. Judges may receive reasonable traveling and other expenses allowed by law.

Section 20 protects the judges of the state against any legislative or executive move to reduce their salary but concomitantly prohibits them from taking on outside work for pay, which includes taking on clients in private practice of the law. This is similar to the federal constitutional guarantee that judges should not suffer diminution of salary while still in office, and has the same function of protecting judges' independence.[106]

> **SECTION 21. Judges—qualifications—age requirements—license to practice law.**—Judges of the supreme court and of the court of appeals shall have been citizens of the United States for at least fifteen years, and qualified voters of the state for nine years next preceding their selection. Such judges shall be at least thirty years of age. Except as provided by section 6, judges of the court of appeals shall be residents of the court of appeals district in which they serve. Circuit judges shall have been citizens of the United States for at least ten years, and qualified voters of this state three years next preceding their selection, and be not less than thirty years of age and residents of the circuit for at least one year. Associate circuit judges shall be qualified voters of this state and residents of the county, at least twenty-five years old, and have such other qualifications as may be provided by law. Every supreme, appellate, circuit, and associate circuit court judge shall be licensed to practice law in this state.

---

[106]Only Article III judges enjoy this guarantee, however; certain other classes of federal judges, such as bankruptcy judges, are considered Article I judges and have fixed terms. Impeachment is the means of removing federal Article III judges and is also available for Missouri judges, but a much easier technique in Missouri is referral of a complaint to the Commission on Retirement, Removal, and Discipline of judges, which may find that the judge should be removed. All decisions of this commission must, however, go the supreme court for approval. Note the commentary at Section 24 of this article about possibly reprimanding the presiding judge of the 21st Circuit in the case of *Matter of Voorhees*.

Section 21 specifies qualifications to be a judge. There is a duration of residency requirement and an age requirement (which is actually quite liberal in that 25-year-olds can aspire to become an associate circuit judge). All judges at all three levels are required to be lawyers, with the exception of municipal judges.

SECTION 22. Court of appeals clerks and personnel—salaries.—Each district of the court of appeals shall appoint a clerk of the court and other personnel to aid in the administration of the business of the court. Their salaries shall be within the limit of the legislative appropriation for that purpose.

Section 22 concerns hiring court staffers; salaries have to be set so they don't exceed the legislature's appropriations for the courts.

SECTION 23. Municipal judges and court personnel—selection—terms—compensation—jurisdiction—appeals—role of associate circuit judges.—Each circuit may have such municipal judges as provided by law and the necessary non-judicial personnel assisting them. The selection, tenure and compensation of such judges and such personnel shall be as provided by law, or in cities having a charter form of government as provided by such charter. A municipal judge may be a part-time judge except where prohibited by ordinance or charter of the municipality. A municipal judge shall hear and determine violations of municipal ordinances in one or more municipalities. Until otherwise provided by law, or supreme court rule, the practice, procedure, right to and method of appeal before and from municipal judges shall be as heretofore provided with respect to municipal courts. Associate circuit judges shall hear and determine violations of municipal ordinances in any municipality with a population of under four hundred thousand within the circuit for which a municipal judge is not provided, or upon request of the governing body of any municipality with a population of under four hundred thousand within the circuit.

Federal vs. Missouri State Judges

FEDERAL JUDGES	MISSOURI STATE JUDGES
865 judges total	408 judges total
Appointed by president	Majority chosen via Missouri Plan; outstate judges primarily elected by popular vote on party ballot
Confirmed by Senate	No confirmation process
Lifetime appointments	Term length: 12 years (appellate judge); 6 years (circuit judge); 4 years (associate circuit judge)
$211,200/year salary	$127,020-$143,883/year circuit court salary

Section 23 covers municipal judges. They can be chosen in a multitude of ways, as dictated by law or municipal ordinance, or if in a charter government (that is, a municipality that has chosen to set up home rule), charter rules take priority over any municipal provision regarding judicial selection to the contrary. (Municipal charters are constitutions for municipalities, and thus have the status of higher law, to which all municipal ordinances are subordinated.) Municipal judges can be part-time; in many instances, municipal judges hold court one or two evenings a week. If a municipality decides against setting up a municipal court, it can refer violations of its ordinances to the prosecuting attorney for prosecution in circuit court. Note that municipal judges are not required to be lawyers, a qualification left out at the behest of the rural interests who worried that there were insufficient lawyers to staff the municipal courts that might spring up.

SECTION 24. **Retirement, removal and discipline of judges, commission on—composition, terms, duties, procedures, reimbursement of expenses—additional duties prohibited.**—1. There shall be a commission on retirement, removal, and discipline, composed of two citizens who are not members of the bar, appointed by the governor, two lawyers appointed by the board of governors of The Missouri Bar, one judge of the court of appeals to be selected by a majority of the judges of the court of appeals, and one judge of the circuit courts to be selected by a majority of the circuit judges of this state. The commission shall receive and investigate all requests and suggestions for retirement for disability, and all complaints concerning misconduct of all judges, members of the judicial commissions, and of this commission. No member of the commission shall participate in any matter in which he has a personal interest. If a member is disqualified to participate in any matter before the commission, the respective selecting authority shall select a substitute to sit during such disqualification. Of the members first appointed, each of the citizen members shall be appointed for a term of two years and each of the lawyer members for a term of four years, and each of the judge members for a term of six years; and thereafter members shall be appointed for a term of six years.

2. Upon recommendation by an affirmative vote of at least four members of the commission, the supreme court en banc shall retire from office any judge or any member of any judicial commission or any member of this commission who is found to be unable to discharge the duties of his office with efficiency because of permanent sickness or physical or mental infirmity. A judge, except a municipal judge so retired shall receive one-half of his regular compensation during the remainder of his term of office. Where a judge subject to retirement under other provisions of law, has been retired under the provisions of this section, the time during which he was retired for disability under this section shall count as time served for purposes of retirement under other provisions of this constitution or of law.

3. Upon recommendation by an affirmative vote of at least four members of the commission, the supreme court en banc, upon concurring with such recommendation, shall remove, suspend, discipline or reprimand any judge of any court or any member of any judicial commission or of this commission, for the commission of a crime, or for misconduct, habitual drunkenness, willful neglect of duty, corruption in office, incompetency or any offense involving moral turpitude, or oppression in office. No action taken under this section shall be a bar to or prevent any other action authorized by law.

4. A judge is disqualified from acting as a judicial officer while there is pending an indictment or information charging him in any court in the United States with a crime punishable as a felony under the laws of Missouri or the United States, or a recommendation to the supreme court by the commission for his removal, or retirement, or after articles of impeachment have been voted by the house of representatives. A judge so disqualified shall continue to receive his salary.

5. On recommendation of the commission, the supreme court shall suspend a judge from office without salary when in any court in the United States he pleads guilty or no contest to, or is found guilty of, an offense punishable as a felony under the laws of Missouri or the United States, or of any other offense that involves moral turpitude. If he is suspended and his conviction becomes final the supreme court shall remove him from office. If his conviction is reversed and he is discharged from that charge by order of court or of the prosecuting officer, whether without further trial or after further trial and a finding of not guilty, his suspension terminates and he shall be paid his salary for the period of suspension.

6. Recommendations to the supreme court by the commission shall be made only after notice and hearing. Rules for the administration of this section and for the procedures thereunder shall be prescribed by supreme court rule unless otherwise provided by law.

7. Members of the commission shall be reimbursed for their actual and necessary expenses incurred in the performance of their duties.

8. Additional duties shall not be imposed by law or supreme court rule upon the commission on retirement, removal and discipline.

Section 24 clarifies the role of the Commission on Retirement, Removal, and Discipline of judges, which here has been given constitutional status after having been initially a statutory reform. This six-member entity considers any complaints about judicial misbehavior through a process of investigation, culminating in a report with recommendations to the supreme court. In reacting to the report, the supreme court has several options. It may find that there is nothing to the charge(s), or it may, in increasing order of harshness, reprimand, discipline, suspend from office, or remove the errant judge. This is an easier process than impeachment (which remains as an awkward alternative). But as the troubles of the 21st Circuit show, it can be used as a cudgel rather than as a judicious means of improving the judiciary.

In the fall of 1985, after the *In re Rules of Circuit Court* decision (see p. 136), the circuit judges of the 21st Circuit elected Judge Voorhees as presiding. He immediately appointed a committee to plan how the circuit could best advance central control over docketing and assignment of cases. But shortly thereafter, four associate circuit judges (referred to as X1, X2, X3, and X4 here) began to obstruct this effort. Judge X1 prepared 40 pill bottles with the label: "Take one pill whenever the urge to worry about reorganization and docket mismanagement occurs" and distributed them to various court employees and judges. Then, Judge X2 took his nameplate down off the door to his courtroom; Judges X3 and X4 followed suit. These judges stated that having their names associated with their disreputable court would hurt their chances for retention in office in the fall 1986 election. More confusion ensued as members of the general public faced difficulty locating the courtrooms where they were supposed to report. Yet further aggravation took place when one of these three judges put up a sign on his courtroom door apologizing for any disruption and referring those with questions to go to the courtrooms of the named judges who served on the committee grappling with establishing central control over docketing and case assignments. The judges on the committee then faced multiple disruptions in their work schedules as lawyers and litigants wandered about the courthouse, complaining about the confusion.

Later, the committee devised a plan to reorganize (centralize) the staff services and procedures of the court, but as the deadline of March 4, 1986, approached those judges supporting the reform began to fear that the four prankster judges would not comply. This became more worrisome when at a meeting two of the recalcitrant judges proclaimed that they would accept no more than 150 cases per annum; another two announced that they would not accept certain kinds of adult abuse cases, and another judge declared that he would not accept any afternoon assignments. Other non-negotiable demands included a claim for additional clerical personnel, a refusal to sign warrants after hours, and a refusal to make docket entries after hearing each case (necessitating the assignment of an additional clerk for that judge's courtroom).

Presiding Judge Voorhees became concerned that the plan for central secretarial control would face immediate resistance and breakdown. At the eleventh hour, Judge X1 sent a letter to all judges of the circuit arguing that the reorganization plan would not work unless the associate circuit judges were allowed to develop their own plans for their divisions "without interference" and suggested that the committee release its claimed control over the associate divisions. A majority of the circuit judges (those supportive of the reform) then met and wrote a letter to the recalcitrant judges suspending their assignments; 14 of the circuit judges signed this document (the six circuit judges unsympathetic to the reorganization did not sign, nor were they asked to). Judge Voorhees considered the document a directive to him to de-activate the four resistant associate judges, but he hesitated at first until the assistant court administrator explained that attempts at subverting the plan might not become obvious for weeks; at this point he had a bailiff deliver identical letters to the four judges relieving each of them of their duties and requiring that they surrender their chambers and courtrooms. The four then filed an application to the supreme court seeking an order setting aside the presiding judge's rulings, but the supreme court instead issued an order directing them to comply with the orders of Presiding Judge Voorhees.

The four resistant judges then filed a complaint with the Commission on Retirement, Removal and Discipline against Judge Voorhees, charging that in removing them from their courtrooms he skipped steps in the Presiding Judges' Handbook. The Commission on Retirement, Removal and Discipline eventually recommended that Judge Voorhees be reprimanded for trying to work with the four recalcitrant judges instead of reporting their misconduct to the commission for its consideration. In short, the commission used the four obstreperous judges' complaint to find that, far from being too hard on them, Judge Voorhees had failed in his duty to be much harder on them! The commission was engaging in empire building for itself. But the commission's findings are always reviewed by the supreme court, which ultimately found that the commission had overlooked the gravity of the situation in the 21st Circuit, that Judge Voorhees had acted with great prudence, and the commission exceeded its authority in recommending that he be reprimanded.[107] This decision of the supreme court can be considered a constitutional interpretation of Article V, Section 24, and serves as a precedent binding the commission's future decision making.

Section 25 establishes the Missouri Plan for judicial selection. Most of this wording was passed in the 1940 and 1942 elections.

Two problems motivated adoption of the Missouri Plan. First, Kansas City and St. Louis (City) both were in the grips of an urban machine type of politics in the 1930s. Judges and many other officials ran for office on party ballots, but the urban political bosses had so much power that they could swing the vote and dominate the outcomes of the primary elections. In this way, the bosses could engineer success at the polls for their political favorites for all elective offices (including the clerks of the various courts in the City of St. Louis). Getting the Democratic nomination was tantamount to sure election in the general election, especially in Jackson County, but slightly less so in St. Louis City (where there were more Republican voters).

The bosses were so confident in their power and so arrogant that they supported non-lawyers for the judgeships. Kansas City's machine was considered the model of total corruption, and Tom Pendergast, the boss, slated some incompetent people for judgeships. Meanwhile, in St. Louis the machine slated a pharmacist for an open judgeship nomination. These candidates, enjoying machine support, won office. Lawyers were aghast at having to argue fine points of law before judges who did not understand the law, so lawyers embraced reforms to improve the courts. Good government groups allied with the lawyers to work toward court reform. Although some idealists wanted to reform courts throughout the entire state (all judges were elected on party ballots before 1940), most supporters realized that they had to concentrate their efforts where the problem was at its worst.

Second, the appellate courts (intermediate courts of appeal and the supreme court) were neither viewed as corrupt nor under the influence of the party bosses, but there was another problem at these levels. Judges would get elected as Democrats or Republicans for terms of 10 years,[108] but 10 years later the winds of politics would blow the other way, and the other party would win the state, carrying with it on its "coattails" new judges of the other party.[109] Judgeships were way down on the ballot, in a time

---

[107]*Matter of Voorhees*, 739 S.W.2d 178 (1987).

[108]Appellate judges' terms were 10 years at the time these provisions were created but were lengthened to 12 years when the new state constitution was adopted in 1945.

[109]For instance, the years 1912–20 were favorable to Democrats, and Democratic judge candidates won the appellate judgeships; but from 1920 to 1932 Republicans trended, and Republican judge candidates beat the Democratic incumbent judges. The same inversion of party dominance on the appellate courts happened during the 1930s, this time favoring the Democrats. (Although Missourians

when the ballots were "party column" ballots. If you cast a vote for the Democratic candidate for president, you could then automatically register votes for Democrats down the line, even if you didn't know who the candidates were (and candidates for appellate courts are fairly obscure). You could split your ticket (vote for some candidates of one party and some of the other party), but that required more effort.

Lawyers found the frequent turnover in judgeships distressing because lawyers want above all stability in judicial rulings and practices. New judges add unpredictability to attorneys' practice of law; the new judges might run the courts slightly differently, might ask more pointed questions, or might replace attorneys' allies among court staffers with new appointees. So lawyers, above and beyond their disgust at the corruption in courts in the two large cities, were open to a way of stabilizing the membership of the appellate courts.

But any reform faced opposition in the legislature, dominated by Democrats allied with the machines, because even any tiny reform would take away machine powers. The solution had to be proposed as an initiative amendment to the constitution.

SECTION 25(a). **Nonpartisan selection of judges—courts subject to plan— appointments to fill vacancies.**—Whenever a vacancy shall occur in the office of judge of any of the following courts of this state, to wit: The supreme court, the court of appeals, or in the office of circuit or associate circuit judge within the city of St. Louis and Jackson county, the governor shall fill such vacancy by appointing one of three persons possessing the qualifications for such office, who shall be nominated and whose names shall be submitted to the governor by a nonpartisan judicial commission established and organized as hereinafter provided. If the governor fails to appoint any of the nominees within sixty days after the list of nominees is submitted, the nonpartisan judicial commission making the nomination shall appoint one of the nominees to fill the vacancy.

SECTION 25(b). **Adoption of plan in other circuits—petitions and elections—form of petition ballots.**—At any general election the qualified voters of any judicial circuit outside of the city of St. Louis and Jackson county, may by a majority of those voting on the question elect to have the circuit and associate circuit judges appointed by the governor in the manner provided for the appointment of judges to the courts designated in section 25(a), or, outside the city of St. Louis and Jackson county, to discontinue any such plan. The question of whether the circuit and associate circuit judges of any such circuit shall be so appointed shall be submitted to the voters of each county in any circuit at the next general election whenever petitions therefor signed by ten percent of the legal voters of each county in the circuit voting for the office of governor at the last election thereof are filed in the office of secretary of state at least 90 days before such election. The question shall be presented as follows: "Shall the circuit and associate circuit judges of the . . . . judicial circuit be selected as provided in Section 25 of Article V of the Missouri Constitution? Yes ¨ No ¨ (Mark One)". The provisions of law with respect to initiative petitions shall apply insofar as applicable relative to the certification of the petitions to local

---

were in general Democratic in their party preferences, there were enough Republicans that if a broad shift occurred, Republicans could win.)

officials by the secretary of state, the preparation, printing, publishing and distribution of the judicial ballots required by this section, the holding and conduct of the election, and the counting, canvassing, return, certification, and proclamation of the votes. If a majority of the votes upon the question are cast in favor of the adoption in each county comprising the circuit, the nonpartisan selection of the circuit and associate judges shall be adopted in the circuit. The question of selection of circuit and associate circuit judges in the manner provided in section 25(a) shall not be submitted more often than once every four years. If any judicial circuit adopts the nonpartisan selection of the circuit and associate circuit judges under the provisions of this section, the question of its discontinuance shall not be submitted more often than once every four years and may be submitted at any general election and shall be proceeded upon insofar as may be applicable in like manner as prescribed in this section for the original adoption of the plan.

The petition shall be in substantially the following form:

To the Honorable Officials in general charge of elections for the county of . . . . for the state of Missouri:

We, the undersigned, legal voters of the state of Missouri, and of the county of . . . ., respectfully demand that the question of the discontinuance of the nonpartisan selection of the circuit and associate circuit judges be submitted to the legal voters of the . . . . judicial circuit, for their approval or rejection, at the general election to be held on the . . . . day of . . . . . , A.D. 19. . . . .

The ballot shall provide as follows:

"Shall the nonpartisan appointment by the governor of the circuit and associate circuit judges be discontinued in the . . . . judicial circuit?

❏ Yes
❏ No

(Place an "X" in one square.)"

If a majority of the votes upon the question are cast in favor of such discontinuance in each county comprising the circuit, the nonpartisan selection of the circuit and associate circuit judges shall be discontinued in such judicial circuit.

If the nonpartisan selection of the judges be discontinued in any such judicial circuit, other than the city of St. Louis and Jackson county, the selection of such judges therein shall be made as otherwise prescribed by law. This section shall be self-enforcing.

SECTION 25(c)(1). Tenure of judges—declaration of candidacy—form of judicial ballot—rejection and retention.—Each judge appointed pursuant to the provisions of sections 25(a)–(g) shall hold office for a term ending December thirty-first following the next general election after the expiration of twelve months in the office. Any judge holding office, or elected thereto, at the time of the election by which the provisions of sections 25(a)–(g) become applicable to his office, shall, unless removed for cause, remain in office for the term to which he would have been entitled had the provisions of sections 25(a)–(g) not become applicable to his office. Not less than sixty days prior to the holding of the general election next preceding the expiration of his term of office, any judge whose office is subject to the provisions of sections 25(a)–(g) may file in the office of the secretary of state a declaration of candidacy for election to succeed himself. If a declaration is not so filed by any judge, the vacancy resulting from the expiration of his term of office shall be filled by appointment as herein provided. If such declaration is filed, his name shall be submitted at said next general election to the voters eligible to vote within the state if his office is that of judge of the supreme court, or within the geographic jurisdiction limit of the district where he serves if his office is that of a judge of the court of appeals, or within the circuit if his office is that of circuit judge, or within the county if his office is that of associate circuit judge on a separate judicial ballot, without party designation, reading:

"Shall Judge. . . . .

(Here the name of the judge shall be inserted)

of the. . . . .

be retained in office?   ❑ Yes ❑ No

(Mark an "X" in the box you prefer.)"

If a majority of those voting on the question vote against retaining him in office, upon the expiration of his term of office, a vacancy shall exist which shall be filled by appointment as provided in section 25(a); otherwise, said judge shall, unless removed for cause, remain in office for the number of years after December thirty-first following such election as is provided for the full term of such office, and at the expiration of each such term shall be eligible for retention in office by election in the manner here prescribed.

(Here the title of the court shall be inserted)

SECTION 25(c)(2). Certification of names upon declaration—law applicable to elections.—Whenever a declaration of candidacy for election to succeed himself is filed by any judge or associate circuit judge under the provisions of this section, the secretary of state shall not less than thirty days before the election certify the name of said judge or associate circuit judge and the official title of his office to the clerks of the county courts, and to the boards of election commissioners in counties or cities having such boards, or to such other officials as may hereafter be provided by law, of all counties and cities wherein the question of retention of such judge in office is to be submitted to the voters, and, until legislation shall be expressly provided otherwise therefor, the judicial ballots required by this section shall be prepared, printed, published and distributed, and the election upon the question of retention of such judge in office shall be conducted and the votes counted, canvassed, returned, certified and proclaimed by such public officials in such manner as is now provided by the statutory law governing voting upon measures proposed by the initiative.

SECTION 25(d). Nonpartisan judicial commissions—number, qualifications, selection and terms of members—majority rule—reimbursement of expenses—rules of supreme court.—Nonpartisan judicial commissions whose duty it shall be to nominate and submit to the governor names of persons for appointment as provided by sections 25(a)–(g) are hereby established and shall be organized on the following basis: For vacancies in the office of judge of the supreme court or of the court of appeals, there shall be one such commission, to be known as "The Appellate Judicial Commission"; for vacancies in the office of circuit judge or associate circuit judge of any circuit court subject to the provisions of sections 25(a)–(g) there shall be one such commission, to be known as "The . . . Circuit Judicial Commission", for each judicial circuit which shall be subject to the provisions of sections 25(a)–(g); the appellate judicial commission shall consist of a judge of the supreme court selected by the members of the supreme court, and the remaining members shall be chosen in the following manner: The members of the bar of this state residing in each court of appeals district shall elect one of their number to serve as a member of said commission, and the governor shall appoint one citizen, not a member of the bar, from among the residents of each court of appeals district, to serve as a member of said commission, and the members of the commission shall select one of their number to serve as chairman. Each circuit judicial commission shall consist of five members, one of whom shall be the chief judge of the district of the court of appeals within which the judicial circuit of such commission, or the major portion of the population of said circuit is situated and the remaining four members shall be chosen in the following manner: The members of the bar of this state residing in the judicial circuit of such commission shall elect two of their number to serve as members of said commission, and the governor shall appoint two citizens, not members of the bar, from among the residents of said judicial circuit to serve as members of said commission, the members of the commission shall select one of their number to serve as chairman; and the terms of office of the members of such commission shall be fixed by law, but no law shall increase or diminish the term of any member then in office. No member of any such commission other than a judge shall hold any public office, and no member shall hold any official position in a political party. Every such commission may act only by the concurrence of a majority of its members. The members of such commission shall receive no salary or other compensation for their services but they shall receive their necessary traveling and other expenses incurred while actually engaged in the discharge of their official duties. All such commissions shall be administered, and all elections provided for under this section shall be held and regulated, under such rules as the supreme court shall promulgate.

SECTION 25(e). Payment of expenses.—All expenses incurred in administering sections 25(a)–(g), when approved by the supreme court, shall be paid out of the state treasury. The supreme court shall certify such expense to the commissioner of administration, who shall draw his warrant therefor payable out of funds not otherwise appropriated.

SECTION 25(f). Prohibition of political activity by judges.—No judge of any court in this state, appointed to or retained in office in the manner prescribed in sections 25(a)–(g), shall directly or indirectly make any contribution to or hold any office in a political party or organization, or take part in any political campaign.

SECTION 25(g). Self-enforceability.—All of the provisions of sections 25(a)–(g) shall be self-enforcing except those as to which action by the general assembly may be required.

The Missouri Plan, or merit selection plan, has a hybrid process for selecting judges, with three steps:

1. When a judicial vacancy occurs, a nonpartisan commission of stakeholders canvasses for meritorious attorneys to fill the vacancy. The commission, chaired by a judge, is comprised of both laypersons and lawyers. This commission comes up with a short list of three attorneys it considers reasonable appointees to the judgeship.

   The commission for a trial court circuit has five members: two lawyers elected (for staggered terms) by members of The Missouri Bar who live in the circuit, two non-lawyers appointed (for staggered terms) by the governor, and the chief judge of the court of appeals within the court of appeals district. The judge presides ex officio and casts a fifth vote (if votes are taken). If the vacancy is on an appellate court (either the court of appeals or the supreme court) the nonpartisan appellate commission picks three candidates for the judgeship.

This commission has seven members: three attorneys, each one elected (for staggered terms) by members of The Missouri Bar living in each of the three districts of the court of appeals, and three laypersons appointed (for staggered terms, one from each of the districts of the court of appeals) by the governor. The chief justice is ex officio a member of the appellate commission and presides over its deliberations.

The membership of these commissions is designed, on the one hand, to provide balance between the lawyers' interest in good judges in particular and the public's concern for good government in general, and on the other hand to provide balance between the governor's subjective politics and the dispassionate and objective collective judgments of the commission. These two sets of concerns check one another. There can't be too much politics, but there can't be too little; we need legal expertise (elitism), and at the same time we need a commonsense approach (populism) too.

Although politics and party consideration are checked somewhat in the history of the commission's functioning, partisanship is not. Nearly 49 years went by under this plan before a clearly nonpartisan appointment (no party ties whatsoever) was made to the supreme court.[110]

2. The second phase begins once the commission has decided on its short list of three persons. Called the "panel," this list is conveyed to the governor, who has 60 days to choose one person on the list. If the governor fails to act, the commission decides.

Occasionally the governor has made common cause with the ex officio judge/chair and loyalist appointees on the commission to "predetermine" a favored name that then "pops up" on the list. This is called "rigging" the list. In 1985, for example, Edward ("Chip") Robertson was included on the list of candidates to fill a vacancy on the supreme court. Robertson was only 33 years old, had worked for the governor (John Ashcroft) since graduating from law school (when the governor had been attorney general of the state), and then became the governor's chief of staff. This nominee was assuredly an atypical choice to rise to the state's highest court at so young an age and with such debatable levels of experience, especially compared with the others on the list: two experienced and respected appellate judges in their 40s. Nevertheless, over the Fourth of July holiday while the general public was otherwise occupied, the word that Robertson had been selected for the supreme court

---

[110]Ann Covington, appointed in 1988, was actually a triple first—she was the first woman appointed to the court of appeals in 1987, then the first woman appointed to the supreme court in 1988, and arguably the first nonpartisan. See Kenyon D. Bunch and Gregory Casey, "Political Controversy on Missouri's Supreme Court: The Case of Merit vs. Politics," *State and Local Government Review* 22.1 (Winter 1990), 5–16; see also Richard Watson and Rondal Downing, *Politics of Bench and the Bar: Judicial Selection under the Missouri Nonpartisan Court Plan* (New York: John Wiley and Sons, 1969). Watson and Downing's work is the seminal study of the plan.

came down.[111] Certainly this appointment violated the spirit of the nonpartisan selection plan.

Still, political machinations have not entirely been eliminated in other cycles of selection; most selections have involved efforts to rig the system by way of alliances between the judge and the lawyers, with the laypersons snowed and set aside by the attorneys' high level of information.

3. The third phase involves the "retention" election. Missouri judges, although originally appointed, had been elected to office on a partisan basis since before the Civil War. They could be held accountable by being voted out of office if the public was displeased with their performance. Elections confer legitimacy and ensure that those who govern rule by popular consent. The supporters of nonpartisan judicial selection wanted to preserve this accountability, even though it didn't help get rid of the corrupt judges in the trial courts of St. Louis City and Jackson County.

Retention elections are special: there can be no competing candidate.[112] The voter is simply asked on the ballot whether he or she wishes to retain the judge in office for another term. A judge needs a simple majority vote (50 percent + 1) to be retained. The term *retention* is used pointedly: the judge will have already been appointed and sworn in, and will have begun his or her service on the bench. Judges are up for retention at the next general election (November of even-numbered years) after they have served for 12 months. For example, if a judge is appointed on November 15 of an odd-numbered year, his or her 12-month anniversary will come after the next general election. So the judge will come up for retention for a full term in office in the election cycle two years later, and will have served nearly three years in office by the time of retention.

Only two judges have failed to be retained since adoption of the plan in 1940. Critics of the plan say that the extraordinarily high retention rate is proof that the plan is not filtering out bad or inadequate judges. But their contention is premised on the notion

[111]Greg Casey, "Public Perceptions of Judicial Scandal: The Missouri Supreme Court 1982–1988," *The Justice System Journal* 13.3 (1988): 284–307.

[112]Many offices are noncompetitive; that is, there is only one candidate. If this occurs in the primary election, there is still legitimacy, because either the voters are satisfied with the candidate running (usually an incumbent) or a potential competitor for the office is convinced that it would be too costly to run against an advantaged candidate. Candidates can be advantaged by being incumbent, having more supporters, having more resources, especially money, and/or being better-spoken, among myriad other factors that work to sway election outcomes. If an office is not contested in the general election, it usually signals that the party not fielding candidates has given up because it is consigned to minority status. From 1876 to 1964, the Democratic party dominated the South; Republicans didn't usually field candidates for office because they saw an effort to win as futile. Being Republican was so stigmatized in many parts of the South that the GOP couldn't get candidates to run because they would have to publicly identify as Republican and might be shunned by friends and neighbors. Now the Democrats are the minority party in the South and don't compete in many local elections. Most outstate Missouri counties are currently majority Republican, and Democrats are unable to field candidates for the General Assembly in many districts.

that the first phase of the plan, developing the short list through the commission process, doesn't bring to the bench meritorious people. However, the screening at initial appointment could mean that only truly good applicants are chosen, and that their performances over the years of their terms lead these judges' constituencies to be quite satisfied with their work in office. If there is a bad judge, or if a good judge turns bad, there is always the possibility of removing that judge through a complaint to the Commission on Retirement, Removal and Discipline of judges. Judges have actually been removed through this process, usually owing to misbehavior and, in some instances, to demonstrated habits of indecision.

It is also notable that the Missouri Plan is in effect for the trial courts in only some circuits (and for the appellate courts). When first adopted in 1940, it only affected the trial courts in Jackson County (16th Circuit) and in the City of St. Louis (22nd Circuit); these courts were the most problematic at the time, and Missourians, skeptical in their outlook (we are the "show me" state, after all), were also profoundly suspicious of large changes in anything ("if it ain't broke, don't fix it"). People thought in 1940 that the trial courts in the outstate area, and even in St. Louis County, were running well, so why change judicial selection in those jurisdictions? Moreover, there was the danger that trying to reform trial courts in more areas would engage more skepticism and undermine the effort to achieve adoption of the plan in the courts it affected. The plan spread to St. Louis County in 1970, to Clay and Platte Counties in 1972, and then to Greene County in 2004. Several counties have considered it but either rejected it at the polls or declined to campaign further for it.

From the mid-1960s, The Missouri Bar began considering the judicial reform that makes up most of the provisions of Article V, and with its work on shaping this proposal also considered trying to campaign for adoption of the Missouri Plan for all trial courts statewide. Again, The Bar and the citizens' committees that worked with it backed off going so far in the final proposal. Even so, considering that the plan is in effect in the urban judicial circuits (the benches with the most judges), more than half of the circuit and associate circuit judges in the state come under it.

The Missouri Plan is called that because Missouri pioneered the creation and application of this reform. Eighteen years later, a neighboring state, Kansas, adopted the reform, also only for its urban trial courts and appellate courts. Now some 25 states have implemented the plan, or some hybridized version of it, either for part of their judiciary or for all courts. The Missouri Plan is currently the most popular model of judicial selection in the United States. Virtually all states that have changed their method of selection in the last 50 years have gone toward the Missouri Plan.

Finally, it's important to point out the hostility that Missouri's political elites have displayed toward the plan. The legislature refused to propose this as a constitutional amendment, so The Bar and good government interests collected enough signatures to put the proposal on the ballot via a citizen initiative. It passed with 55 percent of the votes in the fall of 1940. In the fall of 1942 the legislature countered by referring a constitutional amendment to repeal the reform; this time, the electorate defeated repeal with nearly two-thirds of the votes cast (64.3 percent). This was a sure reproof to Missouri's political class and established the legitimacy of the reform.[113]

SECTION 26. Retirement—assignment as senior judge or commissioner.—1. All judges other than municipal judges shall retire at the age of seventy years, except as provided in the schedule to this article, under a retirement plan provided by law.

2. All judges may retire at an earlier age authorized by law and may participate in a retirement plan provided by law.

3. Any retired judge, associate circuit judge or commissioner, with his consent, may be assigned by the supreme court as a senior judge to any court in this state or as a special commissioner. When serving as a senior judge he shall have the same powers as an active judge.

Section 26 dictates a retirement age of 70 for judges. However, the retirees may come back to the bench as senior judges if they are willing and able, which was not permitted before the reform. A judge may retire early if he or she wishes, and the retirement plan (unmentioned here) is quite attractive.

Schedule

SECTION 27. Effective date and transition provisions.—Except as otherwise provided in this article, the effective date of this article shall be January 2, 1979.

1. All judges elected in 1978 shall be sworn into office on January 1, 1979.

2. All magistrate courts, probate courts, courts of common pleas, the St. Louis court of criminal correction, and municipal corporation courts shall continue to exist until the effective date of this article at which time said courts shall cease to exist. When such courts cease to exist:

a. The jurisdiction of magistrate courts shall be transferred to the circuit court of the circuit and such courts shall become divisions of the circuit court.

b. The jurisdiction of probate courts within the circuit shall be transferred to the circuit court and such courts shall become divisions of the circuit court.

c. The jurisdiction of St. Louis court of criminal correction and all courts of common pleas shall be transferred to the circuit court for the respective circuit and such courts shall become divisions of the circuit court. The provisions of law relating to practice and procedure of the courts of common pleas shall, until otherwise changed by law, remain in effect and the provision of law relating to practice, procedure, venue, jurisdiction, selection of jurors, election of clerk and provisions for deputies and all other provisions of law relating to the Hannibal Court of Common Pleas shall until otherwise changed by law, remain in effect as to such division of the Marion county circuit court and said division shall be known as division number 2 of the Marion county circuit court instead of the Hannibal Court of Common Pleas.

---

[113]The legislature has shown itself utterly out of touch with public opinion in the state on other occasions. See the commentary on the tussle over Section 35 of Article I, the right to farm amendment. This was precipitated when an initiative petition for legislation to regulate dog breeders was adopted, but the legislature, leaning the other way, partially repealed the legislation.

d. The jurisdiction of municipal courts shall be transferred to the circuit court of the circuit in which such municipality or major geographical area thereof shall be located and, such courts shall become divisions of the circuit court. When such courts cease to exist, all records, papers and files shall be transferred to the circuit court which may designate the place where such records may be maintained.

e. Divisions of the circuit court created by this subsection may be changed hereafter by law.

f. After the effective date of this article, in counties with a population of over thirty thousand and less than sixty-five thousand, the office expenses and salaries of associate circuit judges and their clerks who before the effective date of this article were probate judges shall continue to be paid by the counties.

g. After the effective date of this article, in all counties with a population of over sixty-five thousand and in any city not within a county, the office expenses and salaries of the circuit judges who before the effective date of this article were probate judges in said counties or city, shall be paid by the respective counties or city.

3. Until otherwise provided by law associate circuit judges shall hear all cases or matters, civil and criminal, as now provided by law for magistrates within the county and such additional cases or classes of cases as may be provided by law. Until otherwise provided by law, associate circuit judges shall hear all cases or matters as now provided by law for probate courts within the county, except that in the city of St. Louis, in all first class counties, and all second class counties with a population of over sixty-five thousand, the circuit judge of the probate division of the circuit court shall hear all cases and matters as now provided by law for probate courts within such circuits or counties. An associate circuit judge exercising probate jurisdiction shall, in connection therewith, possess general equitable powers. Associate circuit judges of the city of St. Louis shall hear all civil and criminal cases as now provided by law for magistrates and the St. Louis court of criminal correction including appeals and preliminary hearings in felony cases and such additional cases or classes of cases as may hereafter be provided by law. Until otherwise provided by law or supreme court rule the practice, procedure, filing fees and administration of causes heard by associate circuit judges within the jurisdiction of former magistrate and probate courts shall be and remain the same as in the court abolished.

4. a. In 1978, all probate judges except those selected under the nonpartisan selection of judges plan shall be elected as provided by law. On the effective date of this article the probate judge of the city of St. Louis and the probate judges of all first class counties and all second class counties with a population of over sixty-five thousand shall become circuit judges of their respective circuits and thereafter shall be selected or elected from the circuit as in the case of other circuit judges and be entitled to the same compensation as provided by law for circuit judges at the time of the effective date of this article until changed by law, and shall have the same powers and jurisdiction as judges of the circuit court. Each judge who served as probate judge and who is in office on the effective date of this article in such city and counties shall continue to serve in the capacity of judge of the probate division of the circuit court until his successor is selected and qualified, provided that with his consent any circuit or associate circuit judge in the circuit at his request may hear, try and dispose of any matter, case or classes of cases assigned to him by such judge of the probate division, and such judge of the probate division with his consent, may hear, try and determine any case within the jurisdiction of the circuit court. On the

effective date of this article the probate judges of counties with a population of sixty-five thousand or less shall become associate circuit judges of their respective circuits and thereafter shall be selected or elected from the county as in the case of other associate circuit judges and shall be entitled to the same compensation as that to which they were entitled on the effective date of this article until changed by law.

b. On the effective date of this article, judges of the St. Louis court of criminal correction and judges of the courts of common pleas shall become circuit judges and be entitled to the compensation of circuit judges and shall have the same power and jurisdiction as circuit judges.

c. In 1978, all magistrates shall be elected as provided by law. On the effective date of this article all magistrates who are then in office shall become associate circuit judges and shall serve out the remainder of their terms as such. Each such judge shall be entitled to the same compensation as that to which he was entitled on the effective date of this article until otherwise changed by law.

5. The right to and method of review from a final judgment or appealable order of an associate circuit judge, or municipal judge, when so acting within the jurisdiction of cases heretofore within the jurisdiction of the former magistrate or municipal courts shall, until otherwise provided by law, be de novo before a circuit judge or another associate circuit judge within the circuit except that appeals from an associate circuit judge exercising probate jurisdiction in any circuit, and appeals from any cause from an associate circuit judge as provided by law shall be appealed to the appropriate district of the court of appeals upon a record as authorized by law or supreme court rule. Appeals in misdemeanor cases from the associate circuit judge from the city of St. Louis shall be as now provided until changed by law.

6. The costs of judicial proceedings as provided for in all courts existing before the adoption of this article shall remain in effect with respect to cases which would have been within the jurisdiction of those courts until such costs are otherwise changed by law. Until otherwise provided by law, if a cause could have been filed in more than one court before the effective date of this article, the lower cost structure shall be used in calculating costs; provided, however, that a party instituting a civil suit which would have been within the concurrent jurisdiction of the circuit and magistrate courts prior to the effective date of this article may designate the case as being one to be processed in accordance with procedures and rules appertaining before circuit judges, and the court costs heretofore applicable to such cases in circuit court shall apply.

Until the effective date of this article the courts of common pleas, the St. Louis court of criminal corrections, the magistrate courts, the probate courts and the municipal corporation courts shall continue to have the jurisdiction and power provided in the article repealed hereby and provided by the laws and rules enacted thereunder, and shall continue to follow the procedures as provided in such article, laws and rules.

7. Each judge who, on the effective date of this article, becomes a circuit or associate circuit judge in any circuit subject to the provisions of sections 25(a)–(g) of this article shall be eligible for retention in office as a circuit or associate circuit judge respectively by filing in the office of the secretary of state a declaration of candidacy for election not less than sixty days prior to the holding of the general election next preceding the expiration of his term of office. If a majority of those voting on the question vote against retaining him in office, upon the expiration of his term of office, a vacancy shall exist which shall be filled by appointment as provided in section 25(a); otherwise, said judge shall,

unless removed for cause, remain in office for the number of years after December thirty-first following such election as is provided for the full term of such office and at the expiration of each such term shall be eligible for retention in office by election in the same manner prescribed by section 25(c)(1). The secretary of state shall certify the name of such judges in accordance with law or in accordance with section 25(c)(2) of this article.

8. On the effective date of this article the judges of the magistrate court and the judges of the probate court in any circuit which selects judges under the nonpartisan selection of judges shall become nonpartisan judges. The judges of the probate courts of the city of St. Louis and all first class counties, and all second class counties with a population of over sixty-five thousand, when such courts cease to exist, and the judges of the St. Louis court of criminal corrections, shall become circuit judges and receive the compensation payable to circuit judges.

9. a. The judges of all municipal corporations courts in office at the time such courts cease to exist and who qualify for office under the provisions of section 21 of this article shall continue in office until the expiration of the terms to which they have been elected or appointed unless otherwise provided by law. When such courts cease to exist, the judges thereof who continue in office shall become municipal judges and shall serve as such until their terms expire or are otherwise removed. They shall receive the compensation now provided until otherwise changed by law. Such compensation shall be paid by the municipality or municipalities they serve. Upon the expiration of their terms, they shall become eligible for retention in office as municipal judges in the same manner as now provided for the selection of municipal judges in the municipality they serve until otherwise provided by law. In the event the municipal judge now serving shall fail, refuse or be disqualified from continuing in office, the municipality may elect or appoint a municipal judge in the same manner as is now provided in that municipality for selection of a municipal judge unless otherwise provided by law. All expenses incidental to the functioning of municipal judges, including the cost of any staff, and their quarters shall be paid and provided by the respective municipalities as now provided for municipal courts until otherwise provided by law. In municipalities with a population of under four hundred thousand which do not have a municipal judge or for which no municipal judge is provided by law, associate circuit judges shall hear and determine violations of municipal ordinances. No associate circuit judge shall, however, act as a municipal judge in any city with a population of four hundred thousand or more until otherwise provided by law.

10. a. 1. Until otherwise provided by law, circuit clerks in each circuit and county shall be selected in the same manner as provided by law on the effective date of this article, except that in counties having a charter form of government, the circuit clerk shall be selected in the manner as provided in the charter of such county.

2. Upon the expiration of the terms of office of the clerk of the circuit court for criminal causes of the city of St. Louis, and the term of the clerk of the St. Louis court of criminal correction, the offices of such clerks shall cease to exist and thereafter the clerk of the circuit court of the city of St. Louis shall have the powers and perform the duties and functions of such clerks and shall serve all divisions of the circuit court, except the courts presided over by an associate circuit judge, the judge of the probate division of the circuit court and by municipal judges.

3. In any division of the circuit court presided over by an associate circuit judge, in the probate division of the circuit court, and in any division presided over by a municipal judge, the clerks and their deputies of the respective divisions shall continue to be selected

in the same manner as provided for by law on the effective date of this article until otherwise changed by law.

4. There shall continue to be an office of circuit clerk in each county of the circuit, until otherwise changed by law.

b. Upon the effective date of this article, the office of constable serving magistrate courts is abolished. The functions, powers and duties of such constables shall be transferred to and be performed by the sheriff of the county or the sheriff of the city of St. Louis.

c. Upon the effective date of this article the office of prosecuting attorney of the city of St. Louis shall be abolished and all the duties, powers, and functions of such office shall be transferred to the circuit attorney of the city of St. Louis who shall have such powers and perform such functions and duties as the prosecuting attorney of the city of St. Louis.

d. No election shall be held in 1978 for the offices which are abolished by this subsection 10.

11. The commissioners of the supreme court holding office on the effective date of this article shall continue to hold office as commissioners of the court until the end of their terms, and shall be eligible for reappointment thereafter from term to term under existing law until retirement, death, resignation or removal for cause. Upon the occurrence of such vacancy in the office of commissioner of the supreme court, such office shall cease to exist. Commissioners, in addition to their regular duties, shall be subject to temporary assignment for the performance of judicial duties as special judges of the supreme court, court of appeals, or circuit court on order of the supreme court. During such temporary assignments, commissioners sitting as special judges shall have the same powers, duties, and responsibilities as are vested by law in the regular judges of the courts to which they are assigned.

12. The boundaries and territorial jurisdiction of the districts of the court of appeals and of the judicial circuits as they exist on the effective date of this article shall be continued in effect until such time as changed by law.

13. The commission on retirement, removal and discipline and the nonpartisan appellate and circuit judicial commissions in existence on the effective date of this article shall continue to exist, and the terms of office for such commissions shall continue in effect.

14. "Judge" as used in sections 20, 24 and 26 of this article shall include commissioners of the supreme court.

15. Nothing in this article shall deprive any person of any right or privilege to retire and the retirement benefits to which he was entitled immediately prior to the effective date of this article.

16. A municipal corporation with a population of under four hundred thousand shall have the right to enforce its ordinances and to conduct prosecutions before an associate circuit judge in the absence of a municipal judge and in appellate courts under the process authorized or provided by this article and shall receive and retain any fines to which it may be entitled. All court costs shall be paid to and deposited monthly in the state treasury. No filing fees shall be charged in such prosecutions unless and until provided for by a law enacted after the adoption of this article.

17. Until otherwise provided by law, the circuit courts shall continue to have jurisdiction to review administrative decisions, findings, rules, and orders in the manner and practice and pursuant to the laws and rules then in force at the time this article becomes effective.

18. All rights, claims, causes of action and obligations existing and all contracts, prosecutions, recognizances and other instruments executed or entered into and all indictments,

informations, and complaints which shall have been filed and all actions which shall have been instituted and all fines, penalties and forfeitures assessed, due or owing prior to the effective date of this article shall continue to be as valid as if this article had not been adopted.

19. The general assembly may enact such laws and make such appropriations as may be necessary to carry out the provisions of this article.

20. All laws and rules inconsistent with the provisions of this article shall, on the effective date hereof, be and are repealed. Except to the extent inconsistent with the provisions of this article, all provisions of law and rules of court in force on the effective date of this amendment shall continue in effect until superseded in a manner authorized by the constitution or by law.

21. In the event that a new district of the court of appeals is established, the judges presently serving on any district of the court of appeals shall continue to be judges of the court of appeals to which appointed although they are not residents of the court of appeals district in which they serve.

22. Until otherwise provided by law, in any cause heard and determined by an associate circuit judge, the associate circuit judge shall utilize electronic, magnetic, or mechanical sound or video recording devices for the purpose of preserving the record. Electronic, magnetic, or mechanical recording devices shall be approved by the office of state courts administrator prior to their utilization by any associate circuit judge.

23. Each circuit in which judges are selected under the nonpartisan court plan, on the effective date of this article, including the circuits of Platte county, Clay county, and St. Louis county, shall continue under the nonpartisan court plan until and unless such method of selection of judges is discontinued by the voters of the circuit as provided by sections 25(a)–(g) of this article.

24. Judges, other than municipal judges, not selected under the provisions of sections 25(a)–(g) of this article who on the effective day of this article or within six months thereafter, are seventy years of age or older, may petition the commission on retirement, removal and discipline to continue to serve until age seventy-six if he has not completed a total of twelve years of service as a judge. Judges, other than municipal judges, not selected under the provisions of sections 25(a)–(g) of this article who are in office on the effective date of this article, may, within six months before attaining the age of seventy years, petition the commission on retirement, removal, and discipline to be allowed to serve after he has attained that age until age seventy-six or has completed a total of twelve years of service as a judge, whichever shall first occur. If the commission finds the petitioner to be able to perform his duties and approves such service, the petitioner may continue to serve as such a judge until age seventy-six if he has not completed a total of twelve years of service as a judge at such age. No such judge shall be permitted to serve as such a judge beyond the age of seventy-six years regardless of whether or not he has completed a total of twelve years except for the purpose of completing the term to which he was elected or appointed.

Section 27 sets out transition rules for the court reform outlined in Sections 1–24. On January 1, 1979, the day of transition, all trial courts ceased to exist; their judges were readmitted to the judiciary but with different titles and housed administratively in new ways. Special provision was made for the Hannibal Court of Common Pleas in that it did not have to change its procedures, but would now exist as a subordinate division of the circuit court. All municipal courts were metamorphosed into divisions of circuit courts, and magistrate judges became associate circuit judges. All former magistrate (now associate circuit) judges in circuits with the Missouri Plan came under the plan, as did former probate judges (now circuit judges) in jurisdictions under the plan. "Commissioners" of the supreme court were phased out gradually, but the Commission on Retirement, Removal and Discipline and the Missouri Plan commissions were continued. Although the retirement age for judges is set at 70 (see Section 26), for the transitional period judges not under the Missouri Plan could petition to serve until age 76 if they had not spent 12 years as a judge; but they were required to retire at age 76 or when they reach 12 years of service, whichever came first.

This section gave many transitional rules for the City of St. Louis Circuit (22nd). It did away with the clerkships of the abolished courts for criminal causes and of criminal corrections and merged those clerks' offices (stuffed full of patronage appointments of assistant clerks and bailiffs) into the office of the elected circuit clerk. The clerk of the court of criminal corrections, James Lavin, complained: "I don't like one bit the idea of taking the power out of the hands of the many and putting it into the hands of a few appointed demigods," referring to the circuit judges. Under the Missouri Plan, these judges were appointed and would never face a live opponent for their offices, in contrast to Lavin and other head clerks who had, in his opinion, greater legitimacy since they were elected by the voters of the City of St. Louis.[114]

Certainly, Section 27 adds many words to the constitution, and is a baleful change in light of the constitutional ideal of brevity. And most of this wording, having accomplished its transitional purpose, is of no further use or current applicability. But in retrospect, the direct wording specifying shifts of responsibility, especially in the City of St. Louis, helped that circuit and its clerks avoid the troubles that the neighboring 21st Circuit underwent for years after the public vote approving the court reorganization. Usually constitutional analysts plead for short provisions; this section provides counterfactual evidence and suggests that in some cases long and detailed provisions may be needed. Moreover, even though this transitional section is outdated now, perhaps it was worth having for the short time it helped the 22nd Circuit pass through the experience of reform.

In 2012 the General Assembly referred an amendment that would have tinkered with the Missouri Plan. This provision would have removed the judge (the supreme court's choice, usually the chief justice) from the appellate commission, substituting for him or her a fourth layperson appointed by the governor. This measure would exert an uncertain effect but could easily open the way to excessive influence from the governor since his or her appointees would have a 4–3 majority on the commission.[115] The Missouri Bar spoke out strongly against the proposition.

---

[114]Carter Stith, "Amendment No. 6 Would Abolish Complex Court System in St. Louis," *St. Louis Post-Dispatch*, July 19, 1976.
[115]Moreover, the governor would be able to have four appointees in the second year of his or her term.

A conservative reform group called Better Courts for Missouri with 501(c)(4) status was the force behind this plan. The group had been trying for several years to alter the Missouri Plan; other proposals have included increasing the number of judicial nominees on the panel from three to five, allowing the governor to veto the panel of nominees, and requiring Senate confirmation of members of the appellate commission. In 2008 this lobby circulated an initiative drive for voter signatures to put a constitutional amendment on the ballot abolishing the Missouri Plan and substituting for it the federal model of executive nomination and Senate confirmation. That time, Better Courts did not make the deadline for submitting its petitions to the secretary of state (it couldn't get enough signatures). In 2009, Better Courts lobbied for two legislative efforts to tinker with the Missouri Plan; one proposal passed the lower chamber only, and the other didn't make it through either chamber.

In 2012, Better Courts managed to get Amendment 3, this narrower proposal, through both chambers. Good government groups opposed trifling with the Missouri Plan; one group called Missourians for Fair and Impartial Courts put up a spirited campaign in opposition, with support of retired state supreme court judges, yard signs and bumper stickers, and an active Facebook presence. As the election approached, polls showed that the proposal was unlikely to pass, and Better Courts complained that the ballot language to describe the amendment was unflattering, unfair, and stacked the deck against it. Amendment 3's advocates threw in the towel and contemplated their next move. At election the proposition failed utterly, with 76 percent of the voters rejecting it. Significantly for the Missouri Constitution, Missourians continue to believe in and support the nonpartisan judicial selection system at a level approaching virtual consensus. But challenges remain; Governor Eric Greitens and Attorney General Josh Hawley want to change the Missouri Plan to cut back on the influence of trial lawyers, and the legislature may support such a move. Still, the electorate seems strongly supportive of the Plan.

ARTICLE VI
LOCAL GOVERNMENT

Within each state there exist sub-units of government, usually organized at the county and city levels. In what is known as Dillon's Rule—named after a nineteenth-century Iowa judge named John F. Dillon—local governments exercise only those powers expressly granted or delegated to them by the state government. Missouri is one of 39 states that operate under Dillon's Rule.

SECTION 1. Recognition of existing counties.—The existing counties are hereby recognized as legal subdivisions of the state.

SECTION 2. Continuation of existing organization of counties.—The existing organization of counties shall continue until further provisions applicable thereto shall be provided, as authorized in this constitution.

SECTION 3. Consolidation of counties—allocation of liabilities.—Two or more counties may be consolidated by vote of a majority of the qualified electors voting thereon in each county affected, but no such vote shall be taken more than once in five years. The former areas shall be held responsible for their respective outstanding liabilities as provided by law.

SECTION 4. Division or diminution of counties.—No county shall be divided or have any portion stricken therefrom except by vote of a majority of the qualified electors voting thereon in each county affected.

SECTION 5. Dissolution of counties—annexation.—A county may be dissolved by vote of two-thirds of the qualified electors of the county voting thereon, and when so dissolved all or portions thereof may be annexed to the adjoining county or counties as provided by law.

These provisions guarantee the integrity of existing counties, protected unless the electorate decides otherwise by majority rule. It is a democratic, Jacksonian arrangement for these local governments.

SECTION 6. Removal of county seats.—No county seat shall be removed except by vote of two-thirds of the qualified electors of the county voting thereon at a general election, but no such vote shall be taken more than once in five years.

County seats are better protected against the majority than are the counties themselves, in that an extraordinary majority vote is required to move them.

SECTION 7. County courts—number of members—powers and duties.—In each county not framing and adopting its own charter or adopting an alternative form of county government, there shall be elected a county court of three members which shall manage all county business as prescribed by law, and keep an accurate record of its proceedings. The voters of any county may reduce the number of members to one or two as provided by law.

County "councils" or county "commissions" were originally known as county "courts"; all three terms convey the same meaning. When county courts ran counties, the three officers of the county were called "judges." They weren't "judicial" judges, however; they didn't try cases, nor did they proclaim judicial rulings. They were the combined legislative and executive branches of local government. (No checks and balances in local government in early America!) Originally these bodies exercised the judicial function as well, sitting as courts, and on any given day alternated in performing the functions of all three branches of government. Thus, in some states county officials were called "judges." The judicial function was eventually pared away from the county courts and given over to justices of the peace. Because county government was overwhelmingly involved in the care of roads, these officers were often called "road judges." Missouri was the second to last state to abandon the old terminology when it renamed these governmental units county "commissions" in 1985.

While the quaint and archaic term "county court" itself was abandoned 30 years ago, this provision of the constitution still has some current applicability. There are three commissioners (as these officials are now termed); the "presiding commissioner" is elected countywide for a four-year term, while the other two have two-year terms and are elected in districts that are apportioned equally. They are called simply "Commissioner(s) for the Northern/Southern District" (or "Eastern/Western").

SECTION 8. **Classification of counties—revisions to article VI passed by the 88th general assembly to be retroactive.**—Provision shall be made by general laws for the organization and classification of counties except as provided in section 18(a) or section 18(m) of this article or otherwise in this constitution. The number of classes shall not exceed four, and the organization and powers of each class shall be defined by general laws so that all counties within the same class shall possess the same powers and be subject to the same restrictions. The revisions to this article submitted by the first regular session of the eighty-eighth general assembly are intended to be applied retroactively and no law adopted by the general assembly or ordinance or order adopted by the governing body of a county shall be declared unconstitutional if such law, ordinance or order would have been constitutional had this section, as amended, been in effect at the time the law was passed, unless the law is declared unconstitutional pursuant to a different provision of this constitution.

Counties are categorized into four classes depending on property valuation. The metropolitan counties are first class counties, and most urban places are second class if not first class.

SECTION 9. **Alternative forms of county government.**—Alternative forms of county government for the counties of any particular class and the method of adoption thereof may be provided by law.

Counties with a population of at least 85,000 may abandon the constitutional and statutorily imposed form of county government and set up a county constitution or charter with offices and governmental forms that best suit their needs. St. Louis City did this when it became a separate county in 1876, and St. Louis County adopted a charter government in 1950; Jackson County followed suit in 1970. Other qualified counties have written charters only to see them rejected at the polls. Popular consent in the form of majority rule is required to adopt a proposed county constitution.

SECTION 10. **Terms of city and county offices.**—The terms of city or county offices shall not exceed four years.

SECTION 11. **Compensation of county officers—increases in compensation not to require additional services—statement of fees and salaries.—**

1. Except in counties which frame, adopt and amend a charter for their own government, the compensation of all county officers shall either be prescribed by law or be established by each county pursuant to law adopted by the general assembly. A law which would authorize an increase in the compensation of county officers shall not be construed as requiring a new activity or service or an increase in the level of any activity or service within the meaning of this constitution. Every such officer shall file a sworn statement in detail, of fees collected and salaries paid to his necessary deputies or assistants, as provided by law.

2. Upon approval of this amendment by the voters of Missouri the compensation of county officials, or their duly appointed successor, elected at the general election in 1984 or 1986 may be increased during that term in accordance with any law adopted by the general assembly or, in counties which have adopted a charter for their own government, in accordance with such charter, notwithstanding the provisions of section 13 of article VII of the Constitution of Missouri.

County officials in unreformed (non-charter) counties are allowed to adjust their compensation. It always goes up.

SECTION 12. Officers compensated only by salaries in certain counties.—All public officers in the city of St. Louis and all state and county officers in counties having 100,000 or more inhabitants, excepting public administrators and notaries public, shall be compensated for their services by salaries only.

SECTION 13. Compensation of officers in criminal matters—fees.—All state and county officers, except constables and justices of the peace, charged with the investigation, arrest, prosecution, custody, care, feeding, commitment, or transportation of persons accused of or convicted of a criminal offense shall be compensated for their official services only by salaries, and any fees and charges collected by any such officers in such cases shall be paid into the general revenue fund entitled to receive the same, as provided by law. Any fees earned by any such officers in civil matters may be retained by them as provided by law.

Section 13 is another example of a constitutional provision that could use cleaning up. The justices of the peace went out in 1945, and the constables exited in 1979. But the archaic wording remains, because most efforts at fixing the constitution add wording rather than subtract it.

SECTION 14. Joint participation by counties in common enterprises.—By vote of a majority of the qualified electors voting thereon in each county affected, any contiguous counties, not exceeding ten, may join in performing any common function or service, including the purchase, construction and maintenance of hospitals, alms houses, road machinery and any other county property, and by separate vote may join in the common employment of any county officer or employee common to each of the counties. The county courts shall administer the delegated powers and allocate the costs among the counties. Any county may withdraw from such joint participation by vote of a majority of its qualified electors voting thereon.

SECTION 15. Classification of cities and towns—uniform laws—change from special to general law.—The general assembly shall provide by general laws for the organization and classification of cities and towns. The number of such classes shall not exceed four; and the powers of each class shall be defined by general laws so that all such municipal corporations of the same class shall possess the same powers and be subject to the same restrictions. The general assembly shall also make provisions, by general law, whereby any city, town or village, existing by virtue of any special or local law, may elect to become subject to, and be governed by, the general laws relating to such corporations.

This provision forbids legislation aimed at only one city or county, but this is easily avoided by using formulas such as "cities with not more than 200,000 population but less than 300,000 population." Formulas like this are adjustable so, in practice, can be aimed at any one particular city.

SECTION 16. Cooperation by local governments with other governmental units.— Any municipality or political subdivision of this state may contract and cooperate with other municipalities or political subdivisions thereof, or with other states or their municipalities or political subdivisions, or with the United States, for the planning, development, construction, acquisition or operation of any public improvement or facility, or for a common service, in the manner provided by law.

SECTION 17. Consolidation and separation as between municipalities and other political subdivisions.—The government of any city, town or village not in a county framing, adopting and amending a charter for its own government, may be consolidated or separated, in whole or in part, with or from that of the county or other political subdivision in which such city, town or village is situated, as provided by law.

Special Charters

The provisions in Section 18 control the steps through which a county would move to home rule with its own constitution (charter).

SECTION 18(a). County government by special charter—limitations—counties adopting charter or constitutional form shall be a separate class of counties from classification system.—Any county having more than 85,000 inhabitants, according to the census of the United States, may frame and adopt and amend a charter for its own government as provided in this article, and upon such adoption shall be a body corporate and politic. In addition and as an alternative to the foregoing, any county which attains first class county status and maintains such status for at least two years shall be authorized to frame and adopt and amend a charter for its own government as provided by this article, and upon such adoption by a vote of the qualified electors of such county shall be a body corporate and politic. Counties which adopt or which have adopted a charter or constitutional form of government shall be a separate class of counties outside of the classification system established under section 8 of this article.

SECTION 18(b). Provisions required in county charters—exception.—The charter shall provide for its amendment, for the form of the county government, the number, kinds, manner of selection, terms of office and salaries of the county officers, and for the exercise of all powers and duties of counties and county officers prescribed by the constitution and laws of the state; however, such charter shall, except for the charter of any county with a charter form of government and with more than six hundred thousand but fewer than seven hundred thousand inhabitants, require the assessor of the county to be an elected officer.

This is the state plan for county home rule constitutions. Note the use of the population formula that at one time provided only for the County of the City of St. Louis. Now St. Louis City has lost population and it no longer fits the description.

SECTION 18(c). Provisions authorized in county charters—participation by county in government of other local units.—The charter may provide for the vesting and exercise of legislative power pertaining to any and all services and functions of any municipality

Map of Missouri Counties

or political subdivision, except school districts, in the part of the county outside incorporated cities; and it may provide, or authorize its governing body to provide, the terms upon which the county may contract with any municipality or political subdivision in the county and perform any of the services and functions of any such municipality or political subdivision.

The charter may provide for the vesting and exercise of legislative power pertaining to any and all services and functions of any municipality or political subdivision, except school districts, throughout the entire county within as well as outside incorporated municipalities; any such charter provision shall set forth the limits within which the municipalities may exercise the same power collaterally and coextensively. When such a proposition is submitted to the voters of the county the ballot shall contain a clear definition of the power, function or service to be performed and the method by which it will be financed.

SECTION 18(d). Taxation under county charters.—The county shall only impose such taxes as it is authorized to impose by the constitution or by law.

SECTION 18(e). Laws affecting charter counties—limitations.—Laws shall be enacted providing for free and open elections in such counties, and laws may be enacted providing the number and salaries of the judicial officers therein as provided by this constitution and by law, but no law shall provide for any other office or employee of the county or fix the salary of any of its officers or employees.

SECTION 18(f). Petitions for charter commissions—signatures required—procedure.—Whenever a petition for a commission, signed by qualified electors of the county numbering ten percent of the total vote for governor in the county at the last preceding general election, is filed with the county commission or other governing body, the officer or body canvassing election returns shall forthwith finally determine the sufficiency thereof and certify the result to the governing body, which shall give immediate written notice of the petition to the circuit judges of the county.

SECTION 18(g). Charter commission—appointment, number and qualification of members.—Within sixty days thereafter said judges shall appoint a commission to frame the charter, consisting of fourteen qualified electors who shall serve without pay and be equally divided between the two political parties casting the greater number of votes for governor at the last preceding general election.

SECTION 18(h). Adoption of charter—special election—manner of submission.—The charter framed by the commission shall take effect on the day fixed therein and shall supersede any existing charter or government, if approved by vote of a majority of the qualified electors of the county voting thereon at a special election held on a day fixed by the commission and not less than thirty days after the completion of the charter nor more than one year from the day of the selection of the commission. The commission may submit for separate vote any parts of the charter, or any alternative sections or articles, and the alternative sections or articles receiving the larger affirmative vote shall prevail if a charter is adopted.

SECTION 18(i). Notice of special charter election.—The body canvassing election returns shall publish notice of the election at least once a week for at least three weeks in at least two newspapers of general circulation in the county, the last publication to be not more than three nor less than two weeks next preceding the election.

SECTION 18(j). Certificates of adoption of charter—recordation and deposit—judicial notice.—Duplicate certificates shall be made, setting forth the charter adopted and its ratification, signed by the officer or members of the body canvassing election returns; one of such certified copies shall be deposited in the office of the secretary of state and the other, after being recorded in the records of the county, shall be deposited among the archives of the county and all courts shall take judicial notice thereof. This section shall also apply to any amendment to the charter.

SECTION 18(k). Amendments of county charters.—All amendments to such charter approved by the voters shall become a part of the charter at the time and under the conditions fixed in the amendment.

SECTION 18(l). Limitation on resubmission after defeat of charter.—No charter shall be submitted to the electors within the two years next following the election at which a charter was defeated.

SECTION 18(m). County of the first classification may provide a county constitution—content, procedure, limitations.—Any county of the first classification may adopt an alternative form of government to that provided in sections 18(a)–(g) of this article and frame a county constitution as provided in sections 18(m)–(r) of this article. The constitution may provide for the vesting of any and all powers the general assembly has the authority to confer, provided such powers are not limited or denied by laws of this state, except those powers to regulate and provide for free and open elections. A county approving the alternative form of government and adopting a county constitution in the manner prescribed by sections 18(m)–(r) of this article shall only impose such taxes as it is authorized by the constitution and law to impose. The county commission of such a county may authorize the submission of the question by placing it on the ballot on any election day established by law. The circuit judges of the circuit where such county is located shall establish a county constitution commission if the qualified voters of the county approve the question.

SECTION 18(n). Circuit judges may appoint constitution commission, members, qualifications.—If the question is approved, the circuit judges of the circuit where such county is located shall, within sixty days after certification of the election results by the election authority, appoint a commission to frame the county constitution, consisting of fourteen residents of the county who shall serve without pay and be equally divided between the two political parties casting the greater number of votes for governor at the last preceding gubernatorial election.

SECTION 18(o). County constitution, effective when—submission to electorate for separate vote on any part or alternative sections.—The county constitution framed by the commission shall take effect on the day fixed therein and shall supersede any existing charter, county constitution or government, if approved by the majority of the qualified voters of the county voting thereon. The county constitution shall be submitted by the county constitution commission to the election authority of the county not later than thirty days after the completion of the county constitution and not more than one year from the date of the selection of the county constitution commission by the circuit court. The commission may submit for separate vote any part of the county constitution, or any alternative sections or articles, and the alternative sections or articles receiving the larger affirmative vote shall prevail if a constitution is adopted.

SECTION 18(q). Constitution may be adopted or rejected by voters—resubmission procedure.—If a majority of the votes cast by the qualified voters voting on the county constitution are in favor of the proposal, then the county constitution shall be adopted. If a majority of the votes cast by the qualified voters voting thereon are opposed to the proposal, the county constitution shall not be adopted. A proposal to create a county constitution may not be resubmitted to the voters except after the voters approve the selection of a commission to draft a county constitution as provided in section 18(m) of this article and such proposal shall not be resubmitted to the voters until two years after the proposed county constitution has been rejected.

SECTION 18(r). Certified copies of county constitution to be filed, where—amendments to constitution, procedure.—Duplicate certificates shall be made, setting forth the adopted county constitution, and its ratification signed by the election authority of the county after canvassing election returns. One of the certified copies shall be deposited in the office of the secretary of state and the other, after being recorded in the records of the county, shall be deposited among the archives of the county and all courts shall take judicial notice thereof. Amendments shall be certified and deposited in the same way. Amendments to the county constitution shall be approved by the voters and shall become part of the county constitution at the time and under the conditions fixed in each amendment.

Local Government

Cities as well as counties can make the move to home rule with their own constitution (charter).

SECTION 19. **Certain cities may adopt charter form of government—procedure to frame and adopt—notice required—effect of.**—Any city having more than five thousand inhabitants or any other incorporated city as may be provided by law may frame and adopt a charter for its own government. The legislative body of the city may, by ordinance, submit to the voters the question: "Shall a commission be chosen to frame a charter?" If the ordinance takes effect more than sixty days before the next election, the question shall be submitted at such election and if not, then at the next general election thereafter, except as herein otherwise provided. The question shall also be submitted on a petition signed by ten percent of the qualified electors of the city, filed with the body or official in charge of the city elections. If the petition prays for a special election and is signed by twenty percent of the qualified electors, a special election shall be held not less than sixty nor more than ninety days after the filing of the petition. The number of electors required to sign any petition shall be based upon the total number of electors voting at the last preceding general city election. The election body or official shall forthwith finally determine the sufficiency of the petition. The question, and the names or the groups of names of the electors of the city who are candidates for the commission, shall be printed on the same ballot without party designation. Candidates for the commission shall be nominated by petition signed by not less than two percent of the qualified electors voting at the next preceding city election, and filed with the election body or official at least thirty days prior to the election; provided that the signatures of one thousand electors shall be sufficient to nominate a candidate. If a majority of the electors voting on the question vote in the affirmative, the thirteen candidates receiving the highest number of votes shall constitute the commission. On the death, resignation or inability of any member to serve, the remaining members of the commission shall select the successor. All necessary expenses of the commission shall be paid by the city. The charter so framed shall be submitted to the electors of the city at an election held at the time fixed by the commission, but not less than thirty days subsequent to the completion of the charter nor more than one year from the date of the election of the commission. The commission may submit for separate vote any parts of the charter, or any alternative sections or articles, and the alternative sections or articles receiving the larger affirmative vote shall prevail if a charter is adopted. If the charter be approved by the voters it shall become the charter of such city at the time fixed therein and shall supersede any existing charter and amendments thereof. Duplicate certificates shall be made, setting forth the charter adopted and its ratification, signed by the chief magistrate of the city, and authenticated by its corporate seal. One of such certified copies shall be deposited in the office of the secretary of state and the other, after being recorded in the records of the city, shall be deposited among the archives of the city and all courts shall take judicial notice thereof. The notice of the election shall be published at least once a week on the same day of the week for at least three weeks in some daily or weekly newspaper of general circulation in the city or county, admitted to the post office as second class matter, regularly and consecutively published for at least three years, and having a list of bona fide subscribers who have voluntarily paid or agreed to pay a stated price for a subscription for a definite period of time, the last publication to be within two weeks of the election.

SECTION 19(a). **Power of charter cities, how limited.**—Any city which adopts or has adopted a charter for its own government, shall have all powers which the general assembly of the state of Missouri has authority to confer upon any city, provided such powers are consistent with the constitution of this state and are not limited or denied either by the charter so adopted or by statute. Such a city shall, in addition to its home rule powers, have all powers conferred by law.

This provision emphasizes the applicability of Dillon's Rule; cities are a subdivision of the state and as such are completely subject to its constitution and statutes.

SECTION 20. **Amendment to city charters—procedure to submit and adopt.**— Amendments of any city charter adopted under the foregoing provisions may be submitted to the electors by a commission as provided for a complete charter. Amendments may also be proposed by the legislative body of the city or by petition of not less than ten percent of the registered qualified electors of the city, filed with the body or official having charge of the city elections, setting forth the proposed amendment. The legislative body shall at once provide, by ordinance, that any amendment so proposed shall be submitted to the electors at the next election held in the city not less than sixty days after its passage, or at a special election held as provided for a charter. Any amendment approved by a majority of the qualified electors voting thereon, shall become a part of the charter at the time and under the conditions fixed in the amendment; and sections or articles may be submitted separately or in the alternative and determined as provided for a complete charter.

SECTION 21. **Reclamation of blighted, substandard or insanitary areas.**—Laws may be enacted, and any city or county operating under a constitutional charter may enact ordinances, providing for the clearance, replanning, reconstruction, redevelopment and rehabilitation of blighted, substandard or insanitary areas, and for recreational and other facilities incidental or appurtenant thereto, and for taking or permitting the taking, by eminent domain, of property for such purposes, and when so taken the fee simple title to the property shall vest in the owner, who may sell or otherwise dispose of the property subject to such restrictions as may be deemed in the public interest.

SECTION 22. **Laws affecting charter cities—officers and employees.**—No law shall be enacted creating or fixing the powers, duties or compensation of any municipal office or employment, for any city framing or adopting its own charter under this or any previous constitution, and all such offices or employments heretofore created shall cease at the end of the terms of any present incumbents.

Finances

SECTION 23. **Limitation on ownership of corporate stock, use of credit and grants of public funds by local governments.**—No county, city or other political corporation or subdivision of the state shall own or subscribe for stock in any corporation or association, or lend its credit or grant public money or thing of value to or in aid of any corporation, association or individual, except as provided in this constitution.

SECTION 23(a). **Cities may acquire and furnish industrial plants—indebtedness for.**—By vote of two-thirds of the qualified electors thereof voting thereon, any county, city or incorporated town or village in this state may become indebted for and may purchase, construct, extend or improve plants to be leased or otherwise disposed of pursuant to law to private persons or corporations for manufacturing, warehousing and industrial development purposes, including the real estate, buildings, fixtures and machinery; and the indebtedness incurred hereunder shall not be subject to the provisions of sections 26(a), 26(b), 26(c), 26(d) and 26(e) of Article VI of this Constitution; but any indebtedness incurred hereunder for this purpose shall not exceed ten percent of the value of taxable tangible property in the county, city, or incorporated town or village as shown by the last completed assessment for state and county purposes.

This provision shows the high status conferred on the notion of economic development in Missouri. However, the indebtedness is limited; a two-thirds extraordinary majority has to consent, and even then the subordinate unit of state government may not incur debt in excess of 10 percent of property valuation.

SECTION 24. **Annual budgets and reports of local government and municipally owned utilities—audits.**—As prescribed by law all counties, cities, other legal subdivisions of the state, and public utilities owned and operated by such subdivisions shall have an annual budget, file annual reports of their financial transactions, and be audited.

The state auditor's office can be requested to do an audit of local governments, or a private accounting firm can do an audit (in which case the local government entity has to pay for the audit). These audit findings often create scandal, and they are publicly available for the electorate to see and learn from. For example, the state auditor's office has often found multiple defalcations (misappropriations of funds) when auditing municipal courts in St. Louis County.

SECTION 25. **Limitation on use of credit and grant of public funds by local governments—pensions and retirement plans for employees of certain cities and counties.**—No county, city or other political corporation or subdivision of the state shall be authorized to lend its credit or grant public money or property to any private individual, association or corporation except as provided in Article VI, Section 23(a) and except that the general assembly may authorize any county, city or other political corporation or subdivision to provide for the retirement or pensioning of its officers and employees and the surviving spouses and children of deceased officers and employees and may also authorize payments from any public funds into a fund or funds for paying benefits upon retirement, disability or death to persons employed and paid out of any public fund for educational services and to their beneficiaries or estates; and except, also, that any county of the first class is authorized to provide for the creation and establishment of death benefits, pension and retirement plans for all its salaried employees, and the surviving spouses and minor children of such deceased employees; and except also, any county, city or political corporation or subdivision may provide for the payment of periodic cost of living increases in pension and retirement benefits paid under this section to its retired officers and employees and spouses of deceased officers and employees, provided such pension and retirement systems will remain actuarially sound.

SECTION 26(a). **Limitation on indebtedness of local governments without popular vote.**—No county, city, incorporated town or village, school district or other political corporation or subdivision of the state shall become indebted in an amount exceeding in any year the income and revenue provided for such year plus any unencumbered balances from previous years, except as otherwise provided in this constitution.

SECTION 26(b). Limitation on indebtedness of local government authorized by popular vote.—Any county, city, incorporated town or village or other political corporation or subdivision of the state, by vote of the qualified electors thereof voting thereon, may become indebted in an amount not to exceed five percent of the value of taxable tangible property therein as shown by the last completed assessment for state or county purposes, except that a school district by a vote of the qualified electors voting thereon may become indebted in an amount not to exceed fifteen percent of the value of such taxable tangible property. For elections referred to in this section the vote required shall be four-sevenths at the general municipal election day, primary or general elections and two-thirds at all other elections.

SECTION 26(c). Additional indebtedness of counties and cities when authorized by popular vote.—Any county or city, by a vote of the qualified electors thereof voting thereon, may incur an additional indebtedness for county or city purposes not to exceed five percent of the taxable tangible property shown as provided in section 26(b). For elections referred to in this section the vote required shall be four-sevenths at the general municipal election day, primary or general elections and two-thirds at all other elections.

Here the degree of voter consent necessary for local governments to go into debt varies by the timing of the election: if an indebtedness measure comes up for a vote in a high-participation election such as the general, the primary, or the general municipal election (mayoralty, city councilpersons, etc.), only four-sevenths (57.14 percent) is required for passage; but if it is a low-participation election ("other elections"), the higher two-thirds approval is necessary. These requirements seek the fullest possible engagement by the citizenry, even though citizens are often hard to rouse up.

SECTION 26(d). Additional indebtedness of cities for public improvements—benefit districts—special assessments.—Any city, by vote of the qualified electors thereof voting thereon, may become indebted not exceeding in the aggregate an additional ten percent of the value of the taxable tangible property shown as provided in section 26(b), for the purpose of acquiring rights-of-way, constructing, extending and improving the streets and avenues and acquiring rights-of-way, constructing, extending and improving sanitary or storm sewer systems. The governing body of the city may provide that any portion or all of the cost of any such improvement be levied and assessed by the governing body on property benefited by such improvement, and the city shall collect any special assessments so levied and shall use the same to reimburse the city for the amount paid or to be paid by it on the bonds of the city issued for such improvement. For elections referred to in this section the vote required shall be four-sevenths at the general municipal election day, primary or general elections and two-thirds at all other elections.

SECTION 26(e). Additional indebtedness of cities for municipally owned water and light plants—limitations.—Any city, by vote of the qualified electors thereof voting thereon, may incur an indebtedness in an amount not to exceed an additional ten percent of the value of the taxable tangible property shown as provided in section 26(b), for the purpose of paying all or any part of the cost of purchasing or constructing waterworks, electric or other light plants to be owned exclusively by the city, provided the total general obligation indebtedness of the city shall not exceed twenty percent of the assessed valuation. For elections referred to in this section the vote required shall be four-sevenths at the general municipal election day, primary or general elections and two-thirds at all other elections.

SECTION 26(f). Annual tax to pay and retire obligations within twenty years.—Before incurring any indebtedness every county, city, incorporated town or village, school district, or other political corporation or subdivision of the state shall provide for the collection of an annual tax on all taxable tangible property therein sufficient to pay the interest and principal of the indebtedness as they fall due, and to retire the same within twenty years from the date contracted.

SECTION 26(g). Contest of elections to authorize indebtedness.—All elections under this article may be contested as provided by law.

SECTION 27. Political subdivision revenue bonds for utility, industrial and airport purposes—restrictions.—Any city or incorporated town or village in this state, by vote of a majority of the qualified electors thereof voting thereon, and any joint board or commission, established by a joint contract between municipalities or political subdivisions in this state, by compliance with then applicable requirements of law, may issue and sell its negotiable interest bearing revenue bonds for the purpose of paying all or part of the cost of purchasing, construction, extending or improving any of the following projects:

(1) Revenue producing water, sewer, gas or electric light works, heating or power plants;

(2) Plants to be leased or otherwise disposed of pursuant to law to private persons or corporations for manufacturing and industrial development purposes, including the real estate, buildings, fixtures and machinery; or

(3) Airports. The project shall be owned by the municipality or by the cooperating municipalities or political subdivisions or the joint board or commission, either exclusively or jointly or by participation with cooperatives or municipally owned or public utilities, the cost of operation and maintenance and the principal and interest of the bonds to be payable solely from the revenues derived by the municipality or by the cooperating municipalities or political subdivisions or the joint board or commission from the operation of the utility or the lease or operation of the project. The bonds shall not constitute an indebtedness of the state, or of any political subdivision thereof, and neither the full faith and credit nor the taxing power of the state or of any political subdivision thereof is pledged to the payment of or the interest on such bonds. Nothing in this section shall affect the ability of the public service commission to regulate investor-owned utilities.

This provision clarifies that if a local government goes into the businesses mentioned here, mainly including public utilities, but also zones for economic development, and loses money, only that local government is responsible for the debt; the state and other local governments remain uninvolved.

SECTION 27(a). Political subdivision revenue bonds issued for utilities and airports, restrictions.—Any county, city or incorporated town or village in this state, by vote of a majority of the qualified electors thereof voting thereon, may issue and sell its negotiable interest bearing revenue bonds for the purpose of paying all or part of the cost of purchasing, constructing, extending or improving any of the following: (1) revenue producing water, gas or electric light works, heating or power plants; or (2) airports; to be owned exclusively by the county, city or incorporated town or village, the cost of operation and maintenance and the principal and interest of the bonds to be payable solely from the revenues derived by the county, city or incorporated town or village from the operation of the utility or airport.

SECTION 27(b). **Political subdivision revenue bonds issued for industrial development, restriction.**—Any county, city or incorporated town or village in this state, by a majority vote of the governing body thereof, may issue and sell its negotiable interest bearing revenue bonds for the purpose of paying all or part of the cost of purchasing, constructing, extending or improving any facility to be leased or otherwise disposed of pursuant to law to private persons or corporations for manufacturing, commercial, warehousing and industrial development purposes, including the real estate, buildings, fixtures and machinery. The cost of operation and maintenance and the principal and interest of the bonds shall be payable solely from the revenues derived by the county, city, or incorporated town or village from the lease or other disposal of the facility.

SECTION 27(c). **Revenue bonds defined.**—As used in article VI, sections 27(a) and 27(b), the term "revenue bonds" means bonds neither the interest nor the principal of which is an indebtedness or obligation of the issuing county, city or incorporated town or village.

SECTION 28. **Refunding bonds.**—For the purpose of refunding, extending, and unifying the whole or any part of its valid bonded indebtedness any county, city, school district, or other political corporation or subdivision of the state, under terms and conditions prescribed by law may issue refunding bonds not exceeding in amount the principal of the outstanding indebtedness to be refunded and the accrued interest to the date of such refunding bonds. The governing authority shall provide for the payment of interest at not to exceed the same rate, and the principal of such refunding bonds, in the same manner as was provided for the payment of interest and principal of the bonds refunded.

SECTION 29. **Application of funds derived from public debts.**—The moneys arising from any loan, debt, or liability contracted by the state, or any county, city, or other political subdivision, shall be applied to the purposes for which they were obtained, or to the repayment of such debt or liability, and not otherwise.

City and County of St. Louis

SECTION 30(a). **Powers conferred with respect to intergovernmental relations—procedure for selection of board of freeholders.**—The people of the city of St. Louis and the people of the county of St. Louis shall have power (1) to consolidate the territories and governments of the city and county into one political subdivision under the municipal government of the city of St. Louis; or, (2) to extend the territorial boundaries of the county so as to embrace the territory within the city and to reorganize and consolidate the county governments of the city and county, and adjust their relations as thus united, and thereafter the city may extend its limits in the manner provided by law for other cities; or, (3) to enlarge the present or future limits of the city by annexing thereto part of the territory of the county, and to confer upon the city exclusive jurisdiction of the territory so annexed to the city; or, (4) to establish a metropolitan district or districts for the functional administration of services common to the area included therein; or, to formulate and adopt any other plan for the partial or complete government of all or any part of the city and the county. The power so given shall be exercised by the vote of the people of the city and county upon a plan prepared by a board of freeholders consisting of nineteen members, nine of whom shall be electors of the city and nine electors of the county and one an elector of some other county. Upon the filing with the officials in general charge of elections in the city of a petition proposing the exercise of the powers hereby granted, signed by registered voters of the city in such number as shall equal three percent of the total vote cast in the city at the last general election for governor, and the certification thereof by the election officials to the mayor, and to the governor, then, within ten days after the certification the mayor shall, with the approval of a majority of the board of aldermen, appoint the city's nine members of the board, not more than five of whom shall be members of or affiliated with the same political party. Each member so appointed shall be given a certificate certifying his appointment signed by the mayor and attested by the seal of the city. Upon the filing with the officials in general charge of elections in the county of a similar petition signed by registered voters of the county, in such number as shall equal three percent of the total vote cast in the county at the last general election for governor, and the certification thereof by the county election officials to the county supervisor of the county and to the governor, within ten days after the certification, the county supervisor shall, with the approval of a majority of the county council, appoint the county's nine members of the board, not more than five of whom shall be members of or affiliated with the same political party. Each member so appointed shall be given a certificate of his appointment signed by the county supervisor and attested by the seal of the county.

SECTION 30(b). **Appointment of member by governor—meetings of board— vacancies—compensation and reimbursement of members—preparation of plan— taxation of real estate affected—submission at special elections—effect of adoption—certification and recordation—judicial notice.**—Upon certification of the filing of such similar petitions by the officials in general charge of elections of the city and the county, the governor shall appoint one member of the board who shall be a resident of the state, but shall not reside in either the city or the county, who shall be given a certificate of his appointment signed by the governor and attested by the seal of the state. The freeholders of the city and county shall fix reasonable compensation and expenses for the freeholder appointed by the governor and the cost shall be paid equally by the city and county. The appointment of the board shall be completed within thirty days after the certification of the filing of the petition, and at ten o'clock on the second Monday after their appointment the members of the board shall meet in the chamber of the board of aldermen in the city hall of the city and shall proceed with the discharge of their duties, and shall meet at such other times and places as shall be agreed upon. On the death, resignation or inability of any member of the board to serve, the appointing authority shall select the successor. The board shall prepare and propose a plan for the execution of the powers herein granted and for the adjustment of all matters and issues arising thereunder. The members of the board shall receive no compensation for their services as members, but the necessary expenses of the board shall be paid one-half by the county and one-half by the city on vouchers signed by the chairman of the board. The plan shall be signed in duplicate by the board or a majority thereof, and one copy shall be returned to the officials having general charge of elections in the city, and the other to such officials in the county, within one year after the appointment of the board. Said election officials shall cause separate elections to be held in the city and county, on the day fixed by the freeholders, at which the plan shall be submitted to the qualified voters of the city and county separately. The elections shall not be less than ninety days after the filing of the plan with said officials, and not on or within seventy days of any state or county primary or general election day in the city or county. The plan shall provide for the assessment and taxation of real estate in accordance with the use to which it is being put at the time of the assessment, whether agricultural, industrial or other use, giving due regard to the other provisions of this constitution. If a majority of the qualified electors of the city voting thereon, and a majority of the qualified electors of the county voting thereon at the separate elections shall vote for the plan, then, at such time as shall be prescribed therein, the same shall become the organic law of the territory therein defined, and shall take the place of and supersede all laws, charter provisions and ordinances inconsistent therewith relating to said territory. If the plan be adopted, copies thereof, certified to by said election officials of the city and county, shall be deposited in the office of the secretary of state and recorded in the office of the recorder of deeds for the city, and in the office of the recorder of deeds of the present county, and the courts of this state shall take judicial notice thereof.

City of St. Louis

SECTION 31. **Recognition of city of St. Louis as now existing both as a city and as a county.**—The city of St. Louis, as now existing, is recognized both as a city and as a county unless otherwise changed in accordance with the provisions of this constitution. As a city it shall continue for city purposes with its present charter, subject to changes and amendments provided by the constitution or by law, and with the powers, organization, rights and privileges permitted by this constitution or by law. As a county, it shall not be required to adopt a county charter but may, except for the office of circuit attorney, amend or revise its present charter to provide for the number, kinds, manner of selection, terms of office and salaries of its county officers, and for the exercise of all powers and duties of counties and county officers prescribed by the constitution and laws of the state.

The first sentence of this provision marks the "Great Divorce" of 1876 in the history of the St. Louis area (and of our state). St. Louis's then-current boundaries were frozen by this sentence in the constitution. This provision was added at the behest of St. Louis City leaders who did not want to have to pay taxes to provide services and urban amenities for the areas of St. Louis County outside the city limits. Much of what is now St. Louis City was once countryside, undeveloped land, farmland, and woods; vacant lots (where streets actually existed) separated the houses that had been built. But urban growth kept on, and soon the city limits were full of houses, apartment buildings, office buildings, factories, stores, and taverns. This growth eventually spilled over the county line into suburbs such as Clayton, University City, Wellston, Maplewood, Richmond Heights, Webster Groves, and Kirkwood. Note that this list is not inclusive: there are 90 incorporated municipalities in St. Louis County.

The newer dwellings available in the county motivated many St. Louisans to move out of the city. The results were foreseeable as soon as the 1920s; the tax base of St. Louis County was expanding, while that of St. Louis City was set to contract as the energy moved out to the county. Some Missourians supported a constitutional amendment in 1924 to permit "unfreezing" the geographical limits of St. Louis County so that the city and the country could "remarry." This amendment had to be accepted by the entire state, because it modified the statement "as now existing" in the first sentence of this section of the constitution. The amendment was successfully adopted with 55.3 percent of the vote. Its acceptance meant that thenceforth a statewide vote would no longer be necessary on the question of whether or not to merge the city and county; the balloting would be only in St. Louis City and St. Louis County. With this go-ahead, city leaders eventually used the procedures specified in Sections 30(a) and 30(b) to propose a plan for consolidation of the city and county, which was on the ballot in November 1930. It lost by a wide margin, garnering only 36.8 percent of the vote. (The economic woes of the Great Depression probably provoked the negativity.) Beaten back, the proponents of reform took a generation before presenting another plan in November 1962: this proposal went down with only 25.6 percent positive votes, losing by wide margins in both the city and county. This plan had proposed creating in place of the city and county a new municipal county with 22 boroughs, each electing two representatives to a legislature and one mayor as executive. In 1987 a new plan was proposed that would have merged the 90 municipalities in the county into 37. But this too was rejected, although the electorate was warming to the idea of consolidation somewhat: it received 46 percent in the county and 47 percent in the city.

In 1950, St. Louis City attained its peak population of about 857,000. At this time St. Louis County was growing, but only had a population of 403,000. Now St. Louis City has only 315,685 residents, but St. Louis County has a population of just over a million.

SECTION 32(a). Amendment of charter of St. Louis.—The charter of the city of St. Louis now existing, or as hereafter amended or revised, may be amended or revised for city or county purposes from time to time by proposals therefor submitted by the lawmaking body of the city to the qualified voters thereof, at a general or special election held at least sixty days after the publication of such proposals, and accepted by three-fifths of the qualified electors voting for or against each of said amendments or revisions so submitted.

Note the requirement of three-fifths majority for amendments to St. Louis's home rule constitution, whereas amendments to other city charters require only a simple majority vote. This extraordinary majority requirement exemplifies the fact that Missouri has historically been suspicious of self-government in St. Louis. St. Louisans don't even have control over their own police department; it is run by a commission of five members, one the popularly elected mayor, and the other four members all appointed by the governor with senatorial confirmation.

SECTION 32(b). Revision of charter of St. Louis—officers to complete terms and staff given opportunity for city employment.—In the event of any amendment or revision of the charter of the city of St. Louis which shall reorganize any county office and/or transfer any or all of the duties, powers and functions of any county officer who is then in office, the officer shall serve out the remainder of his or her term, and the amendment or revision of the charter of the city of St. Louis shall take effect, as to such office, upon the expiration of the term of such office holder. In the event of any amendment or revision of the charter of the city of St. Louis which shall reorganize any county office and/or transfer any or all of the duties, powers and functions of any county officer, all of the staff of such office shall be afforded the opportunity to become employees of the city of St. Louis with their individual seniority and compensation unaffected and on such other comparable terms and conditions as may be fair and equitable.

Here we see recognition of the need to take care of political (patronage) appointees in case they are removed from their jobs due to reforms. Their transition should be eased by these assurances of continuing their positions as long as possible and helping them obtain other city employment.

SECTION 32(c). Effect of revision on retirement.—An amendment or revision adopted pursuant to section 32(a) of this article shall not deprive any person of any right or privilege to retire and to retirement benefits, if any, to which he or she was entitled immediately prior to the effective date of that amendment or revision.

SECTION 33. Certification, recordation and deposit of amendments and revised charter—judicial notice.—Copies of any new or revised charter of the city of St. Louis or of any amendments to the present, or to any new or revised charter, with a certificate thereto appended, signed by the chief executive and authenticated by the seal of the city, setting forth the submission to and ratification thereof, by the qualified voters of the city shall be made in duplicate, one of which shall be deposited in the office of the secretary of state, and the other, after being recorded in the office of the recorder of deeds of the city, shall be deposited among the archives of the city, and thereafter all courts of this state shall take judicial notice thereof.

The most notable facet of this article of the constitution is that, while it deals with county and city government, mention of Kansas City by name is completely absent. On the other hand, St. Louis, especially the city, is treated *ad infinitum*. Kansas City is among the larger cities in the country in terms of area, having benefited from Missouri's liberal annexation laws to place a large land mass spilling over much of three counties under common rule. The contrasts between the two cities are remarkable: St. Louis, constrained and laboring under Balkanized political authority, and Kansas City, united, marching forward effectively. Kansas City's urban functionality is the foil to St. Louis's dysfunction—and yet Kansas City also confronts many of the problems of a big city.

Currently, there are some efforts to enable the City of St. Louis to rejoin St. Louis County as its 91st municipality. Area leaders express exasperation at the fragmentation of governmental authority in the region; the Ferguson crisis, the concern over scandals in the municipal courts, the decline of St. Louis as an important American city, and the notion that the duplication of so many government services over the entire region is wasteful are coming together in a realization that something should be done.

ARTICLE VII
PUBLIC OFFICERS

SECTION 1. **Impeachment—officers liable—grounds.**—All elective executive officials of the state, and judges of the supreme court, courts of appeals and circuit courts shall be liable to impeachment for crimes, misconduct, habitual drunkenness, willful neglect of duty, corruption in office, incompetency, or any offense involving moral turpitude or oppression in office.

SECTION 2. **Power of impeachment—trial of impeachments.**—The house of representatives shall have the sole power of impeachment. All impeachments shall be tried before the supreme court, except that the governor or a member of the supreme court shall be tried by a special commission of seven eminent jurists to be elected by the senate. The supreme court or special commission shall take an oath to try impartially the person impeached, and no person shall be convicted without the concurrence of five-sevenths of the court or special commission.

SECTION 3. **Effect of judgment of impeachment.**—Judgment of impeachment shall not extend beyond removal from office, but shall not prevent punishment of such officer by the courts on charges growing out of the same matter.

Impeachment is a two-step process through which government officials are removed from office. First, the officer is "impeached," and then he or she is tried. Impeachment is the legal equivalent of being indicted or charged with an offense, while trial is just that—a trial. There are two possible outcomes of the trial: either the officer is removed from office or allowed to stay because too few of the members of the trial body believe he or she is guilty of what he or she has been charged with.

Under the U.S. Constitution, the legislature may impeach executive and judicial branch officials for "Treason, Bribery, or other high Crimes and Misdemeanors" (Art. II, Sec. 4). While the House of Representatives has the power of impeachment, the Senate has the "sole Power to try all Impeachments" (Art. I, Sec. 3) and actually find the person guilty on the charges made by the House. Both Presidents Andrew Johnson and Bill Clinton were impeached during their administrations, for example, but neither was found guilty during the Senate trial and therefore they were allowed to remain in office. President Richard Nixon was facing impeachment and near-certain conviction but resigned before the process could get underway.

The Missouri process of impeachment is similar to the federal model. Rather than facing trial in front of the Senate, however, an impeached official in Missouri must stand trial in front of the Missouri Supreme Court. Since 1825, 10 Missouri officials have been impeached, resulting in four removals from office and two resignations before trial.[116] The most recent impeachment came in 1994 when Secretary of State Judith Moriarty[117] was accused of asking an employee to backdate her son's paperwork to allow him to run for office; she was later found guilty and removed from office.

SECTION 4. Removal of officers not subject to impeachment.—Except as provided in this constitution, all officers not subject to impeachment shall be subject to removal from office in the manner and for the causes provided by law.

SECTION 5. Election contests—executive state officers—other election contests.— Contested elections for governor, lieutenant governor and other executive state officers shall be had before the supreme court in the manner provided by law, and the court may appoint one or more commissioners to hear the testimony. The trial and determination of contested elections of all other public officers in the state, shall be by courts of law, or by one or more of the judges thereof. The general assembly shall designate by general law the court or judge by whom the several classes of election contests shall be tried and regulate the manner of trial and all matters incident thereto; but no law assigning jurisdiction or regulating its exercise shall apply to the contest of any election held before the law takes effect.

SECTION 6. Penalty for nepotism.—Any public officer or employee in this state who by virtue of his office or employment names or appoints to public office or employment any relative within the fourth degree, by consanguinity or affinity, shall thereby forfeit his office or employment.

Nepotism, or favoritism to her son, was the charge against Secretary of State Judith Moriarty. This provision is quite specific—consanguinity to the fourth degree means an officer cannot hire a third cousin. (How many of us are even acquainted with our third cousins?)

SECTION 7. Appointment of officers.—Except as provided in this constitution, the appointment of all officers shall be made as prescribed by law.

This does not exclude patronage appointments.

SECTION 8. Qualifications for public office—nonresidents.—No person shall be elected or appointed to any civil or military office in this state who is not a citizen of the United States, and who shall not have resided in this state one year next preceding his election or appointment, except that the residence in this state shall not be necessary in cases of appointment to administrative positions requiring technical or specialized skill or knowledge.

---

[116]"Impeachment Facts," Missouri First, www.mofirst.org/?page=issues/impeachment/impeachment -facts.php (accessed 1/9/17).

[117]Moriarty was the first female secretary of state; upon accessing her office, she announced that the State Manual (the "Blue Book") and the state constitution would be bound in the color mauve, to celebrate women in Missouri history. When she was removed from office, Governor Carnahan appointed in her place Rebecca "Bekki" Cook.

The only exception to this provision: there are longer durational requirements for running for governor.

SECTION 9. Disqualification by federal employment—exceptions.—No person holding an office of profit under the United States shall hold any office of profit in this state, members of the organized militia or of the reserve corps excepted.

SECTION 10. Equality of sexes in public service.—No person shall be disqualified from holding office in this state because of sex.

SECTION 11. Oath of office.—Before taking office, all civil and military officers in this state shall take and subscribe an oath or affirmation to support the Constitution of the United States and of this state, and to demean themselves faithfully in office.

All civil and military officers in Missouri must take an oath of office. The U.S. Constitution also requires oaths of office for the president (Art. II, Sec. 1) and federal and state legislative, executive, and judicial branch officers (Art. VI). The Missouri Constitution requires that those taking the oath of office support both the U.S. Constitution and that of Missouri. The Missouri Constitution also requires a unique oath for legislators related to public corruption: "I will not knowingly receive, directly or indirectly, any money or other valuable thing for the performance or nonperformance of any act or duty pertaining to my office, other than the compensation allowed by law" (see Article III, Section 15 above).

SECTION 12. Tenure of office.—Except as provided in this constitution, and subject to the right of resignation, all officers shall hold office for the term thereof, and until their successors are duly elected or appointed and qualified.

SECTION 13. Limitation on increase of compensation and extension of terms of office.—The compensation of state, county and municipal officers shall not be increased during the term of office; nor shall the term of any officer be extended.

SECTION 14. Statement of actuary required before retirement benefits substantially changed.—The legislative body which stipulates by law the amount and type of retirement benefits to be paid by a retirement plan covering elected or appointed public officials or both, shall, before taking final action of any substantial proposed change in future benefits, cause to be prepared a statement regarding the cost of such change. Such statement of cost shall be prepared by a qualified actuary with experience in retirement plan financing and such statement shall be available for public inspection. The general assembly shall provide by law applicable standards and requirements governing the preparation, content, and disposition of such statements of cost.

ARTICLE VIII
SUFFRAGE AND ELECTIONS

Elections are one of the most important functions of state governments. Even federal elections are administered at the state level. In Missouri this is done through the secretary of state's office and coordinated by county election clerks.

SECTION 1. Time of general elections.—The general election shall be held on the Tuesday next following the first Monday in November of each even year, unless a different day is fixed by law, two-thirds of all members of each house assenting.

SECTION 2. Qualifications of voters—disqualifications.—All citizens of the United States, including occupants of soldiers' and sailors' homes, over the age of eighteen who are residents of this state and of the political subdivision in which they offer to vote are entitled to vote at all elections by the people, if the election is one for which registration is required if they are registered within the time prescribed by law, or if the election is one for which registration is not required, if they have been residents of the political subdivision in which they offer to vote for thirty days next preceding the election for which they offer to vote: Provided however, no person who has a guardian of his or her estate or person by reason of mental incapacity, appointed by a court of competent jurisdiction and no person who is involuntarily confined in a mental institution pursuant to an adjudication of a court of competent jurisdiction shall be entitled to vote, and persons convicted of felony, or crime connected with the exercise of the right of suffrage may be excluded by law from voting.

SECTION 3. Methods of voting—secrecy of ballot—exceptions.—All elections by the people shall be by ballot or by any mechanical method prescribed by law. All election officers shall be sworn or affirmed not to disclose how any voter voted; provided, that in cases of contested elections, grand jury investigations and in the trial of all civil or criminal cases in which the violation of any law relating to elections, including nominating elections, is under investigation or at issue, such officers may be required to testify and the ballots cast may be opened, examined, counted, and received as evidence.

SECTION 4. Privilege of voters from arrest—exceptions.—Voters shall be privileged from arrest while going to, attending and returning from elections, except in cases of treason, felony or breach of the peace.

SECTION 5. Registration of voters.—Registration of voters may be provided for by law.

Voter registration has been required statewide since the early 1970s; before that, voters were registered only in municipalities, and not if they lived in a county with no other level of civil subdivision over them. In rural areas, election judges would determine, on the basis of their personal knowledge of the local citizens, who was qualified to vote. Election judges (not a member of the judiciary, but rather a citizen appointed to judge the fairness of the election procedures) of both parties were present to prevent any efforts at vote suppression (as might happen if only one party's judges were present).

SECTION 6. Retention of residence for voting purposes.—For the purpose of voting, no person shall be deemed to have gained or lost a residence by reason of his presence or absence while engaged in the civil or military service of this state or of the United States, or in the navigation of the high seas or the waters of the state or of the United States, or while a student of any institution of learning, or kept in a poor house or other asylum at public expense, or confined in public prison.

SECTION 7. Absentee voting.—Qualified electors of the state who are absent, whether within or without the state, may be enabled by general law to vote at all elections by the people.

Note that Sections 8 through 10 are not present.

SECTION 11. A person seeking to vote in person in public elections may be required by general law to identify himself or herself and verify his or her qualifications as a citizen of the United States of America and a resident of the state of Missouri by providing election officials with a form of identification, which may include requiring valid government-issued photo identification. Exceptions to the identification requirement may also be provided for by general law.

Section 11 was approved by 63 percent of the voters in November 2016. This amendment restores to the legislature the power to pass laws to require voters to present proof of their qualifications to vote, which may include photo or picture identification.

This proposal reflects the nationwide effort advanced by conservatives and Republicans to prevent "voter impersonation fraud." This would be a situation in which one person falsely assumes the identity of another voter and votes in his or her place, thereby stealing a vote and compromising the integrity of the election. Verifying the identity of each voter by demanding some form of photo identification would ensure that such fraud would not take place, but opponents of this thrust, largely Democrats and liberals, maintain that voter impersonation is extremely rare and that proposals to reform elections by demanding that each voter provide proof of identity are a solution in search of a problem. While proponents of voter ID argue that the measures they favor prevent undocumented immigrants from voting illegally, detractors maintain that such measures keep the poor, minorities, and the disabled from voting due to the greater difficulty they have in obtaining documentation of their civil status.

This new trend in legislation hit Missouri in mid-June 2006 when the General Assembly passed voter identification requirements, which were enacted and signed by Governor Blunt. The voter ID requirements were short-lived, though; a legal challenge to them immediately rose to the state supreme court, and in its decision in mid-October, the court found them unconstitutional.[118] The court's ruling held that the right to vote was fundamental because it is protected by the state constitution (Section 2 of this Article), and that this provision gave greater protection to the right to vote than does the U.S. Constitution. Since the voter ID measure impinged on a fundamental right by placing a substantial burden on the exercise of that right, it failed to measure up to the standard of the constitution and was declared null and void.

So supporters of voter ID had to amend the state constitution to permit passage of voter ID provisions. They set about doing so; in 2011 a resolution to amend the state constitution passed, and preparations began for placing the proposed amendment on the ballot in November 2012. But litigation took place over the ballot title, which used the terminology "Voter Protection Act." Opponents of voter ID argued

[118]*Weinschenk v. State*, 203 S.W.3d 201 (2006). See Veronica Harwin, "A Tale of Two States: Challenges to Voter ID Ballot Measures in Missouri and Minnesota," *Washington University Journal of Law and Policy* 42 (2013), 203–34.

that it wasn't a voter protection measure but rather a voter shutout measure. The ballot title was thrown out in the circuit court. But the legislature returned to the issue in 2016 and the proposed amendment passed the Senate with 75 percent support and the House with 74.4 percent support. It was placed on the ballot for the fall election, and voters approved the measure with 63.1 percent in favor.

Thus, the Missouri electorate has now decided that it is constitutional for the legislature to set up voter identification requirements. Since the legislature has in the meantime passed a bill doing just that (a bill that would have been unconstitutional if the electorate had not approved the constitutional amendment), the legislation is now constitutional and beyond the reach of the state supreme court. Certainly, given the heavy majorities this idea attracted in both chambers of the legislature and in the popular vote, one can conclude that the General Assembly reflects the views of the majority of Missourians.

SECTIONS 12 to 14 *have been omitted here.*

SECTION 15. Preamble.—The people of Missouri hereby state our intention that this initiative lead to the adoption of the following U.S. Constitutional Amendment.

SECTION 16. Congressional term limits amendment.—(a) No person shall serve in the office of United States Representative for more than three terms, but upon ratification of this amendment no person who has held the office of the United States Representative or who then holds the office shall serve for more than two additional terms.

(b) No person shall serve in the office of United States Senator for more than two terms, but upon ratification of this amendment no person who has held the office of United States Senator or who then holds the office shall serve in the office for more than one additional term.

(c) Any state may enact by state constitutional amendment longer or shorter limits than those specified in section "a" or "b" herein.

(d) This article shall have no time limit within which it must be ratified to become operative upon the ratification of the legislatures of three-fourths of the several States. Therefore, We, the people of the State of Missouri, have chosen to amend the state constitution to inform voters regarding incumbent and non-incumbent federal candidates' support for the above proposed CONGRESSIONAL TERM LIMITS AMENDMENT.

SECTION 17. Voter instruction on term limits for members of congress.—(1) We, the Voters of Missouri, hereby instruct each member of our congressional delegation to use all of his or her delegated powers to pass the Congressional Term Limits Amendment set forth above.

(2) All primary and general election ballots shall have printed the information "DISREGARDED VOTERS' INSTRUCTION ON TERM LIMITS" adjacent to the name of any United States Senator or Representative who:

(a) fails to vote in favor of the proposed Congressional Term Limits Amendment set forth above when brought to a vote or;

(b) fails to second the proposed Congressional Term Limits Amendment set forth above if it lacks for a second before any proceeding of the legislative body or;

(c) fails to propose or otherwise bring to a vote of the full legislative body the proposed Congressional Term Limits Amendment set forth above if it otherwise lacks a legislator who so proposes or brings to a vote of the full legislative body the proposed Congressional Term Limits Amendment set forth above or;

(d) fails to vote in favor of all votes bringing the proposed Congressional Term Limits Amendment set forth above before any committee or subcommittee of the respective house upon which he or she serves or;

(e) fails to reject any attempt to delay, table or otherwise prevent a vote by the full legislative body of the proposed Congressional Term Limits Amendment set forth above or;

(f) fails to vote against any proposed constitutional amendment that would establish longer term limits than those in the proposed Congressional Term Limits Amendment set forth above regardless of any other actions in support of the proposed Congressional Term Limits Amendment set forth above, or;

(g) sponsors or cosponsors any proposed constitutional amendment or law that would increase term limits beyond those in the proposed Congressional Term Limits Amendment set forth above, or;

(h) fails to ensure that all votes on Congressional Term Limits are recorded and made available to the public.

(3) The information "DISREGARDED VOTERS' INSTRUCTION ON TERM LIMITS" shall not appear adjacent to the names of incumbent candidates for Congress if the Congressional Term Limits Amendment set forth above is before the states for ratification or has become part of the United States Constitution.

SECTION 18. Voter instruction on term limit pledge for non-incumbents.—(1) Non-incumbent candidates for United States Senator and Representative shall be given an opportunity to take a "Term Limit" pledge regarding "Term Limits" each time they file to run for such office. Those who decline to take the "Term Limits" pledge shall have the

U.S. Congressional Representatives from Missouri

	DISTRICT	YEAR ELECTED TO FIRST TERM
Senators		
Sen. Claire McCaskill (D)	Statewide	2006
Sen. Roy Blunt (R)	Statewide	2010
Representatives		
Rep. Lacy Clay Jr. (D)	1st	2000
Rep. Ann Wagner (R)	2nd	2012
Rep. Blaine Luetkemeyer (R)	3rd	2010
Rep. Vicky Hartzler (R)	4th	2010
Rep. Emanuel Cleaver II (D)	5th	2004
Rep. Sam Graves (R)	6th	2000
Rep. Billy Long (R)	7th	2010
Rep. Jason Smith (R)	8th	2012

information "DECLINED TO PLEDGE TO SUPPORT TERM LIMITS" printed adjacent to their name on every primary and general election ballot.

(2) The "Term Limits" pledge shall be offered to non-incumbent candidates for United States Senator and Representative until a Constitutional Amendment which limits the number of terms of United States Senators to no more than two and United States Representatives to no more than three shall have become part of our United States Constitution.

(3) The "Term Limits" pledge that each non-incumbent candidate, set forth above, shall be offered is as follows:

I support term limits and pledge to use all my legislative powers to enact the proposed Constitutional Amendment set forth in the Term Limits Act of 1996. If elected, I pledge to vote in such a way that the designation "DISREGARDED VOTERS' INSTRUCTION ON TERM LIMITS" will not appear adjacent to my name.

SECTION 19. Designation.—(1) The Secretary of State shall be responsible to make an accurate determination as to whether a candidate for the federal legislature shall have placed adjacent to his or her name on the election ballot the information "DISREGARDED VOTERS' INSTRUCTION ON TERM LIMITS" or "DECLINED TO PLEDGE TO SUPPORT TERM LIMITS."

(2) The Secretary of State shall consider timely submitted public comments prior to making the determination required in subsection (1) of this section and may rely on such comments and any information submitted by the candidates in making the determination required in subsection (1).

(3) The Secretary of State, in accordance with subsection (1) of this section shall determine and declare what information, if any, shall appear adjacent to the names of each incumbent federal legislator if he or she was to be a candidate in the next election. This determination and declaration shall be made in a fashion necessary to ensure the orderly printing of primary and general election ballots with allowance made for all legal action provided in section (5) and (6) below, and shall be based upon each member of Congress's action during their current term of office and any action taken in any concluded term, if such action was taken after the determination and declaration was made by the Secretary of State in a previous election.

(4) The Secretary of State shall determine and declare what information, if any, will appear adjacent to the names of non-incumbent candidates for the federal legislature, not later than five (5) business days after the deadline for filing for the office.

(5) If the Secretary of State makes the determination that the information "DISREGARDED VOTERS' INSTRUCTION ON TERM LIMITS" or "DECLINED TO PLEDGE TO SUPPORT TERM LIMITS" shall not be placed on the ballot adjacent to the name of a candidate for the federal legislature, any elector may appeal such decision within five (5) business days to the Missouri Supreme Court as an original action or shall waive any right to appeal such decision; in which case the burden of proof shall be upon the Secretary of State to demonstrate by clear and convincing evidence that the candidate has met the requirements set forth in the Act and therefore should not have the information "DISREGARDED VOTERS' INSTRUCTION ON TERM LIMITS" or "DECLINED TO PLEDGE TO SUPPORT TERM LIMITS" printed on the ballot adjacent to the candidate's name.

(6) If the Secretary of State determines that the information "DISREGARDED VOTERS' INSTRUCTION ON TERM LIMITS" or "DECLINED TO PLEDGE TO SUPPORT TERM LIMITS" shall be placed on the ballot adjacent to a candidate's name, the

candidate may appeal such decision within five (5) business days to the Missouri Supreme Court as an original action or shall waive any right to appeal such decision; in which case the burden of proof shall be upon the candidate to demonstrate by clear and convincing evidence that he or she should not have the information "DISREGARDED VOTERS' INSTRUCTION ON TERM LIMITS" or "DECLINED TO PLEDGE TO SUPPORT TERM LIMITS" printed on the ballot adjacent to the candidate's name.

(7) The Supreme Court shall hear the appeal provided for in subsection (5) and issue a decision within 60 days. The Supreme Court shall hear the appeal provided for in subsection (6) and issue a decision not later than 61 days before the date of the elect

SECTION 20. Automatic repeal.—At such time as the Congressional Term Limits Amendment set forth above has become part of the U.S. Constitution, section 15 through section 22 of this Article automatically shall be repealed.

SECTION 21. Legal challenges, jurisdiction.—Any legal challenge to this Amendment shall be filed as an original action before the Supreme Court of this State.

SECTION 22. Severability.—If any portion, clause, or phrase of this Amendment is, for any reason, held to be invalid or unconstitutional by a court of competent jurisdiction, the remaining portions, clauses, and phrases shall not be affected, but shall remain in full force and effect.

The wording in Sections 15–22 was proposed via initiative and approved in November 1996, with 57.7 percent of the votes. A citizens group called Missouri Term Limits sponsored this measure; this group had enjoyed a huge victory in convincing the electorate to adopt term limits for state legislators and state senators in 1992. That measure obtained 75 percent approval. A counterpart measure presented for voter approval in the same election would have imposed term limits on U.S. representatives and U.S. senators, and it received 74 percent approval. (See commentary at Section 45(a) of Article III.)

The state of Arkansas passed a constitutional amendment to prevent federal representatives and senators from appearing on the ballot if they had already served a limited number of terms.[119] The U.S. Supreme Court threw this out as an unconstitutional additional qualification for federal office; since the Constitution lists qualifications, it is unconstitutional for states to add new qualifications (*U.S. Term Limits v. Thornton* [1994]). Missouri Term Limits then reacted with its initiative drive to put this amendment on the ballot in 1996.

Sections 15–22 are now null and void, having been declared unconstitutional by the U.S. Supreme Court in the case of *Cook v. Gralike* (2001). This new wording was clearly a violation of the Court's decision in *U.S. Term Limits v. Thornton*, but the Court reacted to Missouri's claim that the amendment was merely an application of the state's power under Article I, Section 4 of the U.S. Constitution (the election clause).[120] The justices determined that the state's power under this clause

---

[119]If a congressperson or senator had lapsed right to appear on the ballot, he or she could still win office and serve if he or she got enough write-in ballots to win the election without having his or her name on the ballot.

[120]The wording states: "The times, places, and manner of holding elections for senators and representatives shall be prescribed in each state by the Legislature thereof."

related only to the authority to decide the procedural mechanisms involved in such elections. Because this amendment tried to sway the outcome of elections by using language on the ballot as an advertisement (either positive or negative), it went beyond any legitimate state power over national elections.

SECTION 23. 1. This section shall be known as the "Missouri Campaign Contribution Reform Initiative."

2. The people of the State of Missouri hereby find and declare that excessive campaign contributions to political candidates create the potential for corruption and the appearance of corruption; that large campaign contributions made to influence election outcomes allow wealthy individuals, corporations and special interest groups to exercise a disproportionate level of influence over the political process; that the rising costs of campaigning for political office prevent qualified citizens from running for political office; that political contributions from corporations and labor organizations are not necessarily an indication of popular support for the corporation's or labor organization's political ideas and can unfairly influence the outcome of Missouri elections; and that the interests of the public are best served by limiting campaign contributions, providing for full and timely disclosure of campaign contributions, and strong enforcement of campaign finance requirements.

3. (1) Except as provided in subdivisions (2), (3) and (4) of this subsection, the amount of contributions made by or accepted from any person other than the candidate in any one election shall not exceed the following:

(a) To elect an individual to the office of governor, lieutenant governor, secretary of state, state treasurer, state auditor, attorney general, office of state senator, office of state representative or any other state or judicial office, two thousand six hundred dollars.

(2) (a) No political party shall accept aggregate contributions from any person that exceed twenty-five thousand dollars per election at the state, county, municipal, district, ward, and township level combined.

(b) No political party shall accept aggregate contributions from any committee that exceed twenty-five thousand dollars per election at the state, county, municipal, district, ward, and township level combined.

(3) (a) It shall be unlawful for a corporation or labor organization to make contributions to a campaign committee, candidate committee. exploratory committee, political party committee or a political party; except that a corporation or labor organization may establish a continuing committee which may accept contributions or dues from members, officers, directors, employees or security holders.

(b) The prohibition contained in subdivision (a) of this subsection shall not apply to a corporation that:

(i) Is formed for the purpose of promoting political ideas and cannot engage in business activities; and

(ii) Has no security holders or other persons with a claim on its assets or income; and

(iii) Was not established by and does not accept contributions from business corporations or labor organizations.

(4) No candidate's candidate committee shall accept contributions from, or make contributions to, another candidate committee, including any candidate committee, or equivalent entity, established under federal law.

(5) Notwithstanding any other subdivision of this subsection to the contrary, a candidate's candidate committee may receive a loan from a financial institution organized under

state or federal law if the loan bears the usual and customary interest rate, is made on a basis that assures repayments, is evidenced by a written instrument, and is subject to a due date or amortization schedule. The contribution limits described in this subsection shall not apply to a loan as described in this subdivision.

(6) No campaign committee, candidate committee, continuing committee, exploratory committee, political party committee, and political party shall accept a contribution in cash exceeding one hundred dollars per election.

(7) No contribution shall be made or accepted, directly or indirectly, in a fictitious name, in the name of another person, or by or through another person in such a manner as to conceal the identity of the actual source of the contribution or the actual recipient. Any person who receives contributions for a committee shall disclose to that committee's treasurer, deputy treasurer or candidate the recipient's own name and address and the name and address of the actual source of each contribution such person has received for that committee.

(8) No anonymous contribution of more than twenty-five dollars shall be made by any person, and no anonymous contribution of more than twenty-five dollars shall be accepted by any candidate or committee. If any anonymous contribution of more than twenty-five dollars is received, it shall be returned immediately to the contributor, if the contributor's identity can be ascertained, and if the contributor's identity cannot be ascertained, the candidate, committee treasurer or deputy treasurer shall immediately transmit that portion of the contribution which exceeds twenty-five dollars to the state treasurer and it shall escheat to the state.

(9) The maximum aggregate amount of anonymous contributions which shall be accepted per election by any committee shall be the greater of five hundred dollars or one percent of the aggregate amount of all contributions received by that committee in the same election. If any anonymous contribution is received which causes the aggregate total of anonymous contributions to exceed the foregoing limitation, it shall be returned immediately to the contributor, if the contributor's identity can be ascertained, and, if the contributor's identity cannot be ascertained, the committee treasurer, deputy treasurer or candidate shall immediately transmit the anonymous contribution to the state treasurer to escheat to the state.

(10) Notwithstanding the provisions of subdivision (9) of this subsection, contributions from individuals whose names and addresses cannot be ascertained which are received from a fund-raising activity or event, such as defined in section 130.011, RSMo, as amended from time to time, shall not be deemed anonymous contributions, provided the following conditions are met:

(a) There are twenty-five or more contributing participants in the activity or event;

(b) The candidate, committee treasurer, deputy treasurer or the person responsible for conducting the activity or event makes an announcement that it is illegal for anyone to make or receive a contribution in excess of one hundred dollars unless the contribution is accompanied by the name and address of the contributor;

(c) The person responsible for conducting the activity or event does not knowingly accept payment from any single person of more than one hundred dollars unless the name and address of the person making such payment is obtained and recorded pursuant to the record-keeping requirements of section 130.036, RSMo, as amended from time to time;

(d) A statement describing the event shall be prepared by the candidate or the treasurer of the committee for whom the funds were raised or by the person responsible for conducting the activity or event and attached to the disclosure report of contributions and expenditures required by section 130.041, RSMo, as amended from time to time. The following information to be listed in the statement is in addition to, not in lieu of, the requirements elsewhere in this chapter relating to the recording and reporting of contributions and expenditures:

(i) The name and mailing address of the person or persons responsible for conducting the event or activity and the name and address of the candidate or committee for whom the funds were raised;

(ii) The date on which the event occurred;

(iii) The name and address of the location where the event occurred and the approximate number of participants in the event;

(iv) A brief description of the type of event and the fund-raising methods used;

(v) The gross receipts from the event and a listing of the expenditures incident to the event;

(vi) The total dollar amount of contributions received from the event from participants whose names and addresses were not obtained with such contributions and an explanation of why it was not possible to obtain the names and addresses of such participants;

(vii) The total dollar amount of contributions received from contributing participants in the event who are identified by name and address in the records required to be maintained pursuant to section 130.036, RSMo, as amended from time to time.

(11) No candidate or committee in this state shall accept contributions from any out-of-state committee unless the out-of-state committee from whom the contributions are received has filed a statement of organization pursuant to section 130.021. RSMo, as amended from time to time, or has filed the reports required by sections 130.049 and 130.050, RSMo, as amended from time to time, whichever is applicable to that committee.

(12) Political action committees shall only receive contributions from individuals; unions; federal political action committees; and corporations, associations, and partnerships formed under chapters 347 to 360, RSMo, as amended from time to time, and shall be prohibited from receiving contributions from other political action committees, candidate committees, political party committees, campaign committees, exploratory committees, or debt service committees. However, candidate committees, political party committees, campaign committees, exploratory committees, and debt service committees shall be allowed to return contributions to a donor political action committee that is the origin of the contribution.

(13) The prohibited committee transfers described in subdivision (12) of this subsection shall not apply to the following committees:

(a) The state house committee per political party designated by the respective majority or minority floor leader of the house of representatives or the chair of the state party if the party does not have majority or minority party status;

(b) The state senate committee per political party designated by the respective majority or minority floor leader of the senate or the chair of the state party if the party does not have majority or minority party status.

(14) No person shall transfer anything of value to any committee with the intent to conceal, from the Missouri ethics commission, the identity of the actual source. Any violation of this subdivision shall be punishable as follows:

(a) For the first violation, the Missouri ethics commission shall notify such person that the transfer to the committee is prohibited under this section within five days of determining that the transfer is prohibited, and that such person shall notify the committee to which the funds were transferred that the funds must be returned within ten days of such notification;

(b) For the second violation, the person transferring the funds shall be guilty of a class C misdemeanor;

(c) For the third and subsequent violations, the person transferring the funds shall be guilty of a class D felony.

(15) No person shall make a contribution to a campaign committee, candidate committee, continuing committee, exploratory committee, political party committee, and political party with the expectation that some or all of the amounts of such contribution will be reimbursed by another person. No person shall be reimbursed for a contribution made to any campaign committee, candidate committee, continuing committee, exploratory committee, political party committee, and political party, nor shall any person make such reimbursement expect as provided in subdivision (5) of this subsection.

(16) No campaign committee, candidate committee, continuing committee, exploratory committee, political party committee, and political party shall knowingly accept contributions from:

(a) Any natural person who is not a citizen of the United States;

(b) A foreign government; or

(c) Any foreign corporation that does not have the authority to transact business in this state pursuant to Chapter 347, RSMo, as amended from time to time.

(17) Contributions from persons under fourteen years of age shall be considered made by the parents or guardians of such person and shall be attributed toward any contribution limits prescribed in this chapter. Where the contributor under fourteen years of age has two custodial parents or guardians, fifty percent of the contribution shall be attributed to each parent or guardian, and where such contributor has one custodial parent or guardian, all such contributors shall be attributed to the custodial parent or guardian.

(18) Each limit on contributions described in subdivisions (1), (2)(a), and (2)(b) of this subsection shall be adjusted by an amount based upon the average of the percentage change over a four year period in the United States Bureau of Labor Statistics Consumer Price Index for Kansas City, all items, all consumers, or its successor index, rounded to the nearest lowest twenty-five dollars and the percentage change over a four year period in the United States Bureau of Labor Statistics Consumer Price Index for St. Louis, all items, all consumers, or its successor index, rounded to the nearest lowest twenty-five dollars. The first adjustment shall be done in the first quarter of 2019, and then every four years thereafter. The secretary of state shall calculate such an adjustment in each limit and specify the limits in rules promulgated in accordance with Chapter 536, RSMo, as amended from time to time.

4. (1) Notwithstanding the provisions of subsection 3 of section 105.957, RSMo, as amended from time to time, any natural person may file a complaint with the Missouri ethics commission alleging a violation of the provisions of section 3 of this Article by any candidate for elective office, within sixty days prior to the primary election at which such candidate is running for office, until after the general election. Any such complaint shall be in writing, shall state all facts known by the complainant which have given rise to the complaint, and shall be sworn to, under penalty of perjury, by the complainant.

(2) Within the first business day after receipt of a complaint pursuant to this section, the executive director shall supply a copy of the complaint to the person or entity named in the complaint. The executive director of the Missouri ethics commission shall notify

the complainant and the person or entity named in the complaint of the date and time at which the commission shall audit and investigate the allegations contained in the complaint pursuant to subdivision (3) of this subsection.

(3) Within fifteen business days of receipt of a complaint pursuant to this section, the commission shall audit and investigate the allegations contained in the complaint and shall determine by a vote of at least four members of the commission that there are reasonable grounds to believe that a violation of law has occurred within the jurisdiction of the commission. The respondent may reply in writing or in person to the allegations contained in the complaint and may state justifications to dismiss the complaint. The complainant may also present evidence in support of the allegations contained in the complaint, but such evidence shall be limited in scope to the allegations contained in the original complaint, and such complaint may not be supplemented or otherwise enlarged in scope.

(4) If, after audit and investigation of the complaint and upon a vote of at least four members of the commission, the commission determines that there are reasonable grounds to believe that a violation of law has occurred within the jurisdiction of the commission, the commission shall proceed with such complaint as provided by sections 105.957 to 105.963, RSMo, as amended from time to time. If the commission does not determine that there are reasonable grounds to believe that such a violation of law has occurred, the complaint shall be dismissed. If a complaint is dismissed, the fact that such complaint was dismissed, with a statement of the nature of the complaint, shall be made public within twenty-four hours of the commission's action.

(5) Any complaint made pursuant to this section, and all proceedings and actions concerning such a complaint, shall be subject to the provisions of subsection 15 of section 105.961, RSMo, as amended from time to time.

(6) No complaint shall be accepted by the commission within fifteen days prior to the primary or general election at which such candidate is running for office.

5. Any person who knowingly and willfully accepts or makes a contribution in violation of any provision of section 3 of this Article or who knowingly and willfully conceals a contribution by filing a false or incomplete report or by not filing a required report under Chapter 130, RSMo, as amended from time to time, shall be held liable to the state in civil penalties in an amount of at least double and up to five times the amount of any such contribution.

6. (1) Any person who purposely violates the provisions of section 3 of this Article is guilty of a class A misdemeanor.

(2) Notwithstanding any other provision of law which bars prosecutions for any offenses other than a felony unless commenced within one year after the commission of the offense, any offense under the provisions of this section may be prosecuted if the indictment be found or prosecution be instituted within three years after the commission of the alleged offense.

(3) Any prohibition to the contrary notwithstanding, no person shall be deprived of the rights, guarantees, protections or privileges accorded by sections 130.011 to 130.026, 130.031 to 130.068, 130.072, and 130.081, RSMo, as amended from time to time, by any person, corporation, entity or political subdivision.

7. As used in this section, the following terms have the following meanings:

(1) "Appropriate officer" or "appropriate officers", the person or persons designated in section 130.026, or any successor section, to receive certain required statements and reports;

(2) "Candidate", an individual who seeks nomination or election to public office. The term "candidate" includes an elected officeholder who is the subject of a recall election, an individual who seeks nomination by the individual's political party for election to public office, an individual standing for retention in an election to an office to which the individual was previously appointed, an individual who seeks nomination or election whether or not the specific elective public office to be sought has been finally determined by such individual at the time the individual meets the conditions described in paragraph (a) or (b) of this subdivision, and an individual who is a write-in candidate as defined in subdivision (26) of this section. A candidate shall be deemed to seek nomination or election when the person first:

(a) Receives contributions or makes expenditures or reserves space or facilities with intent to promote the person's candidacy for office; or

(b) Knows or has reason to know that contributions are being received or expenditures are being made or space or facilities are being reserved with the intent to promote the person's candidacy for office; except that, such individual shall not be deemed a candidate if the person files a statement with the appropriate officer within five days after learning of the receipt of contributions, the making of expenditures, or the reservation of space or facilities disavowing the candidacy and stating that the person will not accept nomination or take office if elected; provided that, if the election at which such individual is supported as a candidate is to take place within five days after the person's learning of the above-specified activities, the individual shall file the statement disavowing the candidacy within one day; or

(c) Announces or files a declaration of candidacy for office.

(3) "Cash", currency, coin, United States postage stamps, or any negotiable instrument which can be transferred from one person to another person without the signature or endorsement of the transferor.

(4) "Committee", a person or any combination of persons, who accepts contributions or makes expenditures for the primary or incidental purpose of influencing or attempting to influence the action of voters for or against the nomination or election to public office of one or more candidates or the qualification, passage or defeat of any ballot measure or for the purpose of paying a previously incurred campaign debt or obligation of a candidate or the debts or obligations of a committee or for the purpose of contributing funds to another committee.

(5) "Committee", does not include:

(a) A person or combination of persons, if neither the aggregate of expenditures made nor the aggregate of contributions received during a calendar year exceeds five hundred dollars and if no single contributor has contributed more than two hundred fifty dollars of such aggregate contributions;

(b) An individual, other than a candidate, who accepts no contributions and who deals only with the individual's own funds or property;

(c) A corporation, cooperative association, partnership, proprietorship, or joint venture organized or operated for a primary or principal purpose other than that of influencing or attempting to influence the action of voters for or against the nomination or election to public office of one or more candidates or the qualification, passage or defeat of any ballot measure, and it accepts no contributions, and all expenditures it makes are from its own funds or property obtained in the usual course of business or in any commercial or other transaction and which are not contributions as defined by subdivision (7) of this section;

(d) A labor organization organized or operated for a primary or principal purpose other than that of influencing or attempting to influence the action of voters for or against the nomination or election to public office of one or more candidates, or the qualification, passage, or defeat of any ballot measure, and it accepts no contributions, and expenditures made by the organization are from its own funds or property received from membership dues or membership fees which were given or solicited for the purpose of supporting the normal and usual activities and functions of the organization and which are not contributions as defined by subdivision (7) of this section;

(e) A person who acts as an authorized agent for a committee in soliciting or receiving contributions or in making expenditures or incurring indebtedness on behalf of the committee if such person renders to the committee treasurer or deputy treasurer or candidate, if applicable, an accurate account of each receipt or other transaction in the detail required by the treasurer to comply with all record-keeping and reporting requirements; or

(f) Any department, agency, board, institution or other entity of the state or any of its subdivisions or any officer or employee thereof, acting in the person's official capacity.

(6) The term "committee" includes, but is not limited to, each of the following committees: campaign committee, candidate committee, continuing committee and political party committee;

(a) "Campaign committee", a committee, other than a candidate committee, which shall be formed by an individual or group of individuals to receive contributions or make expenditures and whose sole purpose is to support or oppose the qualification and passage of one or more particular ballot measures in an election or the retention of judges under the nonpartisan court plan, such committee shall be formed no later than thirty days prior to the election for which the committee receives contributions or makes expenditures, and which shall terminate the later of either thirty days after the general election or upon the satisfaction of all committee debt after the general election, except that no committee retiring debt shall engage in any other activities in support of a measure for which the committee was formed;

(b) "Candidate committee", a committee which shall be formed by a candidate to receive contributions or make expenditures in behalf of the person's candidacy and which shall continue in existence for use by an elected candidate or which shall terminate the later of either thirty days after the general election for a candidate who was not elected or upon the satisfaction of all committee debt after the election, except that no committee retiring debt shall engage in any other activities in support of the candidate for which the committee was formed. Any candidate for elective office shall have only one candidate committee for the elective office sought, which is controlled directly by the candidate for the purpose of making expenditures. A candidate committee is presumed to be under the control and direction of the candidate unless the candidate files an affidavit with the appropriate officer stating that the committee is acting without control or direction on the candidate's part;

(c) "Continuing committee", a committee of continuing existence which is not formed, controlled or directed by a candidate, and is a committee other than a candidate committee or campaign committee, whose primary or incidental purpose is to receive contributions or make expenditures to influence or attempt to influence the action of voters whether or not a particular candidate or candidates or a particular ballot measure or measures to be supported or opposed has been determined at the time the committee is required to file any statement or report pursuant to the provisions of this chapter. "Continuing committee" includes, but is not limited to, any committee organized or sponsored by a business entity, a labor organization, a professional association, a trade or business association, a club or other organization and whose primary purpose is to solicit, accept and use contributions from the members, employees or stockholders of such entity and any individual or group of individuals who accept and use contributions to influence or attempt to influence the action of voters. Such committee shall be formed no later than sixty days prior to the election for which the committee receives contributions or makes expenditures; and

(d) "Connected organization", any organization such as a corporation, a labor organization, a membership organization, a cooperative, or trade or professional association which expends funds or provides services or facilities to establish, administer or maintain a committee or to solicit contributions to a committee from its members, officers, directors, employees or security holders. An organization shall be deemed to be the connected organization if more than fifty percent of the persons making contributions to the committee during the current calendar year are members, officers, directors, employees or security holders of such organization or their spouses.

(7) "Contribution", a payment, gift, loan, advance, deposit, or donation of money or anything of value for the purpose of supporting or opposing the nomination or election of any candidate for public office or the qualification, passage or defeat of any ballot measure, or for the support of any committee supporting or opposing candidates or ballot measures or for paying debts or obligations of any candidate or committee previously incurred for the above purposes. A contribution of anything of value shall be deemed to have a money value equivalent to the fair market value. "Contribution" includes, but is not limited to:

(a) A candidate's own money or property used in support of the person's candidacy other than expense of the candidate's food, lodging, travel, and payment of any fee necessary to the filing for public office;

(b) Payment by any person, other than a candidate or committee, to compensate another person for services rendered to that candidate or committee:

(c) Receipts from the sale of goods and services, including the sale of advertising space in a brochure, booklet, program or pamphlet of a candidate or committee and the sale of tickets or political merchandise:

(d) Receipts from fund-raising events including testimonial affairs;

(e) Any loan, guarantee of a loan, cancellation or forgiveness of a loan or debt or other obligation by a third party, or payment of a loan or debt or other obligation by a third party if the loan or debt or other obligation was contracted, used, or intended, in whole or in part, for use in an election campaign or used or intended for the payment of such debts or obligations of a candidate or committee previously incurred, or which was made or received by a committee:

(f) Funds received by a committee which are transferred to such committee from another committee or other source, except funds received by a candidate committee as a transfer of funds from another candidate committee controlled by the same candidate but such transfer shall be included in the disclosure reports;

(g) Facilities, office space or equipment supplied by any person to a candidate or committee without charge or at reduced charges, except gratuitous space for meeting purposes which is made available regularly to the public, including other candidates or committees, on an equal basis for similar purposes on the same conditions; and

(h) The direct or indirect payment by any person, other than a connected organization, of the costs of establishing, administering, or maintaining a committee, including legal, accounting and computer services, fund raising and solicitation of contributions for a committee.

(8) "Contribution" does not include:

(a) Ordinary home hospitality or services provided without compensation by individuals volunteering their time in support of or in opposition to a candidate, committee or ballot measure, nor the necessary and ordinary personal expenses of such volunteers incidental to the performance of voluntary activities, so long as no compensation is directly or indirectly asked or given;

(b) An offer or tender of a contribution which is expressly and unconditionally rejected and returned to the donor within ten business days after receipt or transmitted to the state treasurer;

(c) Interest earned on deposit of committee funds; or

(d) The costs incurred by any connected organization listed pursuant to subdivision (4) of subsection 5 of section 130.021, RSMo, as amended from time to time, for establishing, administering or maintaining a committee, or for the solicitation of contributions to a committee which solicitation is solely directed or related to the members, officers, directors, employees or security holders of the connected organization.

(9) "County", any one of the several counties of this state or the city of St. Louis.

(10) "Disclosure report", an itemized report of receipts, expenditures and incurred indebtedness which is prepared on forms approved by the Missouri ethics commission and filed at the times and places prescribed.

(11) "Election", any primary, general or special election held to nominate or elect an individual to public office, to retain or recall an elected officeholder or to submit a ballot measure to the voters, and any caucus or other meeting of a political party or a political party committee at which that party's candidate or candidates for public office are officially selected. A primary election and the succeeding general election shall be considered separate elections.

(12) "Expenditure", a payment, advance, conveyance, deposit, donation or contribution of money or anything of value for the purpose of supporting or opposing the nomination or election of any candidate for public office or the qualification or passage of any ballot measure or for the support of any committee which in turn supports or opposes any candidate or ballot measure or for the purpose of paying a previously incurred campaign debt or obligation of a candidate or the debts or obligations of a committee; a payment, or an agreement or promise to pay, money or anything of value, including a candidate's own money or property, for the purchase of goods, services, property, facilities or anything of value for the purpose of supporting or opposing the nomination or election of any candidate for public office or the qualification or passage of any ballot measure or for the support of any committee which in turn supports or opposes any candidate or ballot measure or for the purpose of paying a previously incurred campaign debt or obligation of a candidate or the debts or obligations of a committee. An expenditure of anything of value

shall be deemed to have a money value equivalent to the fair market value. "Expenditure" includes, but is not limited to:

(a) Payment by anyone other than a committee for services of another person rendered to such committee;

(b) The purchase of tickets, goods, services or political merchandise in connection with any testimonial affair or fund-raising event of or for candidates or committees, or the purchase of advertising in a brochure, booklet, program or pamphlet of a candidate or committee;

(c) The transfer of funds by one committee to another committee: and

(d) The direct or indirect payment by any person, other than a connected organization for a committee, of the costs of establishing, administering or maintaining a committee, including legal, accounting and computer services, fund raising and solicitation of contributions for a committee.

(13) "Expenditure" does not include:

(a) Any news story, commentary or editorial which is broadcast or published by any broadcasting station, newspaper, magazine or other periodical without charge to the candidate or to any person supporting or opposing a candidate or ballot measure:

(b) The internal dissemination by any membership organization, proprietorship, labor organization, corporation, association or other entity of information advocating the election or defeat of a candidate or candidates or the passage or defeat of a ballot measure or measures to its directors, officers, members, employees or security holders, provided that the cost incurred is reported pursuant to subsection 2 of section 130.051. RSMo. as amended from time to time;

(c) Repayment of a loan, but such repayment shall be indicated in required reports;

(d) The rendering of voluntary personal services by an individual of the sort commonly performed by volunteer campaign workers and the payment by such individual of the individual's necessary and ordinary personal expenses incidental to such volunteer activity, provided no compensation is, directly or indirectly, asked or given;

(e) The costs incurred by any connected organization listed pursuant to subdivision (4) of subsection 5 of section 130.021, RSMo, as amended from time to time, for establishing, administering or maintaining a committee, or for the solicitation of contributions to a committee which solicitation is solely directed or related to the members, officers, directors, employees or security holders of the connected organization; or

(f) The use of a candidate's own money or property for expense of the candidate's personal food, lodging, travel, and payment of any fee necessary to the filing for public office, if such expense is not reimbursed to the candidate from any source.

(14) "Exploratory committees", a committee which shall be formed by an individual to receive contributions and make expenditures on behalf of this individual in determining whether or not the individual seeks elective office. Such committee shall terminate no later than December thirty-first of the year prior to the general election for the possible office.

(15) "Fund-raising event", an event such as a dinner, luncheon, reception, coffee, testimonial, rally, auction or similar affair through which contributions are solicited or received by such means as the purchase of tickets, payment of attendance fees, donations for prizes or through the purchase of goods, services or political merchandise.

(16) "In-kind contribution" or "in-kind expenditure", a contribution or expenditure in a form other than money.

(17) "Labor organization", any organization of any kind, or any agency or employee representation committee or plan, in which employees participate and which exists for the purpose, in whole or in part, of dealing with employers concerning grievances, labor disputes, wages, rates of pay, hours of employment, or conditions of work.

(18) "Loan", a transfer of money, property or anything of ascertainable monetary value in exchange for an obligation, conditional or not, to repay in whole or in part and which was contracted, used, or intended for use in an election campaign, or which was made or received by a committee or which was contracted, used, or intended to pay previously incurred campaign debts or obligations of a candidate or the debts or obligations of a committee.

(19) "Person", an individual, group of individuals, corporation, partnership, committee, proprietorship, joint venture, any department, agency, board, institution or other entity of the state or any of its political subdivisions, union, labor organization, trade or professional or business association, association, political party or any executive committee thereof, or any other club or organization however constituted or any officer or employee of such entity acting in the person's official capacity.

(20) "Political action committee", a committee of continuing existence which is not formed, controlled or directed by a candidate, and is a committee other than a candidate committee, political party committee, campaign committee, exploratory committee, or debt service committee, whose primary or incidental purpose is to receive contributions or make expenditures to influence or attempt to influence the action of voters whether or not a particular candidate or candidates or a particular ballot measure or measures to be supported or opposed has been determined at the time the committee is required to file any statement or report pursuant to the provisions of this chapter. Such a committee includes, but is not limited to, any committee organized or sponsored by a business entity, a labor organization, a professional association, a trade or business association, a club or other organization and whose primary purpose is to solicit, accept and use contributions from the members, employees or stockholders of such entity and any individual or group of individuals who accept and use contributions to influence or attempt to influence the action of voters. Such committee shall be formed no later than sixty days prior to the election for which the committee receives contributions or makes expenditures.

(21) "Political merchandise", goods such as bumper stickers, pins, hats, ties, jewelry, literature, or other items sold or distributed at a fund-raising event or to the general public for publicity or for the purpose of raising funds to be used in supporting or opposing a candidate for nomination or election or in supporting or opposing the qualification, passage or defeat of a ballot measure.

(22) "Political party", a political party which has the right under law to have the names of its candidates listed on the ballot in a general election.

(23) "Political party committee", a state, district, county, city, or area committee of a political party, as defined in section 115.603, RSMo, as amended from time to time, which may be organized as a not-for-profit corporation under Missouri law, and which committee is of continuing existence, and has the primary or incidental purpose of receiving contributions and making expenditures to influence or attempt to influence the action of voters on behalf of the political party.

(24) "Public office" or "office", any state, judicial, county, municipal, school or other district, ward, township, or other political subdivision office or any political party office which is filled by a vote of registered voters.

(25) "Write-in candidate", an individual whose name is not printed on the ballot but who otherwise meets the definition of candidate in subdivision (2) of this section.

8. The provisions of this section are self-executing. All of the provisions of this section are severable. If any provision of this section is found by a court of competent jurisdiction to be unconstitutional or unconstitutionally enacted, the remaining provisions of this section shall be and remain valid.

This lengthy (over 6,000 words) amendment imposes regulation in campaign financing, provides better transparency in public understanding of sources of contributions to candidates for office, bans lobbyists from using gifts and entertainment to woo legislators, and prevents other practices that compromise legislators' objectivity. After nearly eight years with the loosest campaign ethics rules in the Union, Missourians rejected the "free-for-all" and showed their appetite for campaign reform by giving the measure 70 percent approval in the November 2016 election. During the period of no regulation, candidates began receiving fewer donations but of much larger sums, meaning that "fat cats" were making even larger donations. Out-of-state money also came to play a larger role; for instance, the gubernatorial candidates in 2016 received 40 percent of their donations from such sources.[121]

Despite its multitude of provisions, Section 13 is already, in its infancy, attracting criticism for ineffectiveness. Travis Brown, chief lobbyist for the conservative mega contributor Rex Sinquefield, observed after its passage that "it won't change large donor fundraising at all. It actually will probably make it more powerful." Big donors and their staff can multiply political action committees, and they can still use independent expenditure committees to give money without limitation.[122]

ARTICLE IX
EDUCATION

Most of the wording in this article stems from the 1875 constitution and has been carried forward to the constitution of 1945.

SECTION 1(a). Free public schools—age limit.—A general diffusion of knowledge and intelligence being essential to the preservation of the rights and liberties of the people, the general assembly shall establish and maintain free public schools for the gratuitous instruction of all persons in this state within ages not in excess of twenty-one years as prescribed by law.

SECTION 1(b). Specific schools—adult education.—Specific schools for any contiguous territory may be established by law. Adult education may be provided from funds other than ordinary school revenues.

---

[121]Walter Moskop, "Political Fix: As campaign spending soars, Missouri voters contemplate reinstating limits," *St. Louis Post-Dispatch*, October 28, 2016.
[122]Editorial Board, "What part of 'get big money out of Missouri politics' do megadonors not understand?" *St. Louis Post-Dispatch*, November 14, 2016.

SECTION 2(a). State board of education—number and appointment of members—political affiliation—terms—reimbursement and compensation.—The supervision of instruction in the public schools shall be vested in a state board of education, consisting of eight lay members appointed by the governor, by and with the advice and consent of the senate; provided, that at no time shall more than four members be of the same political party. The term of office of each member shall be eight years, except the terms of the first appointees shall be from one to eight years, respectively. While attending to the duties of their office, members shall be entitled to receive only actual expenses incurred, and a per diem fixed by law.

This provision establishes the state board of education, which, under the state reorganization discussed at length in Article IV, branched off into two lineal descendants: the state board of elementary and secondary education, and the coordinating board of higher education. The coordinating board has nine non-salaried laypersons appointed by the governor with senatorial confirmation. No more than five may be of the same party.

SECTION 2(b). Commissioner of education—qualification, duties and compensation—appointment and compensation of professional staff—powers and duties of state board of education.—The board shall select and appoint a commissioner of education as its chief administrative officer, who shall be a citizen and resident of the state, and removable at its discretion. The board shall prescribe his duties and fix his compensation, and upon his recommendation shall appoint the professional staff and fix their compensation. The board shall succeed the state board of education heretofore established, with all its powers and duties, and shall have such other powers and duties as may be prescribed by law.

There are now two commissioners of education: the commissioner of elementary and secondary education and the commissioner of higher education.

SECTION 3(a). Payment and distribution of appropriations and income.—All appropriations by the state for the support of free public schools and the income from the public school fund shall be paid at least annually and distributed according to law.

SECTION 3(b). Deficiency in provision for eight-month school year—allotment of state revenue for school purposes.—In event the public school fund provided and set apart by law for the support of free public schools, shall be insufficient to sustain free schools at least eight months in every year in each school district of the state, the general assembly may provide for such deficiency; but in no case shall there be set apart less than twenty-five percent of the state revenue, exclusive of interest and sinking fund, to be applied annually to the support of the free public schools.

The state is constitutionally required to give over at least 25 percent of general state revenue to public schools and has historically been able to achieve this goal. Hardy and Forbis, writing in 1985, conclude that historically the General Assembly has allocated slightly more than 25 percent of revenue for schools.[123] In the 2017 fiscal year, 27 percent of state expenditures were for education.

[123]Richard J. Hardy and Richard R. Dohm, eds., *Missouri Government and Politics* (Columbia, MO: University of Missouri Press, 1985).

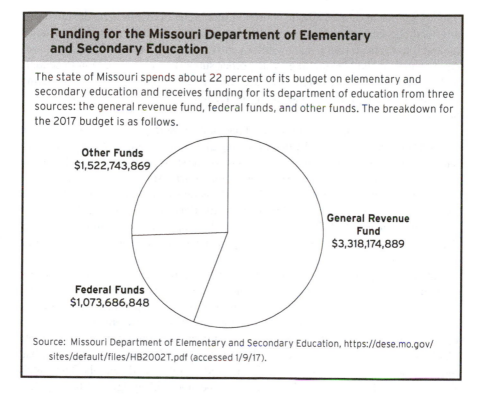

Funding for the Missouri Department of Elementary and Secondary Education

The state of Missouri spends about 22 percent of its budget on elementary and secondary education and receives funding for its department of education from three sources: the general revenue fund, federal funds, and other funds. The breakdown for the 2017 budget is as follows.

Other Funds
$1,522,743,869

General Revenue
Fund
$3,318,174,889

Federal Funds
$1,073,686,848

Source: Missouri Department of Elementary and Secondary Education, https://dese.mo.gov/sites/default/files/HB2002T.pdf (accessed 1/9/17).

SECTION 3(c). Racial discrimination in employment of teachers.—No school district which permits differences in wages of teachers having the same training and experience because of race or color, shall receive any portion of said revenue or fund.

This provision ensures racial fairness in teachers' salaries, but until August 1976 the wording also included the requirement that "separate schools be provided for white and colored children." Missouri had segregated schools by law (what is known as *de jure* segregation), and the wording in Section 3(c) shows early recognition of the separate school systems (although the constitution at least equalized teachers' pay).

The first break in the state's segregated schools came not in the public schools but in the Catholic parochial schools of the St. Louis Archdiocese. Its animator, Joseph Ritter, was appointed archbishop of St. Louis in 1946.[124] When Archbishop Ritter came to St. Louis, one of his first acts was to end racial segregation in all Catholic schools before the beginning of the next fall term. A resistant group of Catholics threatened to sue him for violation of the state constitutional requirement for separation of the races. Ritter then issued a "pastoral" letter to be read at every

---

[124]He came from Indianapolis, where as bishop he desegregated the parochial schools in 1938; the Ku Klux Klan protested outside the cathedral church, and even some of his own priests opposed the change.

Sunday service at every Catholic church in the Archdiocese; in it, he declared that any Catholic who sued him would be thenceforth excommunicated. Resistance melted like a sudden summer snowfall. Legally, only parents with children in parochial schools could get standing to sue; other supporters of segregation in schools had no claim of personal injury, so Ritter was never brought to court for violating the constitutional mandate for segregation. He later also desegregated the Catholic hospitals.

In 1954 the U.S. Supreme Court issued one of its most important rulings in *Brown v. Board of Education*, formally desegregating all public schools. Although Missouri had already tasted desegregation, the response of the state's political leadership to the ruling was tepid and indecisive. Six weeks after *Brown*, Attorney General John Dalton issued a formal clarification: local school districts could allow children of both races to attend the same schools, but the local districts were free to decide "whether [they] must integrate."[125] The General Assembly adopted a resolution to implement the ruling, and Governor Phil M. Donnelly declared that Missouri would not resist the Court's decision.

But little changed; in Kansas City the school district redrew attendance zones every year, making hundreds of adjustments (sometimes only one block at a time) to contain blacks in schools where blacks were already present in high proportions and to preserve white schools' racial uniformity. By the mid-1970s realty practices of "block-busting," "red-lining," and "racial steering" extended the original system of separate black and white schools to the entire Kansas City public school district, so it had mostly black schools, a few white schools, and no integrated schools. The state's Department of Elementary and Secondary Education blithely ignored these policy results. White flight to suburbs, both in Kansas and Missouri, depleted the tax base for the public schools;[126] the city of Kansas City, using Missouri's liberal annexation policies, had grown to cover most of three counties, which assured the city's tax base, but the school districts in the suburbs did not wish to merge with the by-now troubled Kansas City Metropolitan School District (KCMSD) as it faced financial bankruptcy.

Finally the KCMSD school board was taken over by a group of activists, who filed suit in federal district court in 1977 against the state; other plaintiffs in the lawsuit included schoolchildren and members of the school board. Defendants besides the state of Missouri included various federal agencies alleged to have helped cause racial segregation. In court, the judge re-aligned the KCMSD and converted it into

[125]Arthur Benson, *School Segregation and Desegregation in Kansas City*, www.bensonlaw.com /kcmsd/deseg.history.htm (accessed 1/9/17). See also Paul Ciotti, "Money and School Performance: Lessons from the Kansas City Desegregation Experiment," Policy analysis no. 298, Cato Institute, March 16, 1988, https://object.cato.org/sites/cato.org/files/pubs/pdf/pa-298.pdf (accessed 1/9/17) for a conservative viewpoint; and Briana O'Higgins, "How School and District Boundaries Shaped Education in Kansas City," KCUR *Morning Edition*, June 27, 2014, for a more objective evaluation.

[126]The last year that a levy increase or bond issue passed was 1969, which was also the last year the district had a majority white enrollment.

a defendant, due to its complicity in maintaining and extending the system of racially separate schools. This case, *Jenkins v. Missouri*, was to endure for 26 years. In 1985 the federal judge took control of the district and mandated expenditures to build new schools, integrate classrooms, and improve student test scores. The state had to pay for this under court order, and the funds did not ultimately undergo the appropriations process until 1997.

The judicial rulings became quite unpopular as state educational expenditures for KCMSD and the St. Louis area (simultaneously going through its own court-ordered desegregation difficulties) soared to 44 percent of the state budget for elementary and secondary education, benefiting only 9 percent of the state's student enrollment (in the metropolitan school districts). Eventually the judge, finding that the KCMSD was not generating enough revenue, ordered property taxes doubled, then increased again, and then ordered a 1.5 percent surcharge on the income taxes of non-resident Kansas City employees. These moves were even more unpopular, and were appealed; eventually the U.S. Supreme Court decided that the judge could not himself raise taxes but could order the taxing authority to raise them. Finally, in 2003 the federal district court decided that the KCMSD had shown enough improvement in test scores to release it from court control.

The St. Louis area also struggled with desegregation. After the *Brown* decision, housing segregation staved off change; the city school board did permit "intact busing" whereby whole classes of black students would be transferred to white schools with vacant rooms. These students would then eat lunch separately and leave on buses separate from those that the white students rode. During the 1960s predominantly black schools suffered from overcrowding, while white schools suffered sharply declining enrollments. Little progress toward desegregation was noted.

Finally, in 1971, a north St. Louis family sued the school board in U.S. district court, alleging that the city's schools were still segregated, and accusing the board of violating the black students' rights by allowing inner-city schools to deteriorate in comparison to the quality of the predominantly white schools. Thus began the case of *Liddell v. Missouri*. The NAACP joined as a plaintiff and the suburban school districts were added as defendants due to their having bussed their black students to the city prior to 1954. Unlike in Kansas City (where the suburban districts remained utterly uninvolved in desegregation),[127] the judge in St. Louis saw the necessity for an interdistrict solution involving the suburban school districts in St. Louis County. Eventually, the court ordered these districts to accept black transfer students from the city. Because the state had required segregation by constitutional fiat, it was ruled responsible for the transportation costs and other costs of educating the transfer students. An agreement was worked out in 1983 allowing students in

---

[127]Many of the Kansas City suburbs were in Kansas, and therefore subject neither to the jurisdiction of the U.S. District Court for the Western District of Missouri nor to that of the 8th Circuit U.S. Court of Appeals. But in St. Louis the solution did not involve the "East Side" or Illinois; instead, an interdistrict solution in St. Louis would be worked out with the many school districts in St. Louis County.

county school districts to transfer to city magnet schools, with all expenses borne by the state of Missouri. The plan became a political football when gubernatorial candidate John Ashcroft successfully used the busing and cost of the program as a wedge issue in the campaign of 1984. Despite his animadversions, the plan worked fairly well; whereas in 1980, 82 percent of black students attended all-black schools, by 1995 only 41 percent of black students were in all-black schools. Political attacks in the General Assembly continued however, concentrating hostility on costs. The court ordered a revisiting of the plan and a second agreement in 1999 removed the program from court supervision. In summer of 2016 plans were made to shut down the transfer program, which had become the nation's largest and longest.

The removal of the constitutional wording mandating separate schools for the races took place in August 1976. In that election 57.5 percent of Missourians voted for removal, but 42.5 percent voted to keep the wording. The results were embarrassing for Missouri's political leadership. For perspective, consider that Alabama was the last state to put up for a public vote removal of a state constitutional provision banning interracial marriage[128] in the year 2000; more than 40 percent of voters there preferred to keep the ban.

SECTION 4. Public school and seminary funds—certificates of indebtedness— renewals—liquidation—legal investment of funds—tax levy for interest.—All certificates of indebtedness of the state to the public school fund and to the seminary fund are hereby confirmed as sacred obligations of the state to said funds, and they shall be renewed as they mature for such time and at such rate of interest as may be provided by law. The general assembly may provide at any time for the liquidation of said certificates, but all funds derived from such liquidation, and all other funds hereafter accruing to said state school or state seminary funds, except the interest on same, shall be invested only in registered bonds of the United States or the state, bonds of school districts of the state, or bonds or other securities payment of which are fully guaranteed by the United States, of not less than par value. The general assembly may levy an annual tax sufficient to pay the accruing interest of all state certificates of indebtedness.

SECTION 5. Public school fund—sources—payment into state treasury— investment—limitation on use of income.—The proceeds of all certificates of indebtedness due the state school fund, and all moneys, bonds, lands, and other property belonging to or donated to any state fund for public school purposes, and the net proceeds of all sales of lands and other property and effects that may accrue to the state by escheat, shall be paid into the state treasury, and securely invested under the supervision of the state board of education, and sacredly preserved as a public school fund the annual income of which shall be faithfully appropriated for establishing and maintaining free public schools, and for no other uses or purposes whatsoever.

SECTION 6. Seminary fund—sources—payment into state treasury—investment— limitation on use of income.—The proceeds of all certificates of indebtedness due the seminary fund, the net proceeds of all sales of lands granted to the state for the benefit of the

[128]These were called anti-miscegenation laws and were banned by the U.S. Supreme Court in the case of *Loving v. Virginia* (1967). Alabama's action to remove the ban from its constitution happened 33 years after it became null and void.

state university with its several divisions, as provided by law, and all gifts, grants, bequests, or devises to said seminary fund for the benefit of the university, and not otherwise appropriated by the terms of any such gift, grant, bequest or devise, shall be paid into the state treasury, and securely invested by the board of curators of the state university and sacredly preserved as a seminary fund, the annual income of which shall be faithfully appropriated for maintenance of the state university, and for no other uses or purposes whatsoever.

SECTION 7. County and township school funds—liquidation and reinvestment—optional distribution on liquidation—annual distribution of income and receipts.— All real estate, loans, and investments now belonging to the various county and township school funds, except those invested as hereinafter provided, shall be liquidated without extension of time, and the proceeds thereof and the money on hand now belonging to said school funds of the several counties and the city of St. Louis, shall be reinvested in registered bonds of the United States, or in bonds of the state or in approved bonds of any city or school district thereof, or in bonds or other securities the payment of which are fully guaranteed by the United States, and sacredly preserved as a county school fund. Any county or the city of St. Louis by a majority vote of the qualified electors voting thereon may elect to distribute annually to its schools the proceeds of the liquidated school fund, at the time and in the manner prescribed by law.

All interest accruing from investment of the county school fund, the clear proceeds of all penalties, forfeitures and fines collected hereafter for any breach of the penal laws of the state, the net proceeds from the sale of estrays, and all other moneys coming into said funds shall be distributed annually to the schools of the several counties according to law.

SECTION 8. Prohibition of public aid for religious purposes and institutions.— Neither the general assembly, nor any county, city, town, township, school district or other municipal corporation, shall ever make an appropriation or pay from any public fund whatever, anything in aid of any religious creed, church or sectarian purpose, or to help to support or sustain any private or public school, academy, seminary, college, university, or other institution of learning controlled by any religious creed, church or sectarian denomination whatever; nor shall any grant or donation of personal property or real estate ever be made by the state, or any county, city, town, or other municipal corporation, for any religious creed, church, or sectarian purpose whatever.

This is a Blaine-type amendment and is supplemented in Article I, Section 7, by highly similar wording (see p. 14).

SECTION 9(a). State university—government by board of curators—number and appointment.— The government of the state university shall be vested in a board of curators consisting of nine members appointed by the governor, by and with the advice and consent of the senate.

This wording, combined with the wording in Section 9(b), gives the University of Missouri its so-called constitutional status, compared to the statutory basis (i.e., created by passage of a law, rather than being nestled in the constitution) of other state institutions of higher education. Many observers of state politics question whether the general assembly has adequately maintained the University or the other institutions of higher learning.

SECTION 9(b). Maintenance of state university and other educational institutions.— The general assembly shall adequately maintain the state university and such other educational institutions as it may deem necessary.

SECTION 10. Free public libraries—declaration of policy—state aid to local public libraries.—It is hereby declared to be the policy of the state to promote the establishment and development of free public libraries and to accept the obligation of their support by the state and its subdivisions and municipalities in such manner as may be provided by law. When any such subdivision or municipality supports a free library, the general assembly shall grant aid to such public library in such manner and in such amounts as may be provided by law.

The state promotes public libraries but not all counties or other subdivisions (cities, etc.) have free public libraries. If a county or other subdivision does not wish to tax its population for library services, it is not required to do so.

ARTICLE X
TAXATION

SECTION 1. Taxing power—exercise by state and local governments.—The taxing power may be exercised by the general assembly for state purposes, and by counties and other political subdivisions under power granted to them by the general assembly for county, municipal and other corporate purposes.

This comes straight from the constitution of 1875; the constitutional convention carried it forward to the 1945 Constitution. It reflects the consensual belief that governments must tax, and that the state government should exercise its taxing power for "state purposes." Governments below the level of the state (and dependent on the state for their continued existence)—that is, counties and other political subdivisions (all special districts, all cities, towns, villages, etc.)—must also tax and are allowed to tax, provided that the General Assembly explicitly allows them to do so by law.

After the Declaration of Independence was written in 1776, the American Founders set up a constitution called the Articles of Confederation. This constitution did not permit the central government (the United States in Congress Assembled) to tax; it could ask the states to donate money, but it could not impose a tax directly on the people. Government under the Articles of Confederation faltered and then failed, in good measure because the government had no revenue. Eventually, the Founders replaced the ineffectual Congress with a new government under our current U.S. Constitution. The new government had the power to tax citizens directly without going through the administrative apparatus of the state governments. Today, the state governments and the federal government exercise concurrent taxing powers.

One major difference between state and federal public budgeting is that most state constitutions prohibit deficit spending, that is, borrowing money to pay the bills when the budget is not balanced; the federal government is by contrast given the power both to impose taxation and to incur debt.

SECTION 2. Inalienability of power to tax.—The power to tax shall not be surrendered, suspended or contracted away, except as authorized by this constitution.

SECTION 3. Limitation of taxation to public purposes—uniformity—general laws—time for payment of taxes—valuation.—Taxes may be levied and collected for public purposes only, and shall be uniform upon the same class or subclass of subjects within the territorial limits of the authority levying the tax. All taxes shall be levied and collected by general laws and shall be payable during the fiscal or calendar year in which the property is assessed. Except as otherwise provided in this constitution, the methods of determining the value of property for taxation shall be fixed by law.

This phraseology applies to property taxes, which in 1875 were the mainstay of both state and local governments. Taxable property is valued first on its market value, but the market value is then discounted to the assessed value; the assessor is an elected county officer. On family homes, assessed value is currently set at 19 percent of true market value.

Until the late 1970s these value assessments were based on the sales price of a home. However, this method resulted in tax inequities. Many people who had bought their homes 40 or 50 years earlier, before the run-up in housing prices, might have paid $3,000 for their house (which had since grown exponentially in market value). Meanwhile, with inflation, a comparable house next door might have sold for $80,000. If the tax rate were 10 percent of assessed evaluation, the property tax on the former home would be $300, while the tax on the latter would be $8,000.

Eventually the state tax commission ordered reassessment to current market values, and a rolling reassessment has generally kept up with values since. To keep the governments supported by property tax from reaping a windfall of tax revenue, a "rollback" in rates was ordered, so that the tax burden would be revenue-neutral.

SECTION 4(a). Classification of taxable property—taxes on franchises, incomes, excises and licenses.—All taxable property shall be classified for tax purposes as follows: class 1, real property; class 2, tangible personal property; class 3, intangible personal property. The general assembly, by general law, may provide for further classification within classes 2 and 3, based solely on the nature and characteristics of the property, and not on the nature, residence or business of the owner, or the amount owned. Nothing in this section shall prevent the taxing of franchises, privileges or incomes, or the levying of excise or motor vehicle license taxes, or any other taxes of the same or different types.

Tangible personal property includes cars, trucks, and farm animals. While the market value of cars and trucks each year is determined by consulting the October issue of the National Automobile Dealers Association, the number of livestock is self-reported each year by the taxpayer. In 1980, Missouri Farm Facts, published by the Missouri Department of Agriculture, reported that there were 5.5 million head of cattle in the state valued at a little more than $2 billion. On the same date, the Missouri tax commission reported county clerks' certified property tax records showing that only 2.6 million head of cattle were reported to assessors for tax purposes. Half the cattle went unassessed and untaxed.

SECTION 4(b). Basis of assessment of tangible property—real property—taxation of intangibles—limitations.—Property in classes 1 and 2 and subclasses of those classes, shall be assessed for tax purposes at its value or such percentage of its value as may be fixed by law for each class and for each subclass. Property in class 3 and its subclasses shall be taxed only to the extent authorized and at the rate fixed by law for each class and subclass, and the tax shall be based on the annual yield and shall not exceed eight percent thereof. Property in class 1 shall be subclassed in the following classifications:

(1) Residential property;

(2) Agricultural and horticultural property;

(3) Utility, industrial, commercial, railroad, and all other property not included in subclasses (1) and (2) of class 1.

Property in the subclasses of class 1 may be defined by law, however subclasses (1), (2), and (3) shall not be further divided, provided, land in subclass (2) may by general law be assessed for tax purposes on its productive capability. The same percentage of value shall be applied to all properties within any subclass. No classes or subclass shall have a percentage of its true value in money in excess of thirty-three and one-third percent.

SECTION 4(c). Assessment, levy, collection and distribution of tax on intangibles.—All taxes on property in class 3 and its subclasses, and the tax under any other form of taxation substituted by the general assembly for the tax on bank shares, shall be assessed, levied and collected by the state and returned as provided by law, less two percent for collection, to the counties and other political subdivisions of their origin, in proportion to the respective local rates of levy.

The type of property in class 3, such as railroads or utility infrastructure, spans several counties at least (and often goes across the state). Instead of having county tax assessors struggle to figure out the value of the portion of such property in their counties, the state tax commission does it for them, collects the taxes, and returns each county and governmental unit's share to the county for redistribution according to law.

SECTION 4(d). Income tax laws, may incorporate federal laws by reference—rates, how set.—In enacting any law imposing a tax on or measured by income, the general assembly may define income by reference to provisions of the laws of the United States as they may be or become effective at any time or from time to time, whether retrospective or prospective in their operation. The general assembly shall in any such law set the rate or rates of such tax. The general assembly may in so defining income make exceptions, additions, or modifications to any provisions of the laws of the United States so referred to and for retrospective exceptions or modifications to those provisions which are retrospective.

This provision allows the state to "ride" its tax form on the federal income tax forms; the state form, MO-1040, follows the format of the federal 1040 form fairly closely. The taxpayer still must submit both a federal tax return to the IRS and a separate state tax return to the Missouri Department of Revenue (MoDOR), but the state tax return contains the federal 1040 as proof that the taxpayer has not made up those numbers. Note that the state rate of 6 percent applies to all state adjusted gross income over $9,000. This is a low annual income, and the rate hasn't changed since 1971, when it was 4 percent on income above $9,000. At a time when only the very wealthy—the highly salaried bank presidents, physicians, and industrial titans—earned over $9,000, most ordinary people would not even have had to calculate their income tax; they would have earned under $9,000, and they could have taken the number from the grid that was then provided. Now inflation has so devalued the dollar that nearly all taxpayers pay at the highest rate.

Missouri State vs. Federal Income Tax Rates

U.S. TAX BRACKET (SINGLE)

$0–9,075	10%
$9,076–36,900	15%
$36,901–89,350	25%
$89,351–186,350	28%
$186,351–405,100	33%
$405,101–406,750	35%
$406,751 and higher	39.6%

MISSOURI TAX BRACKET (SINGLE)

$0–999	1.5%
$1,000–1,999	2.0%
$2,000–2,999	2.5%
$3,000–3,999	3.0%
$4,000–4,999	3.5%
$5,000–5,999	4.0%
$6,000–6,999	4.5%
$7,000–7,999	5.0%
$8,000–8,999	5.5%
$9,000 and higher	6.0%

SECTION 5. **Taxation on railroads.**—All railroad corporations in this state, or doing business therein, shall be subject to taxation for state, county, school, municipal and other purposes, on the real and personal property owned or used by them, and on their gross earnings, their net earnings, their franchises and their capital stock.

SECTION 6. **Property exempt from taxation.**—1. All property, real and personal, of the state, counties and other political subdivisions, and nonprofit cemeteries, and all real property used as a homestead as defined by law of any citizen of this state who is a former prisoner of war, as defined by law, and who has a total service-connected disability, shall be exempt from taxation; all personal property held as industrial inventories, including raw materials, work in progress and finished work on hand, by manufacturers and refiners, and all personal property held as goods, wares, merchandise, stock in trade or inventory for resale by distributors, wholesalers, or retail merchants or establishments shall be exempt from taxation; and all property, real and personal, not held for private or corporate profit and used exclusively for religious worship, for schools and colleges, for purposes purely charitable, for agricultural and horticultural societies, or for veterans' organizations may be exempted from taxation by general law. In addition to the above, household goods, furniture, wearing apparel and articles of personal use and adornment owned and used by a person in his home or dwelling place may be exempt from taxation by general law but any such law may provide for approximate restitution to the respective political subdivisions of revenues lost by reason of the exemption. All laws exempting from taxation property other than the property enumerated in this article, shall be void. The provisions of this section exempting certain personal property of manufacturers, refiners, distributors, wholesalers, and retail merchants and establishments from taxation shall become effective, unless otherwise provided by law, in each county on January 1 of the year in which that county completes its first general reassessment as defined by law. 2. All revenues lost because of the exemption of certain personal property of manufacturers, refiners, distributors, wholesalers, and retail merchants and establishments shall be replaced to each taxing authority within a county from a countywide tax hereby imposed on all property in subclass 3 of class 1 in each county. For the year in which the exemption becomes effective, the county clerk shall calculate the total revenue lost by all taxing authorities in the county and extend upon all property in subclass 3 of class 1 within the county, a tax at the rate necessary to produce that amount. The rate of tax levied in each county according to this subsection shall not be increased above the rate first imposed and will stand levied at that rate unless later reduced according to the provisions of subsection 3. The county collector shall disburse the proceeds according to the revenue lost by each taxing authority because of the exemption of such property in that county. Restitution of the revenues lost by any taxing district contained in more than one county shall be from the several counties according to the revenue lost because of the exemption of property in each county. Each year after the first year the replacement tax is imposed, the amount distributed to each taxing authority in a county shall be increased or decreased by an amount equal to the amount resulting from the change in that district's total assessed value of property in subclass 3 of class 1 at the countywide replacement tax rate. In order to implement the provisions of this subsection, the limits set in section 11(b) of this article may be exceeded, without voter approval, if necessary to allow each county listed in section 11(b) to comply with this subsection.

3. Any increase in the tax rate imposed pursuant to subsection 2 of this section may be submitted to the voters of a county by the governing body thereof upon its own order, ordinance, or resolution and shall be submitted upon the petition of at least eight percent of the qualified voters who voted in the immediately preceding gubernatorial election.

4. As used in this section, the terms "revenues lost" and "lost revenues" shall mean that revenue which each taxing authority received from the imposition of a tangible personal property tax on all personal property held as industrial inventories, including raw materials, work in progress and finished work on hand, by manufacturers and refiners, and all personal property held as goods, wares, merchandise, stock in trade or inventory for resale by distributors, wholesalers, or retail merchants or establishments in the last full tax year immediately preceding the effective date of the exemption from taxation granted for such property under subsection 1 of this section, and which was no longer received after such exemption became effective.

SECTION 6(a). Homestead exemption authorized.—The general assembly may provide that a portion of the assessed valuation of real property actually occupied by the owner or owners thereof as a homestead, be exempted from the payment of taxes thereon, in such amounts and upon such conditions as may be determined by law, and the general assembly may provide for certain tax credits or rebates in lieu of or in addition to such an exemption, but any such law shall further provide for restitution to the respective political subdivisions of revenues lost, if any, by reason of the exemption, and any such law may also provide for comparable financial relief to persons who are not the owners of homesteads but who occupy rental property as their homes.

SECTION 6(b). Intangible property exempt from taxation, when—local governments may be reimbursed, when.—The general assembly may by general law exempt from taxation all intangible property, including taxation on the yield thereof, when owned by:

(1) Individuals; or

(2) Labor, agricultural or horticultural organizations; or

(3) Corporations or associations organized and operated exclusively for religious, charitable, scientific or educational purposes, no part of the net income of which inures to the benefit of any private stockholder or individual; or

(4) Hospitals which are exempt from payment of Missouri state income tax.

Any such law may provide for approximate reimbursement to the various political subdivisions, by the state, of revenues lost because of the exemption.

SECTION 7. Relief from taxation—forest lands—obsolete, decadent, or blighted areas—limitations—exception.—For the purpose of encouraging forestry when lands are devoted exclusively to such purpose, and the reconstruction, redevelopment, and rehabilitation of obsolete, decadent, or blighted areas, the general assembly by general law may provide for such partial relief from taxation of the lands devoted to any such purpose, and of the improvements thereon, by such method or methods, for such period or periods of time, not exceeding twenty-five years in any instance, and upon such terms, conditions, and restrictions as it may prescribe; provided, however, that in the case of forest lands, the limitation of twenty-five years herein described shall not apply.

SECTION 8. Limitation on state tax rate on tangible property.—The state tax on real and tangible personal property, exclusive of the tax necessary to pay any bonded debt of the state, shall not exceed ten cents on the hundred dollars assessed valuation.

SECTION 9. Immunity of private property from sale for municipal debts.—Private property shall not be taken or sold for the payment of the corporate debt of a municipal corporation.

If a municipality goes bankrupt, ordinarily the property owners in that government unit are ultimately responsible for the debt. This clause excuses property owners from expropriation, though not from financial responsibility through payment of hiked property taxes.

SECTION 10(a). Exclusion of state from local taxation for local purposes.—Except as provided in this constitution, the general assembly shall not impose taxes upon counties or other political subdivisions or upon the inhabitants or property thereof for municipal, county or other corporate purposes.

SECTION 10(b). State aid for local purposes.—Nothing in this constitution shall prevent the enactment of general laws directing the payment of funds collected for state purposes to counties or other political subdivisions as state aid for local purposes.

SECTION 10(c). Reduction in rates of levy may be required by law.—The general assembly may require by law that political subdivisions reduce the rate of levy of all property taxes the subdivisions impose whether the rate of levy is authorized by this constitution or by law. The general assembly may by law establish the method of increasing reduced rates of levy in subsequent years.

SECTION 11(a). Taxing jurisdiction of local governments—limitation on assessed valuation.—Taxes may be levied by counties and other political subdivisions on all property subject to their taxing power, but the assessed valuation therefor in such other political subdivisions shall not exceed the assessed valuation of the same property for state and county purposes.

SECTION 11(b). Limitations on local tax rates.—Any tax imposed upon such property by municipalities, counties or school districts, for their respective purposes, shall not exceed the following annual rates:

For municipalities—one dollar on the hundred dollars assessed valuation;

For counties—thirty-five cents on the hundred dollars assessed valuation in counties having three hundred million dollars, or more, assessed valuation and having by operation of law attained the classification of a county of the first class; and fifty cents on the hundred dollars assessed valuation in all other counties;

For school districts formed of cities and towns, including the school district of the city of St. Louis—two dollars and seventy-five cents on the hundred dollars assessed valuation;

For all other school districts—sixty-five cents on the hundred dollars assessed valuation.

SECTION 11(c). Increase of tax rate by popular vote—further limitation by law—exceptions to limitation.—In all municipalities, counties and school districts the rates of taxation as herein limited may be increased for their respective purposes when the rate and purpose of the increase are submitted to a vote and two-thirds of the qualified electors voting thereon shall vote therefor; provided in school districts the rate of taxation as herein limited may be increased for school purposes so that the total levy shall not exceed six dollars on the hundred dollars assessed valuation, except as herein provided, when the rate and the purpose of the increase are submitted to a vote and a majority of the qualified electors voting thereon shall vote therefor; provided, that in any school district where the board of education is not proposing a higher tax rate for school purposes, the last tax rate approved shall continue and the tax rate need not be submitted to the voters; provided, that in school districts where the qualified voters have voted against a proposed higher tax rate for school purposes, then the rate shall remain at the rate approved in the last previous school election except that the board of education shall be free to resubmit any higher tax rate at any time; provided that any board of education may levy a lower tax rate than approved by the voters as authorized by any provision of this section; and provided, that the rates herein fixed, and the amounts by which they may be increased may be further limited by law; and provided further, that any county or other political subdivision, when authorized by law and within the limits fixed by law, may levy a rate of taxation on all property subject to its taxing powers in excess of the rates herein limited, for library, hospital, public health, recreation grounds and museum purposes.

SECTION 11(d). Tax rate in St. Louis for county purposes.—The city of St. Louis may levy for county purposes, in addition to the municipal rates herein provided, a rate not exceeding the rate allowed for county purposes.

St. Louis City has two levels of government: the county offices and the city offices. The constitution provides that both must be supported.

SECTION 11(e). Exclusion of bonded debt from limitations on tax rates.—The foregoing limitations on rates shall not apply to taxes levied for the purpose of paying any bonded debt.

Through approval of bond issues, citizens of a local governmental unit may fund various projects, and the limitations on tax rates don't apply to them then.

SECTION 11(f). Authorization of local taxes other than ad valorem taxes.—Nothing in this constitution shall prevent the enactment of any general law permitting any county or other political subdivision to levy taxes other than ad valorem taxes for its essential purposes.

SECTION 11(g). Operating levy for Kansas City school districts may be set by school board.—The school board of any school district whose operating levy for school purposes for the 1995 tax year was established pursuant to a federal court order may establish the operating levy for school purposes for the district at a rate that is lower than the court-ordered rate for the 1995 tax year. The rate so established may be changed from year to year by the school board of the district. Approval by a majority of the voters of the district voting thereon shall be required for any operating levy for school purposes equal to or greater than the rate established by court order for the 1995 tax year. The authority granted in this section shall apply to any successor school district or successor school districts of such school district.

This provision pertains to the desegregation litigation in the Kansas City school district (KCMSD) discussed earlier under Article IX, Section 3(c); the provision actually purports to give the Kansas City school board permission to flout potential federal court orders on rate of taxation.

SECTION 12(a). Additional tax rates for county roads and bridges—road districts—reduction in rate may be required, how.—In addition to the rates authorized in section 11 for county purposes, the county court in the several counties not under township organization, the township board of directors in the counties under township organization, and the proper administrative body in counties adopting an alternative form of government, may levy an additional tax, not exceeding fifty cents on each hundred dollars assessed valuation, all of such tax to be collected and turned in to the county treasury to be used for road and bridge purposes; provided that, before any such county may increase its tax levy for road and bridge purposes above thirty-five cents it must submit such increase to the qualified voters of that county at a general or special election and receive the approval of a majority of the voters voting on such increase. In addition to the above levy for road and bridge purposes, it shall be the duty of the county court, when so authorized by a majority of the qualified electors of any road district, general or special, voting thereon at an election held for such purpose, to make an additional levy of not to exceed thirty-five cents on the hundred dollars assessed valuation on all taxable real and tangible personal property within such district, to be collected in the same manner as state and county taxes, and placed to the credit of the road district authorizing such levy, such election to be called and held in the manner provided by law provided that the general assembly may require by law that the rates authorized herein may be reduced.

SECTION 12(b). Refund of road and bridge taxes.—Nothing in this section shall prevent the refund of taxes collected hereunder to cities and towns for road and bridge purposes.

SECTION 13. Tax sales—limitations—contents of notices.—No real property shall be sold for state, county or city taxes without judicial proceedings, unless the notice of sale shall contain the names of all record owners thereof, or the names of all owners appearing on the land tax book, and all other information required by law.

SECTION 14. Equalization commission—appointment—duties.—The general assembly shall establish a commission, to be appointed by the governor by and with the advice and consent of the senate, to equalize assessments as between counties and, under such rules as may be prescribed by law, to hear appeals from local boards in individual cases and, upon such appeal, to correct any assessment which is shown to be unlawful, unfair, arbitrary or capricious. Such commission shall perform all other duties prescribed by law.

SECTION 15. Definition of "other political subdivision".—The term "other political subdivision," as used in this article, shall be construed to include townships, cities, towns, villages, school, road, drainage, sewer and levee districts and any other public subdivision, public corporation or public quasi-corporation having the power to tax.

Everything in this article from this point to Section 24 was added in the fall of 1980 and is termed the Hancock Amendment after its author and enthusiast, Mel Hancock. Hancock ran an initiative campaign along with the Missouri Farm Bureau to put the measure on the ballot, and it won with 55.4 percent of the votes. The measure is, overall, a limitation on the amount of tax revenue the state can collect, and also a constraint on how local governments are allowed to deal with proposed tax increases, fee increases, and charges of all sorts.

Philosophically, Missourians are prone to be suspicious of government and taxation. Missouri was affected by the taxpayers' revolt of the 1970s, which began in California with the passage in 1978 of Proposition 13, a citizen-initiated constitutional amendment, which limited property tax to 1 percent of market value of real property and restricted future increases in assessed value of real property to an inflation factor, not to exceed 2 percent per annum. The proposition also placed in the constitution a requirement for a two-thirds majority for any future increases in either tax rates or amounts collected, applying this cap to income taxation and sales tax rates alike. The passage of this measure was a revolutionary event and signaled that Americans viewed their taxes as too high.

But far earlier, in 1969, there were indications that Missourians were coming to an anti-tax way of thinking. Governor Hearnes, a moderate liberal Democrat who had led the fight for increased spending for many programs, including education and mental health treatment, needed higher taxes to pay the state's bills. His idea was to increase the maximum rate of income taxes from 4 percent on income above $9,000, which had been the rate since 1930, to 6 percent on income above $9,000. At the beginning of his second term, Hearnes was widely popular across the state and able to convince the General Assembly to adopt his proposal. However, some members of the legislature, led by Senator Earl Blackwell, strongly opposed the tax increase. Blackwell was a devotee of tax cuts, a skeptic about expanding government services, and a personal enemy of Hearnes. Upon losing the battle in the legislature, Blackwell vowed revenge and led an initiative drive to put the measure up for a public vote. Repeal of the tax increase was placed on the ballot in April 1970, and Hearnes lost spectacularly; his tax increase received only 43.8 percent of the votes. This demonstrated the appeal of tax-cut and anti-tax fever in the state. Hearnes gave it his all and lost his popularity over the issue. (Later, Hearnes in fact convinced the legislature to raise taxes back up to 6 percent for the maximum rate.)

Other states imitated California after it passed Proposition 13. A similar amendment eventually passed in Michigan, and Mel Hancock was inspired by these vote results. He led an initiative drive to adopt the Michigan wording for the Missouri Constitution. The amendment was on the ballot in the fall of 1980, the same election that chose Ronald Reagan for the presidency, and it won by a large margin. The provision limits both state revenue and state spending, unless overridden by a public vote for a tax put forward as not coming under the limit specified by the "ratio." It limits local governments, too, but they can spend as much as they take in, and they can take in more, but they are constrained to submit any increase in tax, fees, or licenses to the appropriate electorate with a public vote.

> SECTION 16. Taxes and state spending to be limited—state to support certain local activities—emergency spending and bond payments to be authorized.—Property taxes and other local taxes and state taxation and spending may not be increased above the limitations specified herein without direct voter approval as provided by this constitution. The state is prohibited from requiring any new or expanded activities by counties and other political subdivisions without full state financing, or from shifting the tax burden to counties and other political subdivisions. A provision for emergency conditions is established and the repayment of voter approved bonded indebtedness is guaranteed. Implementation of this section is specified in sections 17 through 24, inclusive, of this article.
>
> SECTION 17. Definitions.—As used in sections 16 through 24 of Article X:
>
> (1) "Total state revenues" includes all general and special revenues, license and fees, excluding federal funds, as defined in the budget message of the governor for fiscal year 1980–1981. Total state revenues shall exclude the amount of any credits based on actual tax liabilities or the imputed tax components of rental payments, but shall include the amount of any credits not related to actual tax liabilities.
>
> (2) "Personal income of Missouri" is the total income received by persons in Missouri from all sources, as defined and officially reported by the United States Department of Commerce or its successor agency.
>
> (3) "General price level" means the Consumer Price Index for All Urban Consumers for the United States, or its successor publications, as defined and officially reported by the United States Department of Labor, or its successor agency.

This provision lays the groundwork for how the limiting ratio mentioned above is established: total state revenues in the 1980–81 fiscal year are to be compared with the personal income of Missourians. State revenues in years thereafter cannot go above the percentage of residents' total personal incomes that the ratio dictates. Thus, if personal incomes rise, state revenue can rise; if personal incomes dip, state revenue must dip (if the state over-collects, it must refund the excess to the taxpayers in proportion to the amount of income tax they paid in the prior year).

SECTION 18. Limitation on taxes which may be imposed by general assembly—exclusions—refund of excess revenue—adjustments authorized.—(a) There is hereby established a limit on the total amount of taxes which may be imposed by the general assembly in any fiscal year on the taxpayers of this state. Effective with fiscal year 1981–1982, and for each fiscal year thereafter, the general assembly shall not impose taxes of any kind which, together with all other revenues of the state, federal funds excluded, exceed the revenue limit established in this section. The revenue limit shall be calculated for each fiscal year and shall be equal to the product of the ratio of total state revenues in fiscal year 1980–1981 divided by the personal income of Missouri in calendar year 1979 multiplied by the personal income of Missouri in either the calendar year prior to the calendar year in which appropriations for the fiscal year for which the calculation is being made, or the average of personal income of Missouri in the previous three calendar years, whichever is greater.

(b) For any fiscal year in the event that total state revenues exceed the revenue limit established in this section by one percent or more, the excess revenues shall be refunded pro rata based on the liability reported on the Missouri state income tax (or its successor tax or taxes) annual returns filed following the close of such fiscal year. If the excess is less than one percent, this excess shall be transferred to the general revenue fund.

(c) The revenue limitation established in this section shall not apply to taxes imposed for the payment of principal and interest on bonds, approved by the voters and authorized under the provisions of this constitution.

(d) If responsibility for funding a program or programs is transferred from one level of government to another, as a consequence of constitutional amendment, the state revenue and spending limits may be adjusted to accommodate such change, provided that the total revenue authorized for collection by both state and local governments does not exceed that amount which would have been authorized without such change.

The ratio divides total state revenues (in the 1980–81 fiscal year) by the total personal income of the residents of the state one year earlier (1979). This fraction is converted to a proportion or a percentage. State revenues in the future must be compared in the same way with personal income of state residents; if revenues exceed the percentage figure, there must be refunds to the point where state revenues are within the percentage figure. But these refunds are to be on income tax liability pro rata. This system is quite regressive; it provides for income tax refunds for the wealthy but little for the poor, because the poor pay most of their taxes in the form of sales taxes, while the wealthy pay much more in income tax.

SECTION 18(e). Voter approval required for taxes or fees, when, exceptions—definitions—compliance procedure, remedies.—1. In addition to the revenue limit imposed by section 18 of this article, the general assembly in any fiscal year shall not increase taxes or fees without voter approval that in total produce new annual revenues greater than either fifty million dollars adjusted annually by the percentage change in the personal income of Missouri for the second previous fiscal year, or one percent of total state revenues for the second fiscal year prior to the general assembly's action, whichever is less. In the event that an individual or series of tax or fee increases exceed the ceiling established in the subsection, the taxes or fees shall be submitted by the general assembly to a public vote starting with the largest increase in the given year, and including all increases in descending order, until the aggregate of the remaining increases and decreases is less than the ceiling provided in this subsection.

This provision for no increases in taxes or fees without voter approval signifies a decline in representative government (in which decision-making institutions make policy choices) and an upsurge in plebiscitary democracy (in which the citizens govern more directly by making more policy choices themselves).

2. The term "new annual revenues" means the net increase in annual revenues produced by the total of all tax or fee increases enacted by the general assembly in a fiscal year, less applicable refunds and less all contemporaneously occurring tax or fee reductions in that same fiscal year, and shall not include interest earnings on the proceeds of the tax or fee increase. For purposes of this calculation, "enacted by the general assembly" shall include any and all bills that are truly agreed to and finally passed within that fiscal year, except bills vetoed by the governor and not overridden by the general assembly. Each individual tax or fee increase shall be measured by the estimated new annual revenues collected during the first fiscal year that is fully effective. The term "increase taxes or fees" means any law or laws passed by the general assembly after the effective date of this section that increase the rate of an existing tax or fee, impose a new tax or fee, or broaden the scope of a tax or fee to include additional class of property, activity, or income, but shall not include the extension of an existing tax or fee which was set to expire.

3. In the event of an emergency, the general assembly may increase taxes, licenses or fees for one year beyond the limit in this subsection under the same procedure specified in section 19 of this article.

4. Compliance with the limit in this section shall be measured by calculating the aggregate actual new annual revenues produced in the first fiscal year that each individual tax or fee change is fully effective.

5. Any taxpayer or statewide elected official may bring an action under the provisions of section 23 of this article to enforce compliance with the provisions of this section. The Missouri supreme court shall have original jurisdiction to hear any challenge brought by any statewide elected official to enforce this section. In such enforcement actions, the court shall invalidate the taxes and fees which should have received a public vote as defined in subsection 1 of this section. The court shall order remedies of the amount of revenue collected in excess of the limit in this subsection as the court finds appropriate in order to allow such excess amounts to be refunded or to reduce taxes and/or fees in the future to offset the excess monies collected.

Paragraph 5 permits "taxpayer suits," or going straight to the supreme court to enforce compliance by the legislature and governor in case they fail to observe the requirements of this amendment.

Section 19. Limits may be exceeded, when, how.—The revenue limit of section 18 of this article may be exceeded only if all of the following conditions are met: (1) The governor requests the general assembly to declare an emergency; (2) the request is specific as to the nature of the emergency, the dollar amount of the emergency, and the method by which the emergency will be funded; and (3) the general assembly thereafter declares an emergency in accordance with the specifics of the governor's request by a majority vote for fiscal year 1981–1982, thereafter a two-thirds vote of the members elected to and serving in each house. The emergency must be declared in accordance with this section prior to incurring any of the expenses which constitute the emergency request. The revenue limit may be exceeded only during the fiscal year for which the emergency is declared. In no event shall any part of the amount representing a refund under section 18 of this article be the subject of an emergency request.

SECTION 20. **Limitation on state expenses.**—No expenses of state government shall be incurred in any fiscal year which exceed the sum of the revenue limit established in sections 18 and 19 of this article plus federal funds and any surplus from a previous fiscal year.

SECTION 21. **State support to local governments not to be reduced, additional activities and services not to be imposed without full state funding.**—The state is hereby prohibited from reducing the state financed proportion of the costs of any existing activity or service required of counties and other political subdivisions. A new activity or service or an increase in the level of any activity or service beyond that required by existing law shall not be required by the general assembly or any state agency of counties or other political subdivisions, unless a state appropriation is made and disbursed to pay the county or other political subdivision for any increased costs.

SECTION 22. **Political subdivisions to receive voter approval for increases in taxes and fees—rollbacks may be required—limitation not applicable to taxes for bonds.**—(a) Counties and other political subdivisions are hereby prohibited from levying any tax, license or fees, not authorized by law, charter or self-enforcing provisions of the constitution when this section is adopted or from increasing the current levy of an existing tax, license or fees, above that current levy authorized by law or charter when this section is adopted without the approval of the required majority of the qualified voters of that county or other political subdivision voting thereon. If the definition of the base of an existing tax, license or fees, is broadened, the maximum authorized current levy of taxation on the new base in each county or other political subdivision shall be reduced to yield the same estimated gross revenue as on the prior base. If the assessed valuation of property as finally equalized, excluding the value of new construction and improvements, increases by a larger percentage than the increase in the general price level from the previous year, the maximum authorized current levy applied thereto in each county or other political subdivision shall be reduced to yield the same gross revenue from existing property, adjusted for changes in the general price level, as could have been collected at the existing authorized levy on the prior assessed value.

(b) The limitations of this section shall not apply to taxes imposed for the payment of principal and interest on bonds or other evidence of indebtedness or for the payment of assessments on contract obligations in anticipation of which bonds are issued which were authorized prior to the effective date of this section.

Local governments have to get positive consent in a public vote to increase any tax, license, or fee. That means that if a city wants to raise greens fees for a municipal golf course, it must put the question to a vote in an election. If the charge for a dog license is to increase, it must obtain voter approval. Surprisingly, despite anti-tax fever, virtually all such local tax increases have been approved.

SECTION 23. Taxpayers may bring actions for interpretations of limitations.— Notwithstanding other provisions of this constitution or other law, any taxpayer of the state, county, or other political subdivision shall have standing to bring suit in a circuit court of proper venue and additionally, when the state is involved, in the Missouri supreme court, to enforce the provisions of sections 16 through 22, inclusive, of this article and, if the suit is sustained, shall receive from the applicable unit of government his costs, including reasonable attorneys' fees incurred in maintaining such suit.

Taxpayer suits are permitted against local governments raising fees, taxes, or licenses, and attorneys' fees for a taxpayer litigant who wins in court are paid by the state.

SECTION 24. Voter approval requirements not exclusive—self-enforceability.—
(a) The provisions for voter approval contained in sections 16 through 23, inclusive, of this article do not abrogate and are in addition to other provisions of the constitution requiring voter approval to incur bonded indebtedness and to authorize certain taxes.
(b) The provisions contained in sections 16 through 23, inclusive, of this article are self-enforcing; provided, however, that the general assembly may enact laws implementing such provisions which are not inconsistent with the purposes of said sections.
SECTION 25. Sale or transfer of homes or other real estate, prohibition on imposition of any new taxes, when.—After the effective date of this section, the state, counties, and other political subdivisions are hereby prevented from imposing any new tax, including a sales tax, on the sale or transfer of homes or any other real estate.

This measure protects real-estate interests from any "transfer" tax on the sale of houses. While such taxation would benefit the state treasury, it could add to the costs of buying or selling a home and disincentivize people's mobility. This passed in November 2010 with an impressive 83.7 percent of the vote. Prior to this constitutional barrier, a transfer tax might have been imposed, but it would have had to be by popular vote so it would not count against the Hancock ratio. But these results suggest that a movement to impose a transfer tax is not worth waiting for.

SECTION 26. In order to prohibit an increase in the tax burden on the citizens of Missouri, state and local sales and use taxes (or any similar transaction-based tax) shall not be expanded to impose taxes on any service or transaction that was not subject to sales, use, or similar transaction-based tax on January 1, 2015.

This provision, adopted in the November election of 2016 with 57 percent approval, shows that Missourians' anti-tax attitude is still fairly strong. The wording actually makes it constitutionally impossible to adopt a sales tax on services (day care, rent, health care, car repairs, tutoring, haircuts, tattoos, or other transactions) by a public vote; first an exception to Section 26 would have to be carved out by another constitutional amendment, and then a public vote to increase sales or use tax (not subject to the Hancock ratio) could be held. The Missouri Association of Realtors rallied other professional and trade groups to provide backing for this restriction.

ARTICLE XI
CORPORATIONS

Every provision in this article dates back to 1875, and the only action to make any change has been the repeal of Section 5 in August 1988. This repeal freed up corporations to allow shareholders wider decisional power: they now have a larger role in determining the purpose of the corporation and in deciding how to vote the stock. The repeal was fairly noncontroversial, getting 69.8 percent of the votes cast. Otherwise, the wording of this article reflects nineteenth-century concerns, particularly widespread suspicions of railroads and state banks.

SECTION 1. Definition of "corporation".—The term "corporation," as used in this article, shall be construed to include all joint stock companies or associations having any powers or privileges not possessed by individuals or partnerships.

SECTION 2. Organization of corporations by general law—special laws relating to corporations—invalidation of unexercised charters and franchises.—Corporations shall be organized only under general laws. No corporation shall be created, nor shall any existing charter be extended or amended by special law; nor shall any law remit the forfeiture of any charter granted by special act. All existing charters, or grants of special or exclusive privileges, under which a bona fide organization was not completed, and business was not being done in good faith at the adoption of this constitution, shall thereafter have no validity.

SECTION 3. Exercise of police power with respect to corporations.—The exercise of the police power of the state shall never be surrendered, abridged, or construed to permit corporations to infringe the equal rights of individuals, or the general well-being of the state.

SECTION 4. Corporations subject to eminent domain—trial by jury.—The exercise of the power and right of eminent domain shall never be construed or abridged to prevent the taking by law of the property and franchises of corporations and subjecting them to public use. The right of trial by jury shall be held inviolate in all trials of claims for compensation, when the rights of any corporation are affected by any exercise of said power of eminent domain.

SECTION 5. (Repealed August 2, 1988, L. 1988 HJR 80 Sec. 1)

SECTION 6. Cumulative voting authorized unless alternate method provided by law—exceptions.—In all elections for directors or managers of any corporation, each shareholder shall have the right to cast as many votes in the aggregate as shall equal the number of shares held by him, multiplied by the number of directors or managers to be elected, and may cast the whole number of votes, either in person or by proxy for one candidate, or distribute such votes among two or more candidates; and such directors or managers shall not be elected in any other manner unless an alternative method of electing and removing directors and managers is adopted as provided by law; provided, that this section shall not apply to cooperative associations, societies or exchanges organized under the law.

SECTION 7. Consideration for corporate stock and debts—fictitious issues—antecedent debts—increases of stock or bonds—issuance of preferred stock.—No corporation shall issue stock, or bonds or other obligations for the payment of money, except for money paid, labor done or property actually received; and all fictitious issues or increases of stock or indebtedness shall be void; provided, that no such issue or increase made for valid bona fide antecedent debts shall be deemed fictitious or void. The stock or bonded indebtedness of corporations shall not be increased nor shall preferred stock be issued, except according to general law.

SECTION 8. **Limitation of liability of stockholders.**—No stockholder or subscriber to stock of a corporation shall be individually liable in any amount in excess of the amount originally subscribed on such stock.

Railroads

SECTION 9. **Public highways—common carriers—regulations.**—All railways in this state are hereby declared public highways, and railroad corporations common carriers. Laws shall be enacted to correct abuses and prevent unjust discrimination and extortion in the rates of freight and passenger tariffs on all railroads in this state.

SECTION 10. **Consolidation of domestic with foreign railroad corporations— jurisdiction of Missouri courts—notice of consolidation.**—If any railroad corporation organized under the laws of this state shall consolidate by sale or otherwise, with any railroad corporation organized under the laws of any other state, or of the United States, the same shall not thereby become a foreign corporation, but the courts of this state shall retain jurisdiction in all matters which may arise as if said consolidation had not taken place. No consolidation shall take place, except upon at least sixty days public notice to all stockholders, in the manner provided by law.

SECTION 11. **Local consent for street railroads.**—No law shall grant the right to construct and operate a street railroad within any city, town, village, or on any public highway, without first acquiring the consent of the local authorities having control of the street or highway, and the franchises so granted shall not be transferred without similar assent first obtained.

SECTION 12. **Prohibition of discrimination, favoritism and preferences.**—No discrimination in charges or facilities in transportation shall be made between transportation corporations and individuals, or in favor of either, by abatement, drawback or otherwise; and no common carrier, or any lessee, manager or employee thereof, shall make any preference in furnishing cars or motive power.

Banks

SECTION 13. **Exclusion of state from banking.**—No state bank shall be created, nor shall the state own or be liable for any stock in any corporation, joint stock company, or association for banking purposes.

ARTICLE XII
AMENDING THE CONSTITUTION

The Missouri Constitution is more than 10 times the length of the U.S. Constitution, and annually it continues to grow larger through the amendment process. Compared to the methods of amending the U.S. Constitution, which require supermajorities to propose and ratify new amendments, it is relatively easy to amend the Missouri Constitution. Article XII outlines the three avenues to state-level constitutional amendments: legislative referenda, citizen initiative, and constitutional convention. Every 20 years, Missouri voters are asked whether to hold a new constitutional convention; Missourians will next have to decide whether to rewrite the constitution in the year 2022.

SECTION 1. **Limitation on revision and amendment.**—This constitution may be revised and amended only as therein provided.

SECTION 2(a). **Proposal of amendments by general assembly.**—Constitutional amendments may be proposed at any time by a majority of the members-elect of each house of the general assembly, the vote to be taken by yeas and nays and entered on the journal.

SECTION 2(b). **Submission of amendments proposed by general assembly or by the initiative.**—All amendments proposed by the general assembly or by the initiative shall be submitted to the electors for their approval or rejection by official ballot title as may be provided by law, on a separate ballot without party designation, at the next general election, or at a special election called by the governor prior thereto, at which he may submit any of the amendments. No such proposed amendment shall contain more than one amended and revised article of this constitution, or one new article which shall not contain more than one subject and matters properly connected therewith. If possible, each proposed amendment shall be published once a week for two consecutive weeks in two newspapers of different political faith in each county, the last publication to be not more than thirty nor less than fifteen days next preceding the election. If there be but one newspaper in any county, publication for four consecutive weeks shall be made. If a majority of the votes cast thereon is in favor of any amendment, the same shall take effect at the end of thirty days after the election. More than one amendment at the same election shall be so submitted as to enable the electors to vote on each amendment separately.

SECTION 3(a). **Referendum on constitutional convention—qualifications of delegates—selection of nominees for district delegates and delegates-at-large—election procedure.**—At the general election on the first Tuesday following the first Monday in November 1962, and every twenty years thereafter, the secretary of state shall, and at any general or special election the general assembly by law may, submit to the electors of the state the question "Shall there be a convention to revise and amend the constitution?" The question shall be submitted on a separate ballot without party designation, and if a majority of the votes cast thereon is for the affirmative, the governor shall call an election of delegates to the convention on a day not less than three nor more than six months after the election on the question. At the election the electors of the state shall elect fifteen delegates-at-large and the electors of each state senatorial district shall elect two delegates. Each delegate shall possess the qualifications of a senator; and no person holding any other office of trust or profit (officers of the organized militia, school directors, justices of the peace and notaries public excepted) shall be eligible to be elected a delegate. To secure representation from different political parties in each senatorial district, in the manner prescribed by its senatorial district committee each political party shall nominate but one candidate for delegate from each senatorial district, the certificate of nomination shall be filed in the office of the secretary of state at least thirty days before the election, each candidate shall be voted for on a separate ballot bearing the party designation, each elector shall vote for but one of the candidates, and the two candidates receiving the highest number of votes in each senatorial district shall be elected. Candidates for delegates-at-large shall be nominated by nominating petitions only, which shall be signed by electors of the state equal to five percent of the legal voters in the senatorial district in which the candidate resides until otherwise provided by law, and shall be verified as provided by law for initiative petitions, and filed in the office of the secretary of state at least thirty days before the election. All such candidates shall be voted for on a separate ballot without party designation, and the fifteen receiving the highest number of votes shall be elected. Not less than fifteen days before the election, the secretary of state shall certify to the county clerk of the county the name of each person nominated for the office of delegate from the senatorial district in which the county, or any part of it, is included, and the names of all persons nominated for delegates-at-large.

SECTION 3(b). Convention of delegates—quarters—oath—compensation—quorum—vote required—organization, employees, printing—public sessions—rules—vacancies.—The delegates so elected shall be convened at the seat of government by proclamation of the governor within six months after their election. The facilities of the legislative chambers and legislative quarters shall be made available for the convention and the delegates. Upon convening all delegates shall take an oath or affirmation to support the Constitution of the United States and of the state of Missouri, and to discharge faithfully their duties as delegates to the convention, and shall receive for their services the sum of ten dollars per diem and mileage as provided by law for members of the general assembly. A majority of the delegates shall constitute a quorum for the transaction of business, and no constitution or amendment to this constitution shall be submitted to the electors for approval or rejection unless by the assent of a majority of all the delegates-elect, the yeas and nays being entered on the journal. The convention may appoint such officers, employees and assistants as it may deem necessary, fix their compensation, provide for the printing of its documents, journals, proceedings and a record of its debates, and appropriate money for the expenditures incurred. The sessions of the convention shall be held with open doors, and it shall determine the rules of its own proceedings, choose its own officers, and be the judge of the election, returns and qualifications of its delegates. In case of a vacancy by death, resignation or other cause, the vacancy shall be filled by the governor by the appointment of another delegate of the political party of the delegate causing the vacancy.

SECTION 3(c). Submission of proposal adopted by convention—time of election—effective date.—Any proposed constitution or constitutional amendment adopted by the convention shall be submitted to a vote of the electors of the state at such time, in such manner and containing such separate and alternative propositions and on such official ballot as may be provided by the convention, at a special election not less than sixty days nor more than six months after the adjournment of the convention. Upon the approval of the constitution or constitutional amendments the same shall take effect at the end of thirty days after the election. The result of the election shall be proclaimed by the governor.

Methods of Amendment: The U.S. Constitution vs. the Missouri Constitution

AMENDING METHOD	U.S. CONSTITUTION	MISSOURI CONSTITUTION
Proposal from Congress	✓	✓
Constitutional Convention	✓	✓
Citizen Petition		✓

Schedule

SECTION 1. Supersession of prior constitutional provisions.—The constitution of 1875 and all amendments thereto except as hereinafter provided shall be superseded by this constitution.

Effectively, the constitution of 1945 absorbed the constitution of 1875 because so many provisions of the earlier constitution were presented as wording in the new one. But if a constitutional provision in the earlier constitution was not carried forward explicitly, it is here officially superseded and eliminated.

SECTION 2. Effect on existing laws.—All laws in force at the time of the adoption of this constitution and consistent therewith shall remain in full force and effect until amended or repealed by the general assembly. All laws inconsistent with this constitution, unless sooner repealed or amended to conform with this constitution, shall remain in full force and effect until July 1, 1946.

SECTION 3. Effect on existing terms of office.—The terms of all persons holding public office to which they have been elected or appointed at the time this constitution shall take effect shall not be vacated or otherwise affected thereby.

SECTION 4. Effect on certain existing courts.—All courts of common pleas now existing, the St. Louis courts of criminal correction, and all circuit court circuits as now established, shall continue until changed or abolished by law. The justices of the peace shall continue to hold their offices and receive the emoluments thereof until their terms of office expire, upon which their records shall be transferred to the magistrate courts.

The wording in Section 4 could be removed now; the only courts it mentions still in existence are the circuit courts, and the circuit courts have a solid constitutional foundation in Article V. This provision served to transition to oblivion the justices of the peace who started going away in 1945. The court of criminal corrections and courts of common pleas exited in 1979. Since these transitions have all been accomplished, this clause would be a candidate for removal if a constitutional convention were to clean up the constitution.

SECTION 5. **Effect on existing rights, claims.**—All rights, claims, causes of action and obligations existing and all contracts, prosecutions, recognizances and other instruments executed or entered into and all indictments which shall have been found and informations which shall have been filed and all actions which shall have been instituted and all fines, taxes, penalties and forfeitures assessed, levied, due or owing prior to the adoption of this constitution shall continue to be as valid as if this constitution had not been adopted.

SECTION 6. **Reimbursement for expenses of constitutional election.**—The general assembly shall appropriate out of the general revenue fund of the state a sum sufficient to reimburse the various counties for the sums legally and properly paid by them to the judges and clerks of the special election called for the purpose of adopting or rejecting this constitution.

ARTICLE XIII
PUBLIC EMPLOYEES

This is effectively the youngest and most recent article of the constitution.

SECTION 1. **Medical benefits may be authorized for state officers, employees and their dependents.**—Other provisions of this constitution to the contrary notwithstanding, the general assembly may provide or contract for health insurance benefits, including but not limited to hospital, chiropractic, surgical, medical, optical, and dental benefits, for officers and employees of the state and their dependents, including those employees of entities controlled by boards or commissions created by this constitution.

SECTION 2. **Medical benefits may be authorized for political subdivision officers, employees and their dependents.**—Other provisions of this constitution to the contrary notwithstanding, the general assembly may authorize any county, city or other political corporation or subdivision to provide or contract for health insurance benefits, including but not limited to hospital, chiropractic, surgical, medical, optical, and dental benefits, for officers and employees and their dependents.

These provisions, adopted by the skin of their teeth with only 50 percent[129] of the vote in 1984, enable the legislature to enact laws that would permit counties and cities, at their option, to offer medical benefits not just to employees but also to employees' dependents. Previously, county and city (public) employees had to pay extra to insure their dependents. This amendment allows local governments to recruit employees more effectively by offering medical insurance benefits comparable to those offered in private industry.

SECTION 3. **Compensation of state elected officials, general assembly members and judges to be set by Missouri Citizens' Commission on Compensation—members qualifications, terms, removal, vacancies, duties—procedure.**—1. Other provisions of

---

[129]The final count was Yeas: 918,596; Nays: 917,812. This is a margin of 784 votes! The measure passed, but only grudgingly.

this constitution to the contrary notwithstanding, in order to ensure that the power to control the rate of compensation of elected officials of this state is retained and exercised by the tax paying citizens of the state, after the effective date of this section no elected state official, member of the general assembly, or judge, except municipal judges, shall receive compensation for the performance of their duties other than in the amount established for each office by the Missouri citizens' commission on compensation for elected officials established pursuant to the provisions of this section. The term "compensation" includes the salary rate established by law, mileage allowances, per diem expense allowances.

2. There is created a commission to be known as the "Missouri Citizens' Commission on Compensation for Elected Officials". The Commission shall be selected in the following manner:

(1) One member of the commission shall be selected at random by the secretary of state from each congressional district from among those registered voters eligible to vote at the time of selection. The secretary of state shall establish policies and procedures for conducting the selection at random. In making the selections, the secretary of state shall establish a selection system to ensure that no more than five of the members shall be from the same political party. The policies shall include, but not be limited to, the method of notifying persons selected and for providing for a new selection if any person declines appointment to the commission;

(2) One member shall be a retired judge appointed by the judges of the supreme court, en banc;

(3) Twelve members shall be appointed by the governor, by and with the advice and consent of the senate. Not more than six of the appointees shall be members of the same political party. Of the persons appointed by the governor, one shall be a person who has had experience in the field of personnel management, one shall be a person who is representative of organized labor, one shall be a person representing small business in this state, one shall be the chief executive officer of a business doing an average gross annual business in excess of one million dollars, one shall be a person representing the health care industry, one shall be a person representing agriculture, two shall be persons over the age of sixty years, four shall be citizens of a county of the third classification, two of such citizens selected from a county of the third classification shall be selected from north of the Missouri River and two shall be selected from south of the Missouri River. No two persons selected to represent a county of the third classification shall be from the same county nor shall such persons be appointed from any county represented by an appointment to the commission by the secretary of state pursuant to subdivision (1) of this subsection.

3. All members of the commission shall be residents and registered voters of the state of Missouri. Except as otherwise specifically provided in this section, no state official, no member of the general assembly, no active judge of any court, no employee of the state or any of its institutions, boards, commissions, agencies or other entities, no elected or appointed official or employee of any political subdivision of the state, and no lobbyist as defined by law shall serve as a member of the commission. No immediate family member of any person ineligible for service on the commission under the provisions of this subsection may serve on the commission. The phrase "immediate family" means the parents, spouse, siblings, children, or dependent relative of the person whether or not living in the same household.

4. Members of the commission shall hold office for a term of four years. No person may be appointed to the commission more than once. No member of the commission may be removed from office during the term for which appointed except for incapacity, incompetence, neglect of duty, malfeasance in office, or for a disqualifying change of residence. Any action for removal shall be brought by the attorney general at the request of the governor and shall be heard in the circuit court for the county in which the accused commission member resides.

5. The first appointments to the commission shall be made not later than February 1, 1996, and not later than February first every four years thereafter. All appointments shall be filed with the secretary of state, who shall call the first meeting of the commission not later than March 1, 1996, and shall preside at the first meeting until the commission is organized. The members of the commission shall organize and elect a chairperson and such other officers as the commission finds necessary.

6. Upon a vacancy on the commission, a successor shall be selected and appointed to fill the unexpired term in the same manner as the original appointment was made. The appointment to fill a vacancy shall be made within thirty days of the date the position becomes vacant.

7. Members of the commission shall receive no compensation for their services but shall be reimbursed for their actual and necessary expenses incurred in the performance of their duties from appropriations made for that purpose.

8. The commission shall, beginning in 1996, and every two years thereafter, review and study the relationship of compensation to the duties of all elected state officials, all members of the general assembly, and all judges, except municipal judges, and shall fix the compensation for each respective position. The commission shall file its initial schedule of compensation with the secretary of state and the revisor of statutes no later than the first day of December, 1996, and by the first day of December each two years thereafter. The schedule of compensation shall become effective unless disapproved by concurrent resolution adopted by a two-thirds majority vote the general assembly before February 1 of the year following the filing of the schedule. Each schedule shall be published by the secretary of state as a part of the session laws of the general assembly and may also be published as a separate publication at the discretion of the secretary of state. The schedule shall also be published by the revisor of statutes as a part of the revised statutes of Missouri. The schedule shall apply and represent the compensation for each affected person beginning on the first day of July following the filing of the schedule. In addition to any compensation established by the schedule, the general assembly may provide by appropriation for periodic uniform general cost-of-living increases or decreases for all employees of the state of Missouri and such cost-of-living increases or decreases may also be extended to those persons affected by the compensation schedule fixed by the commission. No cost-of-living increase or decrease granted to any person affected by the schedule shall exceed the uniform general increase or decrease provided for all other state employees by the general assembly.

This measure, passed in 1994 with 57.3 percent of the vote, created the Commission on Compensation of Elected Officials and assigned it the task of determining raises for public officials. Since raises for public officers are tied to raises for state employees, no one will get rich as a public officer; state employees are notoriously underpaid in Missouri compared with other states. Under the 1994 amendment, legislators were able to turn down increased pay by concurrent resolution (i.e., a simple majority vote in each chamber). Legislators fell all over themselves to decline the raises provided by the commission; this made them look public-spirited and avoided giving the impression that they were greedy. But declining the raises for the legislators meant declining the raises for the corps of judges, too. Without raises, judicial salaries were too low to attract good judges; law students entering the labor force at large law firms were earning more money than judges.

To remedy this problem, a legislatively referred constitutional amendment was placed on the 2006 ballot that would impose an extraordinary majority (two-thirds) requirement to turn down the raises. It was thought that with this requirement legislators would be less likely to veto the proposed pay hikes, and therefore that the judges' salaries could rise to reasonable levels. The measure attracted huge support (it passed with 84.1 percent of the votes), but this may be attributable to the strange ballot description, which read: "Shall Article XIII, Section 3 of the Constitution be amended to require that legislators, statewide elected officials, and judges forfeit state pensions upon removal from office following impeachment or for misconduct, and to require that compensation for such persons be set by a citizens' commission subject to voter referendum?" Referendums are obviously popular in the state; Missouri is a plebiscitary democracy. The ballot language, however, ignored the change in wording of Section 8 (the two-thirds majority requirement) and may have actually confused those trying to understand by leading them (possibly falsely) to believe that mainly Section 3 was being changed.[130]

9. Prior to the filing of any compensation schedule, the commission shall hold no less than four public hearings on such schedule, at different geographical locations within the state, within the four months immediately preceding the filing of the schedule. All meetings, actions, hearings, and business of the commission shall be open to the public, and all records of the commission shall be available for public inspection.

10. Until the first day of July next after the filing of the first schedule by the commission, compensation of the persons affected by this section shall be that in effect on the effective date of this amendment.

11. Schedules filed by the commission shall be subject to referendum upon petition of the voters of this state in the same manner and under the same conditions as a bill enacted by the general assembly.

12. Beginning January 1, 2007, any public official subject to this provision who is convicted in any court of a felony which occurred while in office or who has been removed from office for misconduct or following impeachment shall be disqualified from receiving any pension from the state of Missouri.

13. No compensation schedule filed by the commission after the effective date of this subsection shall take effect for members of the general assembly until January 1, 2009.

---

[130]William C. Lhotka, "Passage of Amendment 7 Could Mean Easier Pay Hikes for Judges," *St. Louis Post-Dispatch*, October 30, 2006.